THE MEDITERRANEAN TABLE

THE MEDITERRANEAN TABLE

SIMPLE RECIPES *for* HEALTHY LIVING
ON THE MEDITERRANEAN DIET

SONOMA
PRESS

Illustrations © 2015 by Tom Bingham

Photo credits: Burcu Avsar/Offset, pg. 2; Michela Ravasio/Stocksy, pg. 6; Jelena Jojic/Stocksy, pg. 8; Eckhardt/Diop/Stockfood, pg. 19; Miquel Llonch/Stocksy, pg. 20; Pavel Gramatikov/Stocksy, pg. 30; Jim Scherer/Stockfood, pg. 41; Chris Alack/Stockfood, pg. 48; Ewgenija Schall/StockFood, pg. 54; Ina Peters/Stocksy, pg. 58; Gräfe & Unzer Verlag/Wolfgang Schardt/StockFood, pg. 63; Gräfe & Unzer Verlag/Ulrike Holsten/Stockfood, pg. 68; Valerie Janssen/StockFood, pg. 72; Sandra Eckhardt/StockFood, pg. 78; Rua Castilho/StockFood, pg. 84; Pavel Gramatikov/Stocksy, pg. 90; Valerie Janssen/StockFood, pg. 94; Angie Norwood Browne/StockFood, pg. 100; People Pictures/StockFood, pg. 107; Nataša Mandić/Stocksy, pg. 112; Davide Illini/Stocksy, pg. 118; Great Stock!/StockFood, pg. 125; Renáta Török-Bognár/Stocksy, pg. 130; People Pictures/StockFood, pg. 134; People Pictures/StockFood, pg. 139; Jeff Wasserman/Stocksy, pg. 144; Gräfe & Unzer Verlag/Mona Binner Photographie/StockFood pg. 148; Victoria Firmston/StockFood, pg. 153; Gräfe & Unzer Verlag/Coco Lang/StockFood, pg. 158; Gareth Morgans/StockFood, pg. 164; Eising Studio Food Photo & Video/StockFood, pg. 170; Gareth Morgans/StockFood, pg. 174; People Pictures/StockFood, pg. 181; Rua Castilho/StockFood, pg. 184; Thelma & Louise/StockFood, pg. 189; Tanya Zouev/StockFood, pg. 194; Sara Remington/Stocksy, pg. 200; Michael Wissing/StockFood, pg. 204; Rua Castilho/StockFood, pg. 216; People Pictures/StockFood, pg. 220; People Pictures/StockFood, pg. 227; Gräfe & Unzer Verlag/Melanie Zanin/StockFood, pg. 236; People Pictures/StockFood, pg. 240; Rowena Naylor/Stocksy, pg. 247; Tanya Zouev/StockFood, pg. 252; Renáta Dobránska/StockFood, pg. 258; Lauren Mclean/StockFood, pg. 261; Clinton Hussey/StockFood, pg. 266. All other photos Shutterstock.com.

ISBN: Print 978-1-942411-17-8 | eBook 978-1-942411-18-5

CONTENTS

INTRODUCTION

Warm summers, temperate winters, miles of coastline, and an easygoing attitude characterize the countries surrounding the Mediterranean Sea. Though this region spans many different cultures, including southern Europe, North Africa, and the Middle East, the people of the Mediterranean share a common lifestyle that has made them one of the healthiest populations in the world. Their secret? Lots of outdoor activity, relaxing meals with family and friends, and cuisine based on fresh fruits and vegetables, whole grains, beans and legumes, fish and seafood.

Mediterraneans typically prefer to bike or walk while running errands to and from work. They take time to enjoy the good life each day, heading home for lunch and sipping red wine as they savor the vibrant flavors of traditional home-cooked lunches and suppers. And while people in this region have been eating this way for millennia, it wasn't until the mid-twentieth century that the world caught on to the unmistakable health benefits of the Mediterranean diet and way of life.

In the Seven Countries Study of the 1950s, scientists analyzed the food and lifestyle habits of people in Greece, Italy, Yugoslavia, Finland, the Netherlands, Japan, and the United States. It was the first major study of the affect of diet on human health and concluded that the traditional Mediterranean way of eating—a largely plant-based diet low in saturated fat and high in fiber, monounsaturated fat, and omega-3 fatty acids—could help to lower cholesterol, reduce risk of coronary heart disease, and improve longevity.

In subsequent decades, scientists continued to research the Mediterranean diet and have added even more to its list of benefits, demonstrating that this way of eating can also reduce the risks of obesity, type 2 diabetes, hypertension, metabolic syndrome, cancer, Alzheimer's disease, dementia, depression, and arthritis.

Unlike the many weight loss and diet plans that rely on deprivation and exhaustive lists of restrictions, the Mediterranean diet is all about celebrating fresh, wholesome ingredients and taking the time to appreciate each bite.

1

SECRETS
OF THE
MEDITERRANEAN

From leisurely lunches to light but satisfying dinners, from brisk walks to and from work to bike rides in the countryside, the people of the Mediterranean know how to live. They also know how and what to eat for good health, and the Mediterranean way of eating increases their enjoyment of food, makes them feel better, gives them more energy, and inspires them to fully experience the joys of life with family and friends.

A CLOSER LOOK AT THE MEDITERRANEAN DIET

The Mediterranean diet is based on the cuisines of countries surrounding the Mediterranean Sea, namely Italy, Greece, Spain, Morocco, Cyprus, Croatia, and Portugal, which is on the Atlantic Ocean but influenced by Spanish cuisine and Mediterranean cooking. While these cuisines have wide variations among them, they all omit processed foods, excessive amounts of saturated fat, trans fats, and refined sugar, and they share a focus on fresh vegetables and fruits, whole grains, beans and legumes, lean proteins like fish and poultry, olive oil and other healthy mono-unsaturated fats, and moderate quantities of red meat, cheese and yogurt, and red wine.

Although it is referred to as a diet, the Mediterranean diet is not specifically intended for rapid weight loss. Instead, it is a way of eating that focuses on wholesome, nutritious foods that will satisfy your hunger and appetite while helping you achieve and sustain your optimal weight and improve your overall health. It is a lifestyle that you can adopt today and sustain for the rest of your—hopefully long!—life. If you are worried that you will feel deprived on the Mediterranean diet, don't be. The recipes in this book will prove that you can eat well, thoroughly enjoy your food, and protect your health at the same time.

The History of the Mediterranean Diet

The Mediterranean diet has been around since ancient times, originating in the "cradle of civilization," which is now known as the Mediterranean basin. But it is Ancel Keys, a biologist at the University of Minnesota, who is often credited with "discovering" the Mediterranean diet through his long-range studies of the affects of nutrition on human health begun in the late 1950s.

Keys had noticed that poor people in Southern Italy's small towns were generally healthier than rich people living in New York, including those who had immigrated from the very same Southern Italian towns. Keys hypothesized that the difference had to do with diet, which led him to embark on the now-famous Seven Countries Study of the dietary habits, cardio-vascular health, and longevity of more than 12,000 middle-aged men in Finland, the Netherlands, Italy, United States, Greece, Japan, and Yugoslavia.

While the men from Finland showed a heart disease rate of 28 percent after 10 years, only 2 percent of the men from the Greek Island of Crete had developed heart disease. The difference between the diets of the two cultures was that while both were getting about 30 to 40 percent of their daily calories from fat, the Cretans' saturated fat was much, much lower.

One puzzling result, however, was that while the men from Crete had the lowest blood cholesterol levels of any of the groups, their diets were not the lowest in saturated fat. That prize went to the Japanese, who ate the least saturated fat of any of the groups. According to the research, Greeks were getting close to half of their dietary fat from monounsaturated fats like olive oil, as well as large doses of omega-3 fatty acids from fish, nuts, and seeds. These healthy fats actually help to lower cholesterol levels and reduce the risk of heart disease. Over the course of the study, the men of Crete were shown to live the longest of any of the groups studied.

At its heart, the Cretan diet was and is now very much in line with the diets of other cultures surrounding the Mediterranean—lots of olive oil (which makes up about one-third of the daily caloric intake of people in those regions), as well as whole grains, beans and legumes, fresh vegetables and fruit, fish and other lean protein, and moderate quantities of cheese, milk, eggs, and red wine. The food is generally plant-based, fresh, and unprocessed. This is the essential makeup of the Mediterranean diet: healthy fats, complex carbohydrates, and plenty of fiber, vitamins, minerals, antioxidants, and phytochemicals.

Keys first publicized his findings in 1975, but it wasn't until the 1990s that the Mayo Clinic, the Harvard School of Public Health, and the European Office of the World Health Organization together developed guidelines for the classic Mediterranean diet. The guidelines were based on the dietary habits of people living in Greece and Southern Italy around 1960, during the time Ancel Keys was conducting his studies, and when people there had the world's lowest rates of chronic disease and among the highest life expectancy. In 2013, UNESCO named this diet pattern an "Intangible Cultural Heritage" of Italy, Portugal, Spain, Morocco, Greece, Cyprus, and Croatia.

Lifestyle is Key

Diet is certainly a big part of what makes the Mediterranean region so healthy, but the overall lifestyle of the Mediterranean is also important to the success of this eating plan. People typically enjoy relaxed meals with their families, often accompanied by red wine. They do their errands on foot, buying fresh, locally grown produce from neighborhood shops and markets and stopping to chat with neighbors and friends. Instead of spending hours commuting in traffic, they spend their time out and about in town. Instead of eating lunch hunched over their office computer, most people walk home to enjoy a meal with their families. They take more vacation time than Americans do because they value the importance of leisure.

The Principles of the Mediterranean Diet

The principles of the Mediterranean diet are simple and easy to follow. Unlike quick-fix, rapid weight-loss diets that demand you eliminate certain foods from your daily life to shed pounds, this is a true change in lifestyle in which you overhaul your attitudes toward food and physical activity and enjoy satisfying meals that include the vital nutrients your body needs to thrive and remain healthy. You'll be pleased to discover that the Mediterranean diet is more about what you can and should eat than what you shouldn't eat. Just a handful of rules will help you experience the benefits of this ancient—and delicious—way of eating and living:

Eat a plant-centered diet.

Build meals around fresh fruits, vegetables, beans, and legumes. These whole foods are central to the health benefits of the Mediterranean diet, as they provide energy in the form of complex carbohydrates, vitamins, minerals, antioxidants, phytochemicals, and fiber. These nutrient-dense foods fill you up and keep you satisfied, thus helping to control your weight while providing disease-fighting nutrients.

Choose whole grains.

Stay away from highly refined grains like white flour and rice, which have been stripped of many of their healthful nutrients, and opt instead for whole grains—whole wheat, brown rice, oats, barley, corn, quinoa, farro, bulgur, millet, and so on, including whole-grain breads and pastas. Whole grains are higher in nutrients, including vitamins, minerals, and fiber.

Eat foods that contain healthy fats, including olives, olive oil, nuts, and seeds.

Olives and olive oil are rich in heart-healthy monounsaturated fats and antioxidants. Add olives to salads, pastas, and stews, or have them as a snack. Use olive oil for cooking, dressing vegetables, or dunking whole-wheat bread. Nuts and seeds, such as almonds, cashews, hazelnuts, pine nuts, pistachios, pumpkin seeds, sesame seeds (including tahini), and walnuts, are also good sources of healthy fats. Choose foods that contain these healthy fats over those that are higher in saturated fats such as butter, cream, lard, or red meat. Trans fats, such as those found in hydrogenated oils and margarine, should be avoided altogether.

Eat fish and/or shellfish at least twice a week.

Fish and shellfish are low in saturated fat and give your body beneficial omega-3 fatty acids. In the Mediterranean, popular fish and shellfish include anchovies, bream, clams, cod, herring, mussels, octopus, salmon, sardines, sea bass, shrimp, squid, crab, and tuna.

Limit dairy consumption to moderate portions of cheese and yogurt.

When consumed in moderation, cheese and yogurt are healthy parts of the Mediterranean diet. Low-fat dairy products ensure that you get the calcium you need for healthy bones. Yogurt also contains probiotics that contribute to healthy digestion.

Eat red meat occasionally in small portions.

Red meat is high in saturated fat, so while it can be included in a healthy diet, it should be eaten in small amounts.

Drink wine (especially red) in moderation.

When consumed in moderation, red wine may help reduce the risk of heart disease by boosting levels of "good" (HDL) cholesterol. Some studies have shown that the health benefits are boosted further by certain antioxidant compounds found specifically in red wine. Moderation generally means one five-ounce glass per day for women and two five-ounce glasses per day for men.

Moderation is key.

While no food is strictly off limits on the Mediterranean diet, it's important to keep portion sizes in check when consuming high-calorie and high-saturated-fat foods like cheese, red meat, refined grains, and foods sweetened with refined sugar.

IKARIA: WHERE AGE IS JUST A NUMBER

Ikaria sits in the Mediterranean Sea, about thirty miles off the coast of Turkey, and though it looks like any other Greek island, it bears one important distinction: The people who live there have some of the highest life expectancies in the world. In fact, centenarians—those who have made it to the ripe old age of 100 and beyond—are not uncommon on Ikaria, and these hearty people also boast exceptionally low rates of cancer, heart disease, depression, and dementia. Plus, many of them continue to be physically (and sexually!) active well into their 90s.

A 2009 study conducted by the University of Athens, known as the Ikaria Study, examined this population in an attempt to uncover the secrets of healthy aging. The study compared people living in what are known as "blue zones," places where people live long lives and remain active well into old age. In addition to the island of Ikaria, the researchers studied people in Sardinia (Italy), Okinawa (Japan), Loma Linda (California), and Nicoya Peninsula (Costa Rica). What they found was that certain behaviors were common to all of these blue zones. These behaviors included the habits that make up the Mediterranean diet—an emphasis on family coherence, avoidance of smoking, eating a plant-based diet, engaging in moderate physical activity every day, and remaining engaged socially and in the community.

On Ikaria, this means eating lots of fresh fruits, vegetables, fish, shellfish, olives, olive oil, and goat's milk; drinking wine with friends; climbing up and down the island's rugged hills to get around; and soaking in the local hot springs. Ikarians avoid processed food, smoking, and stress, and they take daily naps. Older people are treated with respect as an important part of the community.

Take time to enjoy life and be physically active. The Mediterranean way of life is more relaxed than the typical American lifestyle. People in this coastal region take the time to enjoy meals with their families. They walk or bike to work instead of driving. They take far more vacation time. And all of these things reduce stress and contribute to good health.

The Health Benefits of the Mediterranean Diet

Since the Seven Countries Study identified the Mediterranean diet and lifestyle in the 1960s, scientists have continued to analyze its benefits, determining that these eating habits, when adopted in middle age, can help ward off heart attack, stroke, and premature death. Eating a wholesome, plant-centered diet that is low in saturated fat and includes monounsaturated fat and omega-3 fatty acids is clearly a powerful health booster. But to be more specific, health benefits of the Mediterranean-style eating pattern can include:

A longer life. A study published in the *British Journal of Medicine* in 2008, which analyzed the results of twelve different studies ranging in length from three to eighteen years and including more than 1 million subjects, found that following a Mediterranean diet reduced overall mortality by 9 percent.

Reduced risk of heart disease. Numerous studies have found that this diet reduces many of the risk factors that can lead to heart disease, including high (LDL) cholesterol, low (HDL) cholesterol, obesity, and high blood pressure. The landmark Seven Countries Study showed that people who eat a plant-based diet that is low in saturated fat reduce the risk of developing dementia, depression, and Alzheimer's disease, and have a lower incidence of heart disease and cancer. The 1999 Lyon Diet Heart Study, which compared two groups of heart attack survivors—a group that consumed a Mediterranean-type diet and one that followed a low-fat, low-cholesterol diet—found that the Mediterranean diet reduced the risk of death by a whopping 56 percent and the risk of recurrent cardiac events by 72 percent. And in 1989 the DART (Diet And Reinfarction Trial) Study showed that eating a moderate portion

of fish, rich in omega-3, twice a week reduced the risk of death from coronary heart disease by 32 percent and the overall risk of death by 29 percent. Eating fish at least twice a week is one of the key recommendations of the Mediterranean diet.

Reduced risk of type 2 diabetes. A study published in *Diabetes Care* in 2011 demonstrates that following the Mediterranean diet can reduce the risk of developing type 2 diabetes by more than 50 percent.

Reduced risk of various types of cancer. Statistics from the World Health Organization have shown that people who live in the Mediterranean basin have significantly lower rates of cancer than people living in northern Europe or the United States. What's more, when these people migrate to other parts of the world and adopt new eating habits, the protective effect disappears. Research conducted by a group of Italian scientists from 1983 to 2001 found that the diet common to the Mediterranean contributed to a significantly reduced rate of mortality from breast, colorectal, lung, and liver cancers.

Improved brain function and reduced risk of Alzheimer's disease. A review of the existing research on the effect of the Mediterranean diet on brain function, published in the journal *Epidemiology* in 2013, found that adherence to a Mediterranean diet can result in improved cognitive function, a lower risk of developing Alzheimer's disease, and a lower rate of cognitive decline.

THE MEDITERRANEAN KITCHEN

Mediterranean cuisine includes a wide range of foods and cooking styles that span the cultures and countries across the Mediterranean basin. Here we focus on the cuisines of Greece, Southern Italy, Spain, Morocco, Portugal, Cyprus, and Croatia. While the styles and specific ingredients vary from country to country and region to region, these cuisines all employ the basic principles of the Mediterranean diet: they are largely plant-based; they employ healthy fats from olives, olive oil, nuts, and seeds; they include fish and seafood, rich in omega-3; and they limit high-saturated fat foods like red meat, cheese, butter, and cream to small portions eaten occasionally. In all of these Mediterranean countries, red wine is often consumed (in moderation) at mealtime, refined sugar and flour are rarely used, and flavor tends to come more from fresh herbs and redolent spices than from salt or butter.

Because the Mediterranean diet includes many of the foods you likely eat already, adapting your kitchen to begin cooking and eating the foods of the Mediterranean is more a matter of adjusting portion sizes (more plants, fewer animal products) than completely overhauling your pantry. And because the hallmark of Mediterranean cuisine as a whole is fresh ingredients prepared simply, the recipes are quick and easy to make.

Foods to Embrace

The key ingredients of Mediterranean cooking can be found throughout the region and will become an integral part of all of the dishes you cook as you adapt to this way of eating. Stocking your pantry with a few basic ingredients will lead you quickly down the path to a healthier diet. By including these key foods and seasonings in your dishes, you will benefit from healthy fats, lean protein, plenty of fiber, vitamins, minerals, and antioxidants. And, of course, you will also enjoy vibrant flavor in every meal and a well-balanced diet that is never tedious.

Chickpeas and other beans

Chickpeas and other beans can be added to soups and stews, tossed with pasta or other grains, or puréed with other ingredients for a satisfying dip or spread. They are full of fiber, which fills you up and helps regulate blood sugar and reduces the risk of colon cancer and heart disease. Cannellini beans, lentils, split peas, fava beans, and black-eyed peas are also common in Mediterranean cooking and offer similar benefits to chickpeas.

Fresh herbs

Fresh herbs are used to flavor dishes throughout the Mediterranean. Saffron is common in Spain; basil in Italy; mint in Greece; fennel seeds in Cyprus; and parsley, oregano, and rosemary are common in all of the cuisines of the Mediterranean. Many fresh herbs have anti-inflammatory or other healing properties, but they are most valuable for adding a bright punch of flavor without using excessive salt or fat.

Garlic

Garlic was first documented as a cooking ingredient 5,000 years ago, back when the pyramids of Giza were being constructed. It is frequently used to flavor savory dishes in the cuisines of the Mediterranean. Researchers at the Jiangsu Provincial Center for Disease Control and Prevention in China found that raw garlic eaten at least twice a week significantly reduces the risk of lung cancer, and other studies have suggested that this pungent allium may also protect against certain forms of arthritis.

Nuts and seeds

Nuts and seeds can be enjoyed as a savory snack, ground into butters, tossed into salads, crushed to coat fish or meat, or used to thicken sauces or dressings. Like olives and olive oil, they contain heart-healthy monounsaturated fat. They also contain protein, fiber, vitamin E, folate, calcium, and magnesium. The arginine in nut protein, an amino acid, contributes to the maintenance of healthy blood vessels. Almonds, walnuts, pistachios, hazelnuts, and sesame seeds (especially sesame tahini) are found in many Mediterranean dishes.

Oily fish

Oily fish contain heart-protecting omega-3 fatty acid, as well as vitamins A and D. This type of fish and shellfish is the source of much of the protein in the traditional Mediterranean diet. Heart-healthy fish commonly used in Mediterranean cuisines include salmon, mackerel, herring, sardines, trout, and fresh tuna. White fish including sole, cod, haddock, hake, halibut, sea bass, turbot, whiting, and mullet are also good choices of lean protein, as are shellfish like mussels, shrimp, crab, and lobster.

Olive oil

Olive oil is the quintessential ingredient in the Mediterranean kitchen. It is added to salad dressings and drizzled over roasted vegetables, infused with herbs and served in place of butter as a dip for bread, tossed with pasta, and used for cooking foods. Unlike butter, olive oil contains no saturated fat, but it is high in monounsaturated fat, which has been shown to lower bad (LDL) cholesterol and raise good (HDL) cholesterol. Olive oil contains oleic acid, squalene, and terpenoid, compounds that have been shown to reduce inflammation in the body and neutralize the damaging effects of free radicals. Extra-virgin olive oil, which is made by simply pressing olives, is the richest, most flavorful olive oil on the market.

Olives

Olives are a prized food throughout the Mediterranean. They are added to stews, tossed with pasta, sprinkled over salads, used to flavor meat and fish, ground and made into flavorful spreads for bread, or enjoyed as a snack. Like olive oil, they contain monounsaturated fat, oleic acid, and other antioxidants that help reduce the risk of disease.

Peppers

Peppers, both sweet and hot, are eaten raw, roasted, added to soups and stews, or dried, ground, and used as a spice. Peppers of all kinds are loaded with vitamins A and C, beta carotene, fiber, folate, and vitamin K. Like

THE MEDITERRANEAN DIET PYRAMID

The Mediterranean Diet Pyramid represents the 1960 dietary traditions of Crete, an island of Greece, and Southern Italy, when the chronic disease rates there were lower than anywhere else in the world and life expectancies were the longest.

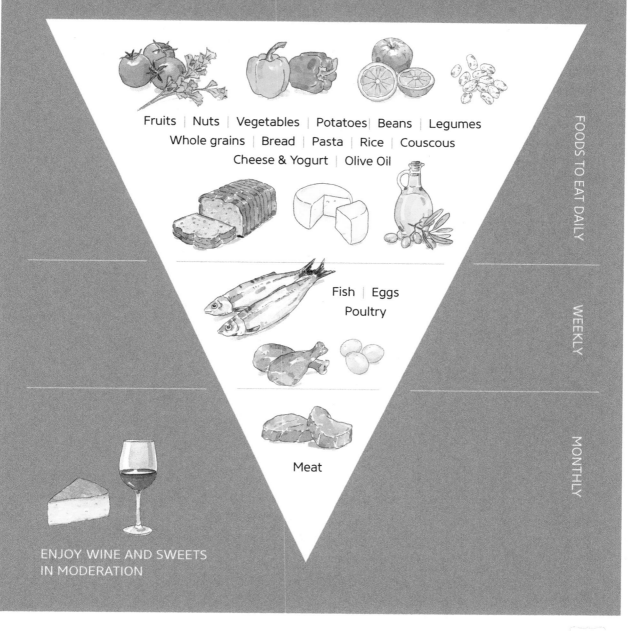

Fruits | Nuts | Vegetables | Potatoes | Beans | Legumes
Whole grains | Bread | Pasta | Rice | Couscous
Cheese & Yogurt | Olive Oil

FOODS TO EAT DAILY

Fish | Eggs
Poultry

WEEKLY

Meat

MONTHLY

ENJOY WINE AND SWEETS
IN MODERATION

tomatoes, red peppers also contain lycopene, lutein, and zeaxanthin, which protect against macular degeneration.

Tomatoes

While tomatoes aren't native to the Mediterranean region (they were brought from the new world by Columbus), they're nonetheless staples in just about every Mediterranean cuisine. They are used fresh and canned, cooked and raw, whole, diced, puréed, and in the form of paste to add color, flavor, and texture to salads, soups, stews, and other savory dishes. Loaded with vitamin C and the heart-healthy antioxidant lycopene, they may help prevent prostate and other cancers.

Whole Grains

Whole grains, including wheat, polenta, bulgur, barley, farro, whole-wheat pasta and couscous, are common in many cuisines of the Mediterranean. Whole, unrefined grains have a lower glycemic index than refined grains, which means they take longer for your body to digest and therefore do not cause blood sugar and insulin spikes the way refined grains and sugars do. Further, they also retain their fiber, minerals like magnesium, vitamins like vitamin E, and other antioxidant phytochemicals. Diets rich in whole grains may protect against heart disease, diabetes, and other chronic diseases.

2

THE MEDITERRANEAN DIET AND YOU

People in the Mediterranean region have been practicing the Mediterranean diet for thousands of years—and enjoying long, healthy lives as a result. Though this way of eating is quite different from the standard American diet, it's easy to follow because it allows for many of the same foods you currently eat, just in different proportions (more plants, fewer animal products). There are no exotic ingredients required, just fresh, wholesome fruits and vegetables, beans, whole grains, fish and shellfish, olives, olive oil, nuts, and seeds—all of which are easy to find at the grocery store or, even better, your local farmers' market. Adopting the Mediterranean diet lifestyle means not only eating more fresh, plant-based foods, healthy fats, and fish, but also including physical activity as a normal part of your day and adjusting your schedule to allow time to cook and enjoy meals. Plus, you get to drink red wine! What could be so hard about that?

ADJUSTING TO THE MEDITERRANEAN DIET

Making significant changes to your eating habits and lifestyle can be challenging when you have to balance shopping, cooking, eating, and exercising with work, family, and other obligations. One of the great things about the Mediterranean diet is that it is meant to make eating as pleasurable as possible, so that you can truly savor your food and spend your mealtimes reconnecting with loved ones. Rather than viewing the dietary changes as an imposition, view this new lifestyle as an opportunity to relax, spend more quality time with family and friends, enjoy your meals, and become more physically active in your day-to-day routines.

Plan Your Week

As with any dietary or lifestyle change, planning ahead is essential to success. Because this diet is so heavily plant based, you'll want to load up on fresh fruits, vegetables, and herbs each week. By keeping your pantry stocked with whole grains like polenta and whole-wheat pasta, dried or canned beans and legumes, olive oil, and even some canned vegetables and fish, you can be sure that you'll always have the ingredients for a healthy meal. If you like to have ready-to-serve meals in the fridge or freezer, cook a big pot of stew, beans, or grains on the weekend and enjoy it throughout the coming week.

Taking your lunch to work will help you stay on track when you can't eat at home. The recent salad-in-a-jar trend is a great way to pack a variety of vegetables and whole grains for days at the office. Add canned tuna or cooked shrimp, chickpeas, or crumbled feta cheese for protein and extra flavor.

If weekday mornings are a scramble for you to get out the door, try making smoothies using fresh or frozen fruit and yogurt (especially Greek yogurt, which contains twice the protein of regular yogurt). Whole grain cereals can be cooked in large batches, then reheated and topped with fruit and nuts for a fast and nutritious breakfast. Or make individual veggie-filled frittatas in a muffin tin and keep them in the fridge or freezer for an easy heat-and-eat breakfast.

Adjust Your Portions

What sets the Mediterranean diet apart from the rest is the fact that, within its parameters, there are really no foods that are completely off limits. The idea is to make up the bulk of your diet with plant-based foods like fruits, vegetables, whole grains, beans, and nuts. Foods like cheese, meat, and sweets are allowed, but they are consumed only occasionally and in small portions.

When many people think of the Mediterranean diet, they think of Italian food, which often brings to mind large bowls of meat-laden pasta and giant, cheesy pizzas, but that is not what Italians and other Mediterraneans typically eat. Pasta, for example, is usually eaten in a small portion as a first course. Pizzas are small and topped with fresh ingredients and a light dusting of cheese. Meat, too, is served in small portions. And just about every meal includes salad along with other vegetables. Dessert, if it is eaten at all, is often a bit of cheese with fresh fruit and honey.

One way to ensure that you are eating enough plant-based foods while following the Mediterranean diet is to fill half your plate with vegetables and fruit, then fill one-quarter with whole grains and the last quarter with lean protein such as beans, fish, shellfish, or poultry. Once every week or two, enjoy a small serving of red meat, such as beef or lamb, or use meat as an accent to add flavor to plant-based stews, sauces, or other dishes.

Here are some guidelines that will help you visualize appropriate portions for the Mediterranean diet:

- One 3-ounce portion of meat (poultry, beef, fish, lamb, or pork) is roughly the size of a deck of cards

- One 1-ounce serving of cheese is about the size of a pair of dice

- One medium piece of fruit is as big as a tennis ball

- 1 cup of vegetables is as big as a baseball

- One ½-cup serving of grains or beans is about the size of the palm of your hand

10 Tips for Sustaining the Mediterranean Diet and Lifestyle

1. Eat your veggies! Choose a rainbow-colored variety of vegetables and work them into every meal you can. Start the day with a veggie-packed omelet or frittata, snack on raw vegetable sticks, have a salad for lunch, and serve sautéed vegetables topped with a small amount of protein for dinner.

2. Replace most red meat with fish or beans. Instead of a burger or steak, have grilled salmon. Instead of beef stew, have Moroccan Red Lentil and Pumpkin Stew (page 160).

3. Dip your bread in olive oil instead of slathering it with butter. Olive oil can also be drizzled over potatoes and other vegetables that you'd normally drench in butter.

4. Visit farmers' markets or a good local grocery store. Seek out high-quality, fresh, locally grown produce whenever possible.

5. Cook your own meals. Mediterranean dishes are known for being straightforward and easy to prepare. Learn to make a handful of key dishes—bean and veggie soups, grilled or roasted fish or poultry, fruit-based desserts, and whole-grain breakfasts and sides—and in no time you'll have meals that are much more delicious and better for you than take-out or frozen dinners.

6. Get to know your spice cabinet and herb garden. Spices and herbs add tons of flavor to meals without excess sodium or saturated fat.

7. Make time to enjoy meals with family and friends. Good, wholesome, delicious food, like that of the Mediterranean diet, isn't meant to be shoveled in while hunched over your computer at work or staring at the television. Try to sit down for at least one meal a day with your family and savor your food along with the conversation.

COMMON FOOD SUBSTITUTIONS

The Mediterranean diet is not about deprivation, but rather about making healthy choices. Here are ten substitutions that you can easily make to transition from a standard American diet to the Mediterranean way of eating.

- INSTEAD OF BUTTER, CHOOSE OLIVE OIL. Use olive oil in place of butter for baking, sautéing, drizzling over cooked or raw vegetables, and serving with bread.

- SUBSTITUTE MASHED AVOCADO FOR CHEESE OR SOUR CREAM. Spread mashed avocado, which is full of monounsaturated fat, on toast, bagels, or sandwiches, or use guacamole in place of sour cream to garnish tacos or chili.

- USE PLAIN YOGURT IN PLACE OF MAYONNAISE OR SOUR CREAM. Yogurt is a much healthier alternative to mayo in pasta and potato salads, creamy salad dressings, and baked goods. It is also delicious dolloped on top of baked potatoes, casseroles, stews, and soups.

- REPLACE SALTY, FATTY CHIPS AND FRENCH FRIES WITH CRUNCHY FRUITS AND VEGETABLES. Since often it is just the texture you crave, you'll find that munching on carrot or celery sticks, or sliced apples or bell peppers can be just as satisfying.

- USE WHOLE-WHEAT FLOUR INSTEAD OF WHITE FLOUR. Whole-wheat flour is a healthy substitute for white flour in breads, muffins, and other baked goods.

- SUBSTITUTE MEAT WITH PLANT-BASED PROTEIN. Replace meat in stuffed peppers or squash recipes with a mixture of beans and whole grains. Try lentils, garbanzo beans, or white beans.

- WHEN BAKING, REPLACE BUTTER WITH APPLESAUCE OR MASHED BANANA. Both butter and mashed banana make a great substitute for butter or oil in a variety of baked goods, including muffins and cakes.

- ENJOY FRESH FRUIT IN PLACE OF SUGARY DESSERTS. Fruits are a healthy way to satisfy your sweet tooth.

- INSTEAD OF FRUIT-FLAVORED YOGURT, BUY PLAIN YOGURT AND ADD YOUR OWN FLAVORING. Store bought fruit-flavored yogurt is usually loaded with sugar and even high-fructose corn syrup. Mix plain yogurt with a drizzle of honey or fresh fruit for a healthy alternative.

- SUBSTITUTE WHOLE-WHEAT PASTA FOR WHITE PASTA. Whole grains like polenta, farro, or bulgur also work well.

8. Move your body more. You don't have to run out and join a gym or train for a marathon. Just commit to walking to work, taking a bike ride around the neighborhood, or walking the dog. Aim for a minimum of 30 minutes a day of physical activity.

9. Drink red wine in moderation. Women should drink no more than one 5-ounce glass of wine per day and men should drink no more than two 5-ounce glasses per day.

10. Don't deprive yourself. If you love steak or cheese or chocolate ice cream, don't cut yourself off. You can still enjoy those foods in small servings on occasion. Just make sure you get the bulk of your sustenance from the healthy recommended foods—fish, olives, olive oil, beans, whole grains, nuts, seeds, vegetables, and fruit.

The Countries of the Mediterranean Diet

The Mediterranean encompasses a very large region and a wide range of culinary traditions, including countries in southern Europe, North Africa, and the Middle East. And regardless of the differences between these cultures, their traditional cuisines share very similar foundations—plant-based, high in monounsaturated fat and omega-3 fatty acids, and low in saturated fat—and these common threads form the fabric of what is now known as "the Mediterranean diet."

Based on dishes and preparations from Croatia, Cyprus, Greece, Morocco, Portugal, Southern Italy, and Spain—with a few key contributions from Lebanon, southern France, and Turkey—the Mediterranean diet reflects the warm temperature and coastal environment of these regions, where plant-based foods flourish, seafood is plentiful, and olive groves dot the landscape.

Croatia Croatia is just across the Adriatic Sea from Italy and its cuisine is heavily influenced by Italian cuisine. Fresh seafood, tomatoes, eggplant, peppers, chiles, olives, and olive oil are abundant. Cheese is a staple, especially *paški sir*, the prized cheese from Pag island, made from the milk of a sheep breed only found there. Croatia is also a major producer of red wine.

Cyprus The island of Cyprus borrows culinary influences from both Greece and Turkey. Locally sourced foods—whole grains, beans, fruit (apricots, dates, figs), vegetables (zucchini and other squash, peppers, eggplant, cucumbers), herbs and spices (oregano, mint, thyme, cinnamon), and seafood—make up the bulk of the diet. Olives and olive oil are used frequently. Whole wheat is used in the form of bulgur, and to make bread. Semolina, the hard grains left after milling wheat into flour, is used in desserts. Halloumi is Cypriot cheese made from mostly goat's milk, mixed with sheep's milk, and sometimes cow's milk. This unique, flavorful cheese is often served fried or grilled.

Greece Often referred to as the original Mediterranean diet, Greek cuisine showcases a wide range of colorful vegetables (peppers, squash, onions, garlic, eggplant, leafy greens, artichokes, fennel), fruits (figs, grapes, dates, cherries, apples, plums), citrus, and fresh herbs (bay leaves, parsley, oregano, dill, mint, thyme). Olive and olive oil are used in many

COUNTRY	COMMON INGREDIENTS	FLAVOR PROFILE
CROATIA	Seafood, olive oil, olives, tomatoes, eggplant, peppers, chiles, sheep's milk cheese, crusty bread	Fresh, herby, warm spices, citrus
CYPRUS	Seafood, olive oil, olives, fruit (apricots, dates, figs), vegetables (zucchini, peppers, eggplant, cucumbers), herbs and spices (oregano, mint, thyme, cinnamon), wheat (semolina and bulgur), halloumi cheese made of sheep's and goat's milk	Fresh, herby, warm spices
GREECE	Seafood, olive oil, olives, lemon, fresh herbs (oregano, thyme, mint), yogurt, feta cheese, vegetables (tomatoes, cucumbers, eggplant, zucchini, peppers), wheat, rice, honey, walnuts, pistachios	Bright, fresh, herby, citrus
MOROCCO	Seafood, olive oil, olives, garlic, dates, figs, citrus, vegetables (peppers, greens, tomatoes, potatoes), spices (turmeric, saffron, ginger, paprika, cayenne, cumin, cardamom, cinnamon, mace, nutmeg), fresh herbs (parsley, cilantro, mint), couscous, bread, honey, almonds	Fruity, warm spices, herby, spicy
PORTUGAL	Seafood, olive oil, garlic, vegetables (tomatoes, leafy greens, onions, potatoes), spiced sausage, coriander, rice, beans, almonds	Hearty, rich
SOUTHERN ITALY	Seafood, olive oil, olives, tomatoes, garlic, parsley, peppers, chiles, sheep's milk cheeses, dried pasta, bread, rice, beans, honey, hazelnuts	Robust, hearty, spicy
SPAIN	Seafood, olive oil, olives, garlic, spiced sausage, cured ham, paprika (sweet, spicy, and smoked), saffron, citrus, peppers, rice, beans, almonds	Robust, spicy

different dishes, and the proteins of choice come from the sea (squid, octopus, tuna, sardines) and are often grilled or roasted. Chicken, pork, lamb, and rabbit are eaten occasionally. Dairy is consumed mostly in the form of yogurt and cheese, particularly feta, which is usually made from a combination of goat's and sheep's milk. Rice is common and wheat is a staple used to make pasta, bulgur, pita bread, and crusty peasant bread. Desserts are often sweetened with honey, and nuts like walnuts and pistachios are used frequently. Red wine and ouzo (anise-flavored liqueur) are popular beverages.

Morocco   Moroccan cuisine features a wide array of available fruits (oranges, melons, dates, figs), vegetables (peppers, greens, tomatoes, potatoes), nuts (especially almonds), grains, seafood, beans (chickpeas), and olives. The food is heavily spiced with a range of seasonings including turmeric, saffron, ginger, paprika, cayenne, cumin, cardamom, cinnamon, mace, and nutmeg, along with fresh herbs like parsley, cilantro, mint, oregano, and garlic. Staple grains are couscous, tiny pasta made from durum wheat, and round, flat Moroccan bread. Desserts usually include almonds and honey.

Portugal   The Portuguese eat more fish than any other Europeans. Cod that has been preserved in salt—called bacalhau—is the most commonly eaten fish in Portugal, but other popular seafood include squid, sardines, octopus, crab, shrimp, lobster, mackerel, sea bass, clams, mussels, oysters, and scallops. Beans and potatoes are often cooked in hearty stews or soups like caldo verde, an iconic Portuguese soup of potato, onion, olive oil, kale, and chouriço, Portugal's version of the Spanish sausage called chorizo. Chouriço and linguiça sausage are used to flavor beans and stews. Leafy greens, potatoes, cabbage, tomatoes, and onions are common vegetables. Olive oil is the cooking fat of choice, and garlic and coriander are common seasonings.

Southern Italy   Southern Italy's cuisine has roots in peasant-style cooking and relies heavily on ingredients plucked from the surrounding sea (octopus, squid, sardines, anchovies), or raised on hardscrabble mountain farms (broccoli rabe, cauliflower). Hot chile peppers, garlic, eggplant, fava beans, chickpeas, and other vegetables that grow well in warm climates are prominent. Dried pastas, thin-crust pizzas, and crusty breads are staples. Sheep's milk cheeses, like Pecorino and ricotta salata, are also common as well as mozzarella di bufala, made from the milk of the domestic water buffalo. Olive oil is the fat of choice for both cooking and dressings, and, as in Greece, desserts often feature honey and nuts. The region is renowned for its wines.

Spain   Spain's long coastline and warm climate make for a cuisine heavy on fish, seafood, fruits, and vegetables. Meat, especially pork, is popular. Jamón serrano, Spain's version of prosciutto, and chorizo, a well-seasoned sausage, are often served as snacks or appetizers, and added to seafood dishes, soups, or stews for the flavor. Olive oil is used liberally, and the predominant flavors come from paprika (sweet, spicy, and smoked versions), saffron, citrus, and peppers. Rice, beans, and almonds are common. Spain is famous for its wines as well as its sherry (fortified wine).

Cuisine from Other Mediterranean Cultures (Lebanon, southern France, and Turkey)   Though they are not always named specifically in association with the Mediterranean diet, Lebanon, southern France, and Turkey also share this way of eating, as well as many common ingredients and cooking techniques.

Adopting any big lifestyle changes can be challenging. The Mediterranean diet includes plenty of delicious, satisfying foods, but if you're not used to eating this way, you may feel a bit lost at first. Having a detailed plan is a great way to get you started on the right track. It's like a road map that shows you exactly where to turn every step of the way.

This 14-day meal plan is designed to help you through the first two weeks of your Mediterranean diet. The menus are just suggestions, however, so you should feel free to switch out any meals that don't appeal to you with other recipes in this book.

WEEK ONE

	BREAKFAST	LUNCH	DINNER
SUNDAY	Mixed Vegetable Frittata with Ricotta Cheese	Flatbread with Ricotta and Orange-Raisin Relish	Spanish Orzo with Shrimp, Chorizo, and Peas
MONDAY	Breakfast Polenta with Pears and Hazelnuts	Leftover Mixed Vegetable Frittata with Ricotta Cheese	Baked Chicken with Olives and Raisins
TUESDAY	Sweet Spiced Couscous with Dried Fruit	Italian Tuna and Olive Salad	Seared Steak with Fig and Garlic Sauce
WEDNESDAY	Greek yogurt with honey, almonds, and fruit	Bocadillo with Herbed Tuna and Piquillo Peppers	Greek Pan-Seared Chicken with Roasted Lemon and Fresh Oregano
THURSDAY	Leftover Sweet Spiced Couscous with Dried Fruit	Classic Hummus with Tahini, with pita bread and salad	Southern Italian Seafood Stew in Tomato Broth
FRIDAY	Greek Yogurt, Fig, and Almond Phyllo Tarts	Portuguese Greens and Sausage Soup (Caldo Verde)	Eggplants Stuffed with Walnuts and Feta
SATURDAY	Baked Eggs with Chorizo, White Beans, and Tomatoes	Roasted Vegetable Bocadillo with Romesco Sauce	Grilled Whole Chicken with Piri Piri Sauce

WEEK TWO

	BREAKFAST	LUNCH	DINNER
SUNDAY	Spanish Tortilla with Potatoes and Peppers	Moroccan Lamb Wrap with Harissa	Whole-Wheat Spaghetti à la Puttanesca
MONDAY	Breakfast Panini with Eggs, Olives, and Tomatoes	Chicken Gyros with Tzatziki and Garlic-Herb Oil	Spiced Lamb Stew with Fennel and Dates
TUESDAY	Leftover Spanish Tortilla with Potatoes and Peppers	Falafel Wraps with Tahini Sauce	Sicilian Baked Cod with Herbed Breadcrumbs
WEDNESDAY	Greek yogurt with honey, almonds, and berries	Saffron-Scented Chickpea Soup with Crispy Pasta	Whole-Wheat Capellini with Sardines, Olives, and Manchego
THURSDAY	Grilled Halloumi with Whole-Wheat Pita Bread, Tomatoes, Cucumbers, and Olives	Sautéed Mushroom, Onion, and Pecorino Panini	Turkish Chicken Kabobs with Aleppo Pepper and Yogurt
FRIDAY	Omelet with Tomatoes, Red Onion, Olives, and Feta	Greek Lemon-Rice Soup with Fish	Tomato, Olive, Caper, and Anchovy Pizza
SATURDAY	Greek Yogurt, Fig, and Almond Phyllo Tarts	Pear, Manchego, and Spanish Chorizo Bocadillo	Vegetarian Paella with Green Beans and Chickpeas

SNACKS   Choose one or two of the following snacks each day (* Recipes included)

Warm Olives with Rosemary and Garlic*

Celery sticks with nut butter (almond, peanut, hazelnut)

Greek Yogurt Labneh with Preserved Lemon and Mint Pesto*

Charred Eggplant Dip with Feta and Mint*, with whole-wheat pita bread

Grilled Halloumi with Watermelon, Cherry Tomatoes, Olives, and Herb Oil*

Classic Hummus with Tahini*, with veggie sticks for dipping

Hard-boiled egg sprinkled with smoked paprika

Thin slices of jamón serrano or prosciutto with melon wedges

Cherry tomatoes with goat cheese, basil leaves, and olives

Plain Greek yogurt with honey, fruit, and toasted nuts

Mixed toasted nuts

3

BREAKFAST

GREECE

GREEK YOGURT, FIG, AND ALMOND
PHYLLO TARTS

Serves 6   Prep time: 15 minutes   Cook time: 6 minutes

VEGETARIAN | QUICK & EASY   *Crispy phyllo tartlets layered with a bit of rich butter and sliced almonds topped with creamy Greek yogurt and luscious sliced figs turns a fruit-and-yogurt breakfast into an experience that's worth waking up for. You can substitute berries or another fruit for the figs if they are out of season.*

6 tablespoons unsalted butter, melted
12 (9-by-13-inch) sheets phyllo dough
6 tablespoons sliced almonds, divided
24 ounces Greek yogurt
12 large mission figs, stemmed and sliced
2 tablespoons honey

1. Preheat the oven to 400°F.

2. Brush two baking sheets lightly with butter.

3. Lay a sheet of phyllo dough on one of the baking sheets and brush it lightly with the melted butter. Lay a second phyllo sheet on top of the first, brushing again with the melted butter.

4. Sprinkle 1 tablespoon of sliced almonds over the phyllo. Add two more sheets of phyllo, brushing each with butter. Sprinkle the fourth phyllo sheet with 1 tablespoon of almonds.

5. Top with two more sheets of phyllo, each brushed with butter, and top with 1 tablespoon of almonds. Repeat the process with the remaining butter, phyllo, and almonds on the second baking sheet.

6. Bake in the preheated oven for about 6 minutes, until golden brown and crisp. Remove from the oven and cool the phyllo mixture on the baking sheets.

7. Cut the stacks into 6 squares each. Place one square on each serving plate. Top each square with about 4 ounces of the yogurt (dividing the yogurt evenly among the six servings).

8. Divide the fig slices among the six servings, laying them on top of the yogurt. Top each stack with one of the remaining phyllo squares, drizzle honey over the top, and serve immediately.

PER SERVING: CALORIES: 427; TOTAL FAT: 19G; SATURATED FAT: 10G; CARBS: 52G; PROTEIN: 17G; SODIUM: 272MG; FIBER: 5G

GREECE

HONEY-VANILLA GREEK YOGURT
WITH BLUEBERRIES

Serves 2 to 3   Prep time: 2 minutes

VEGETARIAN | GLUTEN-FREE | QUICK & EASY   *Greek yogurt may seem like just the latest passing fad, but it is actually a healthy way to start the day. To make Greek yogurt, the watery part of the milk is strained off, giving the yogurt a thick, creamy consistency. Besides just making it taste great, even a bit decadent, straining off the whey also removes much of the sugar and carbohydrates and it also means that a typical serving has far more protein than the usual stuff. Sweeten it with honey and top it with fresh fruit for a simple and delicious breakfast.*

2 cups plain Greek yogurt
¼ to ½ cup honey
¾ teaspoon vanilla extract
1 cup blueberries

1. In a medium bowl, stir together the yogurt, honey (start with the smaller amount; you can always add more later), and vanilla. Taste and add additional honey, if needed.

2. To serve, spoon the sweetened yogurt mixture into bowls and top with the blueberries.

PER SERVING: CALORIES: 295; TOTAL FAT: 0G; SATURATED FAT: 0G; SODIUM: 82MG; CARBS: 55G; FIBER: 2G; PROTEIN: 23G

BREAKFAST POLENTA
WITH PEARS AND HAZELNUTS

Serves 4   Prep time: 5 minutes   Cook time: 40 minutes

GLUTEN-FREE | VEGETARIAN   *Polenta, the Italian version of cornmeal grits, is usually served in savory preparations, but it also makes a fantastic hot breakfast cereal. Simmered with milk and butter, sweetened with honey, and topped with juicy sweet pears and crunchy hazelnuts, it is a creamy, satisfying, and nutritious breakfast.*

4 cups water
½ teaspoon salt
1 cup yellow polenta
1 tablespoon butter
¼ cup milk
2 tablespoons honey, plus additional
   for serving if desired
¼ teaspoon cinnamon
1 ripe pear, thinly sliced
2 tablespoons coarsely
   chopped hazelnuts

★ TIP: For a quicker version, start with precooked polenta in a tube. Dice small and heat in a saucepan with ½ cup water over medium heat. Stir frequently and mash the polenta cubes with the back of a spoon to break them down, until the mixture is smooth and heated through, about 5 minutes. Add the remaining ingredients according to the recipe steps and serve.

1. In a medium saucepan, bring the water to a boil over high heat. Add the salt and reduce the heat so that the water is just simmering.

2. Add the polenta in a thin stream while whisking constantly. Continue to whisk until the mixture is smooth and without lumps. Continue to cook over low heat, stirring frequently, for 5 minutes. The polenta will become very thick.

3. Stir in the butter and milk, cover, and continue to cook, stirring occasionally, until the mixture reaches the desired thickness, about 30 more minutes.

4. Remove from the heat and stir in the honey and cinnamon.

5. To serve, ladle the hot polenta into serving bowls and top with the pear slices, hazelnuts, and additional honey, if desired.

PER SERVING: CALORIES: 309; TOTAL FAT: 11G; SATURATED FAT: 3G; CARBS: 48G; PROTEIN: 6G; SODIUM: 328MG; FIBER: 4G

GREECE

OMELET WITH TOMATOES,
RED ONION, OLIVES, AND FETA

Serves 2   Prep time: 5 minutes   Cook time: 10 minutes

VEGETARIAN | GLUTEN-FREE | QUICK & EASY   *The flavors of Greece—briny Kalamata olives, bright tomatoes, herby oregano, and salty-tangy feta cheese—come together in this simple egg breakfast. Omelets are a quick and easy way to get helpings of vegetables, healthy fats, and protein early in the day. For a complete breakfast, serve these omelets with slices of wholegrain toast.*

1 tablespoon olive oil, divided
2 tablespoons finely diced red onion
8 to 10 cherry tomatoes, halved
4 to 6 Kalamata olives, sliced
4 large eggs, lightly beaten
½ teaspoon minced fresh oregano
½ teaspoon salt
¼ teaspoon freshly ground black pepper
½ cup crumbled feta cheese

★ TIP: If you wish to serve four people, double all of the ingredients, but cook two separate two-egg omelets, each with half of the vegetable filling and cheese.

1. Heat ½ tablespoon olive oil in a medium skillet set over medium-high heat. Add the diced onion and cook, stirring, until it begins to soften, about 2 minutes.

2. Add the tomatoes and cook, stirring, until they begin to blister and break down, about 2 minutes more. Stir in the olives and transfer the mixture to a small bowl or plate. Wipe out the pan.

3. In a medium bowl, combine the eggs, oregano, salt, and pepper and whisk to combine.

4. Heat the remaining ½ tablespoon of oil in the skillet over medium heat. Add the egg mixture. As the egg begins to set around the edges, use a spatula to push the edges in towards the center and tilt the pan this way and that to allow the unset egg mixture to spread under and around the set egg. Continue until all of the egg is just set.

5. Sprinkle the cheese and the vegetable mixture over one half of the omelet. Using the spatula, flip the other half of the omelet over the vegetables and cheese. Cut in half and serve immediately.

PER SERVING: CALORIES: 457; TOTAL FAT: 31G; SATURATED FAT: 13G; CARBS: 24G; PROTEIN: 25G; SODIUM: 1,455MG; FIBER: 7G

FETA AND HERB FRITTATA
IN A PHYLLO CRUST

Serves 6   Prep time: 10 minutes   Cook time: 30 minutes

VEGETARIAN   Frittata *is really an Italian invention—a sort of crustless quiche—but here it takes on a decidedly Greek flare with fresh basil and parsley, tangy feta cheese, and a crisp phyllo crust. The frittata can be served either warm or at room temperature.*

¼ cup olive oil, divided

1 medium onion, halved and thinly sliced

1 clove garlic, minced

8 sheets phyllo dough

8 eggs

¼ cup chopped fresh basil, plus additional for garnish

¼ cup chopped flat-leaf parsley, plus additional for garnish

1 teaspoon salt

½ teaspoon freshly ground black pepper

4 ounces crumbled feta cheese

1. Preheat the oven to 400°F.

2. Heat 2 tablespoons of the olive oil in a medium skillet over medium-high heat. Add the onions and cook, stirring frequently, until softened, about 5 minutes. Add the garlic and cook, stirring, for 1 minute more. Remove from the heat and set aside to cool.

3. While the onion mixture is cooling, make the crust. Place a damp towel on the counter and cover with a sheet of parchment paper. Lay the phyllo sheets in a stack on top of the parchment and cover with a second sheet of parchment and then a second damp towel.

4. Brush some of the remaining olive oil in a 9-by-9-inch baking dish or a 9-inch pie dish. Layer the softened phyllo sheets in the prepared dish, brushing each with some of the olive oil before adding the next phyllo sheet.

5. Next, make the filling. In a large bowl, whisk the eggs with the onion mixture, basil, parsley, salt, and pepper. Add the feta cheese and mix well. Pour the egg mixture into the prepared crust, folding any excess phyllo inside the baking dish.

6. Bake in the preheated oven for about 25 to 30 minutes, until the crust is golden brown and the egg filling is completely set in the center. Cut into rectangles or wedges and serve garnished with basil and parsley.

★ TIP: If you don't have phyllo dough, you can use a premade pie crust instead or omit the crust all together. To make a gluten-free crust, press hash brown potatoes into the baking dish and parbake them until they are lightly browned; fill and bake the frittata according to the recipe steps.

PER SERVING: CALORIES: 415; TOTAL FAT: 20G; SATURATED FAT: 6G; CARBS: 43G; PROTEIN: 17G; SODIUM: 1,070MG; FIBER: 2G

BREAKFAST PANINI
WITH EGGS, OLIVES, AND TOMATOES

Serves 4 Prep time: 5 minutes Cook time: None

VEGETARIAN | DAIRY-FREE | QUICK & EASY Pagnotta foggiana *is a rustic, round Italian bread from the southern region of Puglia. It is the perfect size and shape for this recipe, but any rustic Italian bread will do. You could use ciabatta, ciabatta rolls, or focaccia. Even a baguette would work in a pinch.*

1 (12-ounce) round whole-wheat pagnotta foggiana or other round, crusty bread

2 tablespoons olive oil

½ cup sliced pitted cured olives, such as Kalamata

8 hard-boiled eggs, peeled and sliced into rounds

2 medium tomatoes, thinly sliced into rounds

12 large leaves fresh basil

1. Split the bread horizontally and brush the cut sides with the olive oil.

2. Arrange the sliced olives on the bottom half of the bread in a single layer. Top with a layer of the egg slices, then the tomato slices, and finally the basil leaves. Cut the sandwich into quarters and serve immediately.

★ TIP: For perfect hard-boiled eggs, choose a saucepan that is large enough to hold all of the eggs in a single layer. Fill the saucepan two-thirds full with water and bring the water to a boil over high heat. Reduce the heat to low and use a long-handled spoon to gently lower the eggs into the water. Simmer for 13 minutes, drain, and immediately place the eggs in an ice water bath to cool.

PER SERVING: CALORIES: 427; TOTAL FAT: 21G; SATURATED FAT: 5G; CARBS: 39G; PROTEIN: 23G; SODIUM: 674MG; FIBER: 7G

MIXED VEGETABLE FRITTATA
WITH RICOTTA CHEESE

Serves 6   Prep time: 5 minutes, plus 15 minutes to soak bread   Cook time: 40 minutes

VEGETARIAN   *Frittata is the Italians' answer to the omelet. Instead of cooking eggs in a thin layer and then gingerly folding them around a filling, the ingredients are mixed right into the egg in the skillet and the whole thing is put into a hot oven to finish.*

12 eggs

¼ cup milk

1 teaspoon salt

½ teaspoon freshly ground black pepper

1⅓ cups day-old whole-wheat bread cubes (crusts removed, cut into 1-inch cubes)

2 tablespoons olive oil

1 onion, cut into ½-inch strips

1 red bell pepper, cored, seeded, and cut into ¼-inch-wide slices

1 green bell pepper, cored, seeded, and cut into ¼-inch-wide slices

1⅓ cups whole-milk ricotta cheese

1. Preheat the oven to 350°F.

2. In a large bowl, whisk together the eggs, milk, salt, and pepper. Add the bread and stir to coat. Let the bread soak in the egg mixture for about 15 minutes.

3. In a large (10-inch), oven-safe skillet, heat the olive oil over medium heat. When the oil is hot, add the onion and cook, stirring frequently, until softened, about 5 minutes.

4. Stir in the red and green bell peppers and continue to cook, stirring, for 5 minutes more.

5. Spread the vegetables out into an even layer in the skillet and then pour the egg mixture over the top. Cook without stirring for about 5 minutes, until the bottom just begins to brown. Dollop the ricotta onto the top by large spoonfuls.

6. Place the skillet in the preheated oven and bake for about 25 minutes, until the center is set. Serve the frittata hot or at room temperature.

PER SERVING: CALORIES: 334; TOTAL FAT: 20G; SATURATED FAT: 7G; CARBS: 18G; PROTEIN: 21G; SODIUM: 705MG; FIBER: 3G

SPAIN

BAKED EGGS
WITH CHORIZO, WHITE BEANS, AND TOMATOES

Serves 4   Prep time: 5 minutes   Cook time: 20 minutes

DAIRY-FREE | GLUTEN-FREE | QUICK & EASY   *A quick tomato sauce with white beans makes a flavorful nest for perfectly cooked eggs. Topped with slices of chorizo that crisp up in the oven, this dish looks fancy, but requires minimal effort. Best of all, it's got vegetables, protein, and heart-healthy fats. Feel free to sprinkle a bit of grated manchego cheese over the top just before serving.*

2 tablespoons olive oil
1 shallot, diced
1 clove garlic, minced
1 (14-ounce) can diced tomatoes,
    with juice
1 (14-ounce) can white beans, such as
    cannellini beans, drained and rinsed
½ teaspoon smoked paprika
¼ teaspoon ground cumin
¼ teaspoon cayenne
1 teaspoon salt
½ teaspoon freshly ground black pepper
1 link Spanish chorizo, thinly sliced
4 eggs

1. Preheat the oven to 400°F.

2. In a medium skillet, heat the olive oil over medium heat. Add the shallot and garlic and cook, stirring, until softened, about 3 minutes.

3. Add the tomatoes along with their juice, beans, paprika, cumin, cayenne, salt, and pepper. Cook, stirring frequently, until the sauce begins to thicken, about 8 minutes.

4. Place four 6- or 8-ounce ramekins on a baking sheet. Spoon the tomato mixture into the ramekins, dividing equally. Top with the slices of chorizo, dividing them between the ramekins. Make a well in the middle of each ramekin and break an egg into the middle of each one. Bake in the preheated oven for about 10 to 12 minutes, until the egg white is set, but the yolk is still runny. Serve immediately.

PER SERVING: CALORIES: 605; TOTAL FAT: 23G; SATURATED FAT: 7G; CARBS: 66G; PROTEIN: 37G; SODIUM: 1,105MG; FIBER: 17G

SPAIN

SPANISH TORTILLA
WITH POTATOES AND PEPPERS

Serves 6   Prep time: 5 minutes   Cook time: 50 minutes

VEGETARIAN | GLUTEN-FREE | DAIRY-FREE   *In Spain,* tortilla *refers to the Spanish version of an omelet or frittata, sort of an egg-and-potato skillet casserole. The traditional versions are incredibly simple—with just eggs, potatoes, and seasonings cooked in olive oil—but variations like this one including onions and peppers are common as well.*

½ cup olive oil, plus 2 tablespoons, divided

2 pounds baking potatoes, peeled and cut into ¼-inch slices

2 onions, thinly sliced

1 roasted red pepper, drained and cut into strips

6 eggs

2 teaspoons salt

1 teaspoon freshly ground black pepper

1. In a large skillet over medium heat, heat ½ cup of the olive oil. Add the potatoes and cook, stirring occasionally, until the potatoes are tender, about 20 minutes. Remove the potatoes from the pan with a slotted spoon and discard the remaining oil.

2. In a medium skillet over medium heat, heat the remaining 2 tablespoons of olive oil. Add the onions and cook, stirring frequently, until softened and golden brown, about 10 minutes. Remove the onions from the pan with a slotted spoon, leaving the oil in the pan, and add them to the potatoes. Add the pepper slices to the potatoes as well.

3. In a large bowl, whisk together the eggs, salt, and pepper. Add the cooked vegetables to the egg mixture and gently toss to combine.

4. Heat the medium skillet over low heat. Add the egg-vegetable mixture to the pan and cook for about 10 minutes, until the bottom is lightly browned. Use a spatula to loosen the tortilla and transfer the whole thing to a large plate, sliding it out of the pan so that the browned side is on the bottom. Invert the skillet over the tortilla and then lift the plate to flip it back into the skillet with the browned side on top. Return to the stove and continue to cook over low heat until the tortilla is fully set in the center, about 5 more minutes.

5. Serve the tortilla warm or at room temperature.

PER SERVING: CALORIES: 370; TOTAL FAT: 26G; SATURATED FAT: 5G; CARBS: 29G; PROTEIN: 9G; SODIUM: 876MG; FIBER: 5G

GREECE

WARM FAVA BEANS
WITH WHOLE-WHEAT PITA

Serves 4   Prep time: 5 minutes   Cook time: 10 minutes

VEGETARIAN | DAIRY-FREE | QUICK & EASY   *Beans are an important part of the Mediterranean diet, and warm, stewed bean dishes are common breakfast fare in many parts of the region. This Greek recipe uses canned fava beans and classic Greek flavors—onion, garlic, tomato, parsley, and lemon. A bit of crushed red pepper flakes adds a little kick, and a crumble of feta cheese would not be unwelcome.*

1½ tablespoons olive oil
1 large onion, diced
1 large tomato, diced
1 clove garlic, crushed
1 (15-ounce) can fava beans, not drained
1 teaspoon ground cumin
¼ cup chopped fresh parsley
¼ cup lemon juice
Salt
Freshly ground black pepper
Crushed red pepper flakes
4 whole-grain pita bread pockets

1. Heat the olive oil in a large skillet set over medium-high heat. Add the onion, tomato, and garlic and cook, stirring, for about 3 minutes, until the vegetables soften.

2. Add the fava beans, along with the liquid from the can, and bring to a boil.

3. Lower the heat to medium and stir in the cumin, parsley, and lemon juice. Season with salt, pepper, and crushed red pepper.
Simmer over medium heat, stirring occasionally, for 5 minutes.

4. While the beans are simmering, heat the pitas in a toaster oven or in a cast-iron skillet over medium heat. To serve, cut the pitas into triangles for dipping into and scooping the bean mixture, or halve the pitas and fill the pockets up with beans.

★ TIP: This recipe uses canned fava beans, which can be found in ethnic markets or in the international foods aisle of many supermarkets. If you can't find fava beans, substitute canned lima beans or butter beans.

PER SERVING: CALORIES: 524; TOTAL FAT: 8G; SATURATED FAT: 1G; CARBS: 86G; PROTEIN: 32G; SODIUM: 394MG; FIBER: 31G

SPICED POTATOES
WITH CHICKPEAS

Serves 4   Prep time: 10 minutes   Cook time: 10 minutes

VEGETARIAN | GLUTEN-FREE | QUICK & EASY   *This simple one-pot breakfast is full of flavor from a mix of Moroccan spices and herbs. The chickpeas add plenty of protein, but feel free to top the hash with poached or fried eggs if you like. Also, feel free to play with other greens here instead of spinach: chard or kale will work just as well.*

¼ cup olive oil

3 medium potatoes, peeled and shredded

2 cups finely chopped baby spinach

1 medium onion, finely diced

1 tablespoon minced fresh ginger

1 teaspoon ground cumin

1 teaspoon ground coriander

½ teaspoon ground turmeric

½ teaspoon salt

1 (15-ounce) can chickpeas, drained and rinsed

1 medium zucchini, diced

¼ cup chopped cilantro

1 cup plain yogurt

1. Heat the olive oil in a large skillet over medium heat. Add the potatoes, spinach, onions, ginger, cumin, coriander, turmeric, and salt and stir to mix well. Spread the mixture out into an even layer and let cook, without stirring, for about 5 minutes until the potatoes are crisp and browned on the bottom.

2. Add the chickpeas and zucchini and mix to combine, breaking up the layer of potatoes. Spread the mixture out again into an even layer and continue to cook, without stirring, for another 5 minutes or so, until the potatoes are crisp on the bottom.

3. To serve, garnish with cilantro and yogurt.

★ TIP: Substituting 4 cups frozen shredded hash browned potatoes for the whole potatoes shaves most of the prep time from this recipe. Look for hash brown potatoes without additives or seasonings.

PER SERVING: CALORIES: 679; TOTAL FAT: 20G; SATURATED FAT: 3G; CARBS: 100G; PROTEIN: 28G; SODIUM: 388MG; FIBER: 24G

MOROCCO

SWEET SPICED COUSCOUS
WITH DRIED FRUIT

Serves 4   Prep time: 5 minutes   Cook time: 15 minutes

VEGETARIAN | QUICK & EASY   *Here, couscous is cooked in cinnamon-infused milk, studded with dried apricots and currants, and sweetened with honey. Feel free to change it up, adding whatever dried fruits you have on hand or topping it with a handful of chopped nuts.*

3 cups milk

1 cinnamon stick

1 cup uncooked whole-wheat couscous

½ cup chopped dried apricots

¼ cup dried currants

2 tablespoons honey, plus additional for serving if desired

¼ teaspoon salt

4 teaspoons melted butter

1. In a medium saucepan, combine the milk and the cinnamon stick and heat over medium-high heat until just beginning to simmer (do not boil).

2. Remove the pan from the heat and stir in the couscous, apricots, currants, honey, and salt. Cover the pan and let the mixture stand for 15 minutes, until the couscous is tender.

3. Discard the cinnamon stick and fluff the couscous with a fork.

4. To serve, spoon the mixture into serving bowls, top each with a teaspoon of melted butter, and drizzle additional honey over, if desired.

PER SERVING: CALORIES: 333; TOTAL FAT: 8G; SATURATED FAT: 5G; CARBS: 54G; PROTEIN: 12G; SODIUM: 266MG; FIBER: 3G

SAVORY BREAKFAST POLENTA
WITH ITALIAN SAUSAGE, TOMATOES, AND PECORINO

Serves 4   Prep time: 5 minutes   Cook time: 50 minutes

GLUTEN-FREE   *More commonly associated with dinner than breakfast, polenta—a sort of porridge of coarsely ground cornmeal—makes a fitting base for sausage and vegetables for a satisfying morning meal. Top with a bit of freshly grated Parmesan or Pecorino cheese if you like.*

3¼ cups water

1 cup uncooked polenta

1 (16-ounce) bag frozen yellow corn kernels, thawed

1 teaspoon salt

½ teaspoon pepper

4 ounces Pecorino cheese, divided

1 pound bulk Italian sausage

1 pound cherry tomatoes (about 3½ cups)

½ cup chopped fresh basil

1. Preheat the oven to 425°F.

2. In a 13-by-9-inch glass baking dish, stir together the water, polenta, corn, salt, and pepper. Cook in the preheated oven for about 40 minutes, until the polenta is soft. Stir in 3 ounces of the cheese and return the polenta to the oven for another 10 minutes or so.

3. While the polenta bakes, brown the sausage in a large skillet over medium-high heat, about 5 minutes. Stir in the tomatoes, cover, lower the heat to medium, and let simmer until the tomatoes begin to break down, about 6 minutes more. Remove the lid and continue to simmer for about 10 more minutes, until the juice evaporates and the sauce begins to thicken. Remove from the heat and stir in the basil.

4. To serve, spoon the polenta onto serving plates and top with the sausage mixture. Sprinkle some of the remaining cheese over the top and serve hot.

PER SERVING: CALORIES: 778; TOTAL FAT: 45G; SATURATED FAT: 16G; CARBS: 57G; PROTEIN: 40G; SODIUM: 2,239MG; FIBER: 5G

SPAIN

PAN CON TOMATE
WITH JAMÓN SERRANO

Serves 4   Prep time: 5 minutes   Cook time: 8 minutes

QUICK & EASY   *This traditional Spanish dish is so simple that it hardly needs a recipe. In its simplest form, it is just bread rubbed with garlic and ripe tomato, drizzled with olive oil, and sprinkled with flaky sea salt. This recipe includes a bit of the Spanish ham* jamón serrano*, but you could substitute thinly sliced Spanish chorizo or, for a vegetarian version, manchego cheese.*

4 slices thick, crusty whole-wheat bread, or 4-inch lengths baguette halved lengthwise

4 cloves garlic, peeled and halved crosswise

2 medium, very ripe tomatoes, grated into a bowl on the large holes of a box grater

2 tablespoons best quality olive oil (ideally from Spain)

1 teaspoon flaky sea salt

4 thin slices jamón serrano

1. Preheat the oven to 500°F.

2. Place the bread (cut-side up if using baguette) on a baking sheet and bake in the preheated oven until golden brown, about 6 to 8 minutes.

3. Rub the cut side of the garlic over the cut side of the bread. Spoon some of the grated tomato onto each piece of bread, spreading it with the back of the spoon.

4. Drizzle a bit of the olive oil over each slice, sprinkle with salt, and top with a slice of jamón serrano. Serve immediately.

PER SERVING: CALORIES: 267; TOTAL FAT: 15G; SATURATED FAT: 4G; CARBS: 15G; PROTEIN: 18G; SODIUM: 1,295MG; FIBER: 3G

CYPRUS

GRILLED HALLOUMI
WITH WHOLE-WHEAT PITA BREAD, TOMATOES, CUCUMBERS, AND OLIVES

Serves 4   Prep time: 5 minutes   Cook time: 10 minutes

VEGETARIAN | QUICK & EASY   *Halloumi is a Cypriot cheese that is made from a combination of sheep's and goat's milk. Its flavor is salty but mild and its texture slightly springy. It holds its shape well when cooked, making it perfect for grilling.*

2 teaspoons olive oil

8 (½-inch-thick) slices of halloumi cheese

4 whole-wheat pita rounds

1 Persian cucumber, thinly sliced

1 large tomato, sliced

½ cup pitted Kalamata olives

1. Brush a bit of olive oil on a grill pan and heat it over medium-high heat.

2. Brush the cheese slices all over with olive oil. Add the cheese slices in a single layer and cook until grill marks appear on the bottom, about 3 minutes. Flip the slices over and grill until grill marks appear on the second side, about 2 to 3 minutes more.

3. While the cheese is cooking, heat the pita bread, either in a skillet or in a toaster.

4. Serve the cheese inside of the pita pockets with the sliced cucumber, tomato, and olives.

★ TIP: If you don't have a grill pan, you can fry the cheese in a skillet with a little olive oil.

PER SERVING: CALORIES: 449; TOTAL FAT: 24G; SATURATED FAT: 13G; CARBS: 41G; PROTEIN: 21G; SODIUM: 1,191MG; FIBER: 6G

SPAIN

WHOLE-WHEAT TOAST
WITH APRICOTS, BLUE CHEESE, AND HONEY

Serves 2   Prep time: 5 minutes   Cook time: 5 minutes

VEGETARIAN | QUICK & EASY   *This delicious toast makes a satisfying and simple breakfast, where sweet apricots and honey balance creamy, salty blue cheese. Choose a Spanish blue cheese like cabrales, which is made from a combination of raw cow, goat, and sheep's milk. You can substitute another fruit, such as figs or peaches for the apricots, and walnuts or hazelnuts for the almonds.*

2 thick slices crusty whole-wheat bread
1 tablespoon olive oil
2 apricots, halved and cut into
   ¼-inch-thick slices
2 ounces blue cheese
2 tablespoons honey
2 tablespoons toasted slivered almonds

1. Preheat the broiler to high.

2. Brush the bread on both sides with the olive oil. Arrange the slices on a baking sheet and broil until lightly browned, about 2 minutes per side.

3. Arrange the apricot slices on the toasted bread, dividing equally. Sprinkle the cheese over the top, dividing equally. Return the baking sheet to the broiler and broil for 1 to 2 minutes until the cheese melts and just begins to brown. Remove from the oven and serve drizzled with honey and garnished with the toasted almonds.

PER SERVING: CALORIES: 379; TOTAL FAT: 20G; SATURATED FAT: 7G; SODIUM: 595MG; CARBS: 40G; FIBER: 4G; PROTEIN: 13G

4

SOUPS AND SALADS

SOUTHERN ITALY

CALABRIAN
TOMATO AND ONION SOUP

Serves 6   Prep time: 5 minutes   Cook time: 1 hour and 15 minutes

VEGETARIAN   *This is a Southern Italian version of France's* soupe a l'oignon *(onion soup). Rich with San Marzano tomatoes and made hearty with cheesy toast buried in each bowl, this soup makes a great late night meal or a substantial first course to precede grilled meat or fish.*

½ cup extra-virgin olive oil

2 cloves garlic, sliced

2 large yellow onions, halved and thinly sliced crosswise

1 tablespoon salt

1 (28-ounce) can San Marzano tomatoes

4 cups water

6 slices hearty whole-wheat bread

6 thin slices provolone cheese

⅓ cup grated Pecorino Romano cheese

1. Heat the olive oil in a stockpot over medium heat. Add the garlic, onion, and salt and cook, stirring frequently, for about 15 minutes, until they are very soft and golden.

2. Add the tomatoes and water and bring to a boil. Reduce the heat to low, cover, and simmer for 45 minutes. Remove the lid and continue to simmer for another 15 minutes to thicken the soup.

3. Just before serving, toast the bread slices. Place one slice of bread in the bottom of each of 6 soup bowls and top each with a slice of the provolone. Ladle the soup into the bowls, being careful to include a good portion of the onions in each.

4. Serve hot, garnished with the Pecorino Romano cheese.

PER SERVING: CALORIES: 364; TOTAL FAT: 26G; SATURATED FAT: 7G; CARBS: 22G; PROTEIN: 13G; SODIUM: 1,640MG; FIBER: 5G

MOROCCO

CARROT SOUP
WITH YOGURT AND SPICES

Serves 4   Prep time: 10 minutes   Cook time: 20 minutes

GLUTEN-FREE | QUICK & EASY   *A velvety and bright purée of fresh carrots shot through with the vibrant kick of ginger, cinnamon, cumin, and coriander—this soup is like a bowlful of Mediterranean sunshine. The tangy, creamy yogurt and sharp, herby cilantro add both visual and flavor contrasts that really make this simple soup sing.*

2 tablespoons olive oil
1 medium onion, diced
6 medium carrots, peeled, cut into
    ½-inch dice
1 teaspoon salt
1 teaspoon ground coriander
1 teaspoon ground cumin
½ teaspoon ground cinnamon
¼ teaspoon ground ginger
¼ teaspoon ground turmeric
4 cups chicken broth
1 tablespoon honey
Juice of ½ lemon
1 cup plain yogurt
¼ cup chopped cilantro

1. Heat the oil in a stockpot over medium-high heat. Add the onion and cook, stirring frequently, until softened, about 5 minutes. Add the carrots, salt, coriander, cumin, cinnamon, ginger, turmeric, and broth and bring to a boil.

2. Lower the heat to low, cover, and simmer for about 15 minutes, until the carrots are tender.

3. Using an immersion blender or in batches in a countertop blender, purée the soup until smooth. Reheat if needed and stir in the honey and lemon juice.

4. Serve hot, drizzled with yogurt and garnished with cilantro.

PER SERVING: CALORIES: 214; TOTAL FAT: 9G; SATURATED FAT: 2G; CARBS: 22G; PROTEIN: 10G; SODIUM: 1,456MG; FIBER: 3G

SPAIN

CLASSIC GAZPACHO

Serves 4   Prep time: 10 minutes, plus 3 hours to chill   Cook time: None

VEGETARIAN | DAIRY-FREE   *Classic gazpacho—a chilled soup made with ripe summer tomatoes and cucumber—is spiked with sherry vinegar and thickened with bread. This version sticks to tradition for a refreshing soup that is perfect for a warm day. If you don't have sherry vinegar, you can substitute red wine vinegar.*

2 cups cubed day-old whole-wheat bread
2 cloves garlic
2 teaspoons salt
2 pounds ripe tomatoes, seeded
1 medium cucumber, peeled and seeded
¼ green bell pepper, seeded
1 tablespoon sherry vinegar
½ cup olive oil, plus more for garnish
Freshly ground black pepper, for garnish

1. In a medium bowl, cover the bread with water and soak for about 10 minutes. Drain and squeeze out the excess water.

2. While the bread is soaking, bring a small pot of water to a boil. Add the garlic and let simmer for 2 to 3 minutes. Remove the garlic and discard the water.

3. In a blender, combine the garlic, soaked bread, salt, tomatoes, cucumber, bell pepper, and vinegar. Process until smooth. With the blender running, slowly add ½ cup of the olive oil in a thin stream. Process until the soup is emulsified. Taste and add additional seasoning if needed.

4. Cover and refrigerate the soup for at least 3 hours to chill thoroughly and let the flavors meld.

5. Serve chilled, garnished with a drizzle of olive oil and freshly ground pepper.

PER SERVING: CALORIES: 447; TOTAL FAT: 28G; SATURATED FAT: 4G; CARBS: 42G; PROTEIN: 12G; SODIUM: 1,507MG; FIBER: 8G

SAFFRON-SCENTED
CHICKPEA SOUP WITH CRISPY PASTA

Serves 4   Prep time: 5 minutes   Cook time: 15 minutes

DAIRY-FREE | QUICK & EASY   *This soup, from the region of Puglia in Southern Italy, takes a handful of simple ingredients and magically transforms them into a very special—and delicious—soup. If you prefer to use dried chickpeas, soak them in water overnight and cook them in the broth until tender before proceeding with the recipe as written.*

4 cups chicken broth

2 (15-ounce) cans chickpeas, drained and rinsed

1 teaspoon salt

Pinch of saffron

⅓ cup olive oil

6 ounces pappardelle or other wide ribbon-shaped pasta, cooked according to the package instructions, divided

1. In a stockpot, combine the broth and chickpeas and bring to a boil over medium-high heat. Reduce the heat to medium-low and simmer for about 5 minutes, until the chickpeas are nice and tender. Add the salt and saffron. Continue to simmer the soup over low heat.

2. Meanwhile, heat the olive oil in a large skillet over medium-high heat. Dry ⅓ of the cooked noodles well with paper towels or a clean dishtowel and add them to the hot oil. Cook, flipping as needed with a spatula, until the noodles are crisp and golden brown, about 2 minutes. Transfer the fried noodles to a paper towel-lined plate, reserving the oil in the pan.

3. Stir the remaining cooked noodles into the soup. Serve the soup hot, garnished with the fried noodles and a drizzle of the olive oil from the skillet.

PER SERVING: CALORIES: 690; TOTAL FAT: 25G; SATURATED FAT: 4G; CARBS: 89G; PROTEIN: 30G; SODIUM: 1,381MG; FIBER: 19G

PORTUGUESE GREENS AND SAUSAGE SOUP (CALDO VERDE)

Serves 4 to 6   Prep time: 10 minutes   Cook time: 20 minutes

GLUTEN-FREE | DAIRY-FREE | QUICK & EASY   Caldo verde, *or "green soup" is, unofficially at least, the national dish of Portugal. True to the peasant cooking roots of most Mediterranean cuisine, it is made from humble ingredients—a bit of sausage, lots of greens, potatoes, onions, and garlic—but makes a satisfying and flavorful meal. You can substitute collard greens, Swiss chard, or any other hearty, dark, leafy green vegetable for the kale.*

8 ounces Portuguese chouriço or linguiça, cut into ¼-inch-thick rounds

2–3 tablespoons olive oil

1 large yellow onion, diced

2 cloves garlic, sliced

4 medium potatoes, peeled and thinly sliced

1 pound kale, thick center ribs removed, leaves julienned

4 cups chicken broth

4 cups water

1 teaspoon salt

★ TIP: This soup is quick to make, but it is even better on the second day. Let it cool to room temperature before refrigerating. Bring it back to a boil just before serving.

1. In a stockpot over medium heat, cook the sausage for about 3 to 5 minutes, until lightly browned. Transfer the sausage to a plate.

2. Add 2 to 3 tablespoons of olive oil to the rendered fat in the pot and heat over medium heat. Add the onion and cook, stirring frequently, until softened, about 5 minutes. Add the garlic and cook about 1 minute more. Add the potatoes, greens, broth, water, and salt. Bring to a boil, cover, and reduce the heat to low. Simmer until the potatoes are tender, about 10 minutes. Add half of the sausage.

3. Using an immersion blender, or in batches in a countertop blender, purée the soup. Return to medium heat and bring back to a boil. Taste and add additional seasoning if needed.

4. Serve the soup hot, garnished with the remaining slices of sausage.

PER SERVING: CALORIES: 436; TOTAL FAT: 23G; SATURATED FAT: 6G; CARBS: 41G; PROTEIN: 17G; SODIUM: 1,451MG; FIBER: 6G

GREECE

GREEK LEMON-RICE SOUP WITH FISH

Serves 8   Prep time: 10 minutes   Cook time: 30 minutes

DAIRY-FREE | GLUTEN-FREE *Greek cuisine is known for its simple, fresh flavors. This classic lemon-rice soup, traditionally made with chicken, is bright with fresh lemon juice and thickened with rice and eggs. It makes a great starter or a light meal.*

2 tablespoons olive oil

1 medium onion, finely diced

⅔ cup Arborio rice

10 cups chicken broth

1 pound firm white fish fillet, such as tilapia, cod, or haddock, cut into 2-inch pieces

½ cup lemon juice

2 eggs

1 teaspoon freshly ground black pepper

2 tablespoons chopped flat-leaf parsley, for garnish

1. In a stockpot, heat the olive oil over medium-high heat. Add the onion and cook, stirring frequently, until softened, about 5 minutes. Stir in the rice until the grains are well coated with oil.

2. Add the broth and bring to a boil. Reduce the heat to medium-low and simmer for about 18 minutes, until the rice is just tender.

3. Add the fish and simmer until the fish is just cooked through, about 5 minutes.

4. In a heat-safe glass measuring cup with a spout, whisk together the lemon juice, eggs, and pepper. While whisking, add a few ladles full of the hot broth to the egg mixture. Stir the egg mixture into the soup. Taste and add additional seasoning if needed. Serve immediately, garnished with the parsley.

★ TIP: Instead of fish, you can make this soup with leftover roasted or grilled chicken breast, or even store-bought rotisserie chicken. Just dice the skinned chicken breast and add it to the soup at the end of step two and cook just until heated through, about 3 minutes.

PER SERVING: CALORIES: 221; TOTAL FAT: 7G; SATURATED FAT: 2G; CARBS: 16G; PROTEIN: 22G; SODIUM: 1,019MG; FIBER: 1G

ARUGULA AND FENNEL SALAD
WITH FRESH BASIL

Serves 4   Prep time: 5 minutes, plus 10 minutes to marinate   Cook time: None

VEGETARIAN | GLUTEN-FREE | QUICK & EASY   *Fennel grows abundantly throughout the Mediterranean where it has been used in cooking since ancient times. Because pretty much the whole plant can be eaten—the dried seeds, the fresh bulb and fronds, and even the pollen—it is amazingly versatile. Raw and thinly sliced, the bulb is crunchy with a mild licorice-like flavor that pairs beautifully with a salty cheese like feta and tangy lemon dressing.*

3 tablespoons olive oil

3 tablespoons lemon juice

1 teaspoon honey

½ teaspoon salt

1 medium bulb fennel,
   very thinly sliced

1 small cucumber, very thinly sliced

2 cups arugula

¼ cup toasted pine nuts

½ cup crumbled feta cheese

¼ cup julienned fresh basil leaves

1. In a medium bowl, whisk together the olive oil, lemon juice, honey, and salt. Add the fennel and cucumber and toss to coat and let sit for 10 minutes or so.

2. Put the arugula in a large salad bowl. Add the marinated cucumber and fennel, along with the dressing, to the bowl and toss well. Serve immediately, sprinkled with pine nuts, feta cheese, and basil.

★ TIP: Trim the feathery fronds from the fennel bulb and reserve them to use as an herb in salad dressings and other sauces.

PER SERVING: CALORIES: 237; TOTAL FAT: 21G; SATURATED FAT: 5G; CARBS: 11G; PROTEIN: 6G; SODIUM: 537MG; FIBER: 3G

CYPRUS

ROASTED CAULIFLOWER SALAD
WITH TAHINI-YOGURT DRESSING AND TOASTED WALNUTS

Serves 8 to 10   Prep time: 10 minutes   Cook time: 35 minutes

VEGETARIAN | DAIRY-FREE | GLUTEN-FREE   *Tahini is a thick paste made of ground sesame seeds, which is common in some Mediterranean cuisines, especially Cypriot, Syrian, Lebanese, and Israeli. Look for it near the nut butters in Middle Eastern markets, large-chain supermarkets, and health food stores. In this recipe, a rich tahini sauce is paired with sweet and earthy roasted cauliflower.*

10 cups cauliflower florets (1- to 2-inch florets, from 1 to 2 heads)

1½ tablespoons olive oil

¾ teaspoon kosher salt, divided

½ cup walnuts

½ cup yogurt

¼ cup tahini, at room temperature

¼ cup lemon juice, plus more to taste

¼ cup water

1 tablespoon honey

¼ cup chopped fresh dill

1 tablespoon minced shallot

★ TIP: This salad can be made up to one day in advance, minus the walnuts. Keep the walnuts in a covered container at room temperature, and keep the salad in an airtight container in the refrigerator. When you're ready to serve it, bring the salad to room temperature and sprinkle the walnuts over the top.

1. Preheat the oven to 450°F.

2. On a large baking sheet, toss the cauliflower with the olive oil and ¼ teaspoon of the salt. Spread the cauliflower out in a single layer and roast in the preheated oven for about 30 minutes, until it is tender and browned on the bottom. Place the cooked cauliflower in a large bowl and set aside to cool while you prepare the rest of the salad.

3. Toast the walnuts in a skillet over medium heat until fragrant and golden, about 5 minutes. Chop and set aside.

4. In a blender or food processor, combine the yogurt, tahini, lemon juice, water, and honey and process until smooth. If the mixture is too thick, add a tablespoon or two of additional water.

5. Add the dill, shallot, and the remaining ½ teaspoon of salt to the cauliflower and toss to combine. Add the dressing and toss again to coat well.

6. Serve the salad at room temperature, garnished with the toasted walnuts.

PER SERVING: CALORIES: 153; TOTAL FAT: 10G; SATURATED FAT: 1G; CARBS: 12G; PROTEIN: 6G; SODIUM: 249MG; FIBER: 4G

LEBANON

TOASTED PITA BREAD SALAD
WITH FRESH MINT AND LEMON DRESSING

Serves 4   Prep time: 10 minutes   Cook time: None

VEGETARIAN | DAIRY-FREE | QUICK & EASY   *Fattoush is a popular bread salad enjoyed all over the Middle East, especially in Lebanon. Crispy pieces of pita bread are tossed with tomatoes, lettuce, cucumber, and other vegetables and coated with a tangy lemon dressing. Sumac is a tart Mediterranean berry that grows in Southern Italy and throughout the Middle East. It is usually dried, ground, and sprinkled over vegetables and other foods. Here it enhances the tanginess of the lemon dressing.*

For the dressing
½ cup lemon juice
½ cup olive oil
1 small clove garlic, minced
1 teaspoon salt
½ teaspoon ground sumac
¼ teaspoon freshly ground black pepper

For the salad
2 cups shredded Romaine lettuce
1 large or 2 small cucumbers, seeded and diced
2 medium tomatoes, diced
½ cup chopped fresh flat-leaf parsley leaves
¼ cup chopped fresh mint leaves
1 small green bell pepper, diced
1 bunch scallions, thinly sliced
2 whole-wheat pita bread rounds, toasted and broken into quarter-sized pieces
Ground sumac for garnish

1. To make the dressing, whisk together the lemon juice, olive oil, garlic, salt, sumac, and pepper in a small bowl.

2. To make the salad, in a large bowl, combine the lettuce, cucumber, tomatoes, parsley, mint, bell pepper, scallions, and pita bread. Toss to combine. Add the dressing and toss again to coat well.

3. Serve immediately sprinkled with sumac.

★ TIP: Ground sumac is available in Middle Eastern markets or online. If you can't find it, however, you can substitute the finely grated zest of one-half lemon.

PER SERVING: CALORIES: 359; TOTAL FAT: 27G; SATURATED FAT: 4G; CARBS: 29G; PROTEIN: 6G; SODIUM: 777MG; FIBER: 6G

SOUTHERN ITALY

ITALIAN TUNA AND OLIVE SALAD

Serves 4   Prep time: 5 minutes, plus 1 hour to chill   Cook time: None

DAIRY-FREE | GLUTEN-FREE   *Tuna imported in jars from Italy, Spain, and other parts of the Mediterranean is meatier and more flavorful than the canned stuff we're used to. If you can't find it, just be sure to use solid white tuna packed in olive oil instead of water. Canned or jarred tuna and a few other simple ingredients are all you need to make this salad, and it makes for a satisfying lunch, especially when served with a side of crusty whole-wheat bread.*

¼ cup olive oil
3 tablespoons white wine vinegar
1 teaspoon salt
1 cup pitted green olives
1 medium red bell pepper, seeded and diced
1 small clove garlic, minced
2 (6-ounce cans or jars) tuna in olive oil, well drained
Several leaves curly green or red lettuce

1. In a large bowl, whisk together the olive oil, vinegar, and salt.

2. Add the olives, bell pepper, and garlic to the dressing and toss to coat. Stir in the tuna, cover, and chill in the refrigerator for at least 1 hour to let the flavors meld.

3. To serve, line a serving bowl with the lettuce leaves and spoon the salad on top. Serve chilled.

PER SERVING: CALORIES: 343; TOTAL FAT: 28G; SATURATED FAT: 4G; CARBS: 6G; PROTEIN: 21G; SODIUM: 1,217MG; FIBER: 2G

SOUTHERN ITALY

CAPRESE SALAD
WITH FRESH MOZZARELLA, BALSAMIC VINEGAR, AND PESTO

Serves 6 to 8   Prep time: 10 minutes

VEGETARIAN | GLUTEN-FREE | QUICK & EASY   *Basil pesto and balsamic vinegar are both northern Italian specialties, but they so perfectly complement the rich red summer tomatoes that grow throughout the southern regions and the creamy mozzarella cheese that also originated in the south. Mozzarella was originally made of buffalo's milk, but now is often made with cow's milk. If you can find mozzarella di bufala—made with Italian buffalo's milk—it's worth the extra cost.*

For the pesto

2 cups (packed) fresh basil leaves, plus more for garnish

⅓ cup pine nuts

3 garlic cloves, minced

½ cup (about 2 ounces) freshly grated Parmesan cheese

½ cup extra-virgin olive oil

Salt

Freshly ground black pepper

For the salad

4 to 6 large, ripe tomatoes, cut into thick slices

1 pound fresh mozzarella, cut into thick slices

3 tablespoons balsamic vinegar

Salt

Freshly ground black pepper

1. To make the pesto, in a food processor combine the basil, pine nuts, and garlic and pulse several times to chop. Add the Parmesan cheese and pulse again until well combined. With the food processor running, add the olive oil in a slow, steady stream. Transfer to a small bowl, taste, and add salt and pepper as needed. Slice, quarter, or halve the tomatoes, based on your preferred salad presentation.

2. To make the salad, on a large serving platter arrange the tomato slices and cheese slices, stacking them like fallen dominoes.

3. Dollop the pesto decoratively on top of the tomato and cheese slices. (You will likely have extra pesto. Refrigerate the extra in a tightly sealed container and use within 3 days, or freeze it for up to 3 months.)

4. Drizzle the balsamic vinegar over the top, garnish with basil leaves, sprinkle with salt and pepper to taste, and serve immediately.

PER SERVING: CALORIES: 398; TOTAL FAT: 32G; SATURATED FAT: 11G; SODIUM: 474MG; CARBS: 8G; FIBER: 1G; PROTEIN: 23G

BACALHAU
AND BLACK-EYED PEA SALAD

Serves 4   Prep time: 10 minutes, plus 24 hours soaking time   Cook time: 10 minutes

DAIRY-FREE | GLUTEN-FREE   *Black-eyed peas are common in Portuguese cuisine, often mixed with potatoes or fish in salads. This simple salad uses* bacalhau, *the beloved Portuguese salt-preserved cod. Garnish this salad with chopped hard-boiled eggs or cured black olives if you like.*

1 pound bacalhau (salt cod) fillets

¼ cup olive oil, plus 1 tablespoon, divided

3 tablespoons white wine vinegar

1 teaspoon salt

¼ teaspoon freshly ground black pepper

1 (15-ounce) can black-eyed peas, drained and rinsed

1 small yellow onion, halved and thinly sliced crosswise

1 small clove garlic, minced

¼ cup chopped fresh flat-leaf parsley leaves, divided

1. Rinse the cod under cold running water to remove any surface salt. Place the fish pieces in a large nonreactive pot, cover with water and refrigerate (covered) for 24 hours, changing the water several times.

2. Pour off the water, refill the pot with clean water and gently boil the cod until it flakes easily with a fork, about 7 to 10 minutes (or longer), depending on the thickness. Drain and set aside to cool.

3. To make the dressing, whisk together the oil, vinegar, salt, and pepper in a small bowl.

4. In a large bowl, combine the beans, onion, garlic, and ¾ of the parsley. Add the dressing and mix to coat well. Stir in the salt cod, cover, and chill in the refrigerator for at least 2 hours to let the flavors meld. Let sit on the countertop for 30 minutes before serving.

5. Serve garnished with the remaining parsley.

★ TIP: Canned chickpeas, butter beans, or even white beans like cannellini can be substituted for the black-eyed peas.

PER SERVING: CALORIES: 349; TOTAL FAT: 18G; SATURATED FAT: 2G; CARBS: 16G; PROTEIN: 32G; SODIUM: 8,401MG; FIBER: 4G

GREECE

MARINATED GREEK SALAD
WITH OREGANO AND GOAT CHEESE

Serves 4   Prep time: 10 minutes, plus 1 hour to marinate   Cook time: none

GLUTEN-FREE | VEGETARIAN   *Marinating cucumbers, onions, and banana peppers infuses them with the flavor of the herbs and vinegar and mellows the bite of the onions and peppers. If you can't find small banana peppers, use any mild pepper, such as sliced red or orange bell peppers or other small mild chiles. Serve this salad alongside grilled meat or fish, or stuff it into pita bread with a falafel patty for a healthy lunch.*

½ cup white wine vinegar

1 small garlic clove, minced

1 teaspoon crumbled dried
    Greek oregano

½ teaspoon salt

¼ teaspoon freshly ground black pepper

2 Persian cucumbers, sliced thinly

4 to 6 long, skinny red or yellow banana
    peppers or other mild peppers

1 medium red onion, cut into rings

1 pint mixed small heirloom tomatoes,
    halved

2 ounces crumbled goat cheese or feta

1. In a large, nonreactive (glass, ceramic, or plastic) bowl, whisk together the vinegar, garlic, oregano, salt, and pepper. Add the cucumbers, peppers, and onion and toss to mix. Cover and refrigerate for at least 1 hour.

2. Add the tomatoes to the bowl and toss to coat. Serve topped with the cheese.

PER SERVING: CALORIES: 98; TOTAL FAT: 4G; SATURATED FAT: 2G;
CARBS: 13G; PROTEIN: 4G; SODIUM: 460MG; FIBER: 3G

5

SMALL PLATES AND SNACKS

GREECE

WARM OLIVES
WITH ROSEMARY AND GARLIC

Serves 4   Prep time: 5 minutes   Cook Time: 3 minutes

VEGETARIAN | DAIRY-FREE | GLUTEN-FREE | QUICK & EASY   *Meals in Greece almost always include olives in some form or another. Here they are warmed in garlic- and herb-infused olive oil, enhancing their already irresistible flavor.*

1 tablespoon olive oil

1 clove garlic, chopped

2 sprigs fresh rosemary

¼ teaspoon salt

1 cup whole cured black olives, such as Kalamata

1. Heat the olive oil in a medium saucepan over medium heat. Add the garlic, rosemary, and salt. Reduce the heat to low and cook, stirring, for 1 minute.

2. Add the olives and cook, stirring occasionally, for about 2 minutes, until the olives are warm.

3. To serve, scoop the olives from the pan using a slotted spoon into a serving bowl. Pour the rosemary and garlic over the olives and serve warm.

PER SERVING: CALORIES: 71; TOTAL FAT: 7G; SATURATED FAT: 1G; CARBS: 3G; PROTEIN: 1G; SODIUM: 441MG; FIBER: 1G

GREECE

GREEK YOGURT LABNEH
WITH PRESERVED LEMON AND MINT PESTO

Serves 4 to 6   Prep time: 5 minutes, plus 24 hours to drain   Cook time: None

VEGETARIAN | GLUTEN-FREE   *Labneh is a rich, creamy thickened yogurt that is eaten throughout the Middle East. It makes a luscious topping for toast or fruit. Here it's combined with an intensely flavored pesto of fresh herbs and Preserved Lemons with Moroccan Spices (page 246), delicious scooped up with warm whole-wheat pita bread.*

2 cups plain whole-milk or
   2% Greek yogurt

½ teaspoon salt

Juice of 1 lemon

1 small clove garlic, minced

1 cup chopped fresh flat-leaf
   parsley leaves

½ cup chopped fresh mint leaves

1 Preserved Lemons with Moroccan
   Spices (page 246), flesh removed
   and discarded, rind rinsed and
   coarsely chopped, divided

¼ teaspoon ground cumin

⅓ cup olive oil

★ TIP: Preserved Lemon is easy to make and keeps for months in the refrigerator, but it can also be purchased at Middle Eastern or European markets or online.

1. To make the labneh, in a small bowl, stir together the yogurt and salt.

2. Layer 2 layers of cheesecloth in a fine-meshed sieve and set the sieve over a medium bowl. Put the yogurt mixture into the sieve, cover, and refrigerate for at least 24 to 48 hours.

3. Pour off the excess water from the labneh and place it in a medium bowl. Stir in the lemon juice and about 1 tablespoon of water. Continue adding water in small amounts until the mixture is the consistency of a thick sour cream.

4. In a food processor, combine the garlic, parsley, mint, 2 tablespoons preserved lemon rind, cumin, and olive oil and process until smooth. Taste and add additional seasoning if needed. Spoon ⅔ of the pesto mixture into the labneh and stir to mix. Place the labneh into a serving bowl and spoon the remaining pesto over the top. Serve at room temperature, garnished with the remaining preserved lemon.

PER SERVING: CALORIES: 200; TOTAL FAT: 15G; SATURATED FAT: 3G; CARBS: 10G; PROTEIN: 7G; SODIUM: 314MG; FIBER: 1G

CROATIA

CROATIAN RED PEPPER DIP
(AJVAR)

Serves 4 to 6   Prep time: 10 minutes, plus time to cool   Cook time: 30 minutes

VEGETARIAN | DAIRY-FREE | GLUTEN-FREE   *In Croatia and other parts of Eastern Europe, this smoky, savory roasted pepper and eggplant dip (called* ajvar*) is enjoyed every fall, when red peppers are harvested. The only accompaniment it needs is some crusty bread, but it also makes a fantastic sauce for grilled meat or fish and can be used as a sandwich spread.*

4 or 5 medium red bell peppers
1 medium eggplant (about ¾ pound)
¼ cup olive oil, divided
1 teaspoon salt, divided
½ teaspoon freshly ground black
    pepper, divided
4 cloves garlic, minced
1 tablespoon white vinegar

1. Preheat the broiler to high.

2. Line a large baking sheet with aluminum foil.

3. Brush the peppers and eggplant all over with 2 tablespoons of the olive oil and sprinkle with ½ teaspoon of the salt and ¼ teaspoon of the pepper. Place the peppers and the eggplant on the prepared baking sheet and broil, turning every few minutes, until the skins are charred on all sides. The peppers will take about 10 minutes and the eggplant will take about 20 minutes.

4. When the peppers are fully charred, remove them from the baking sheet, place them in a bowl, cover with plastic wrap, and let them steam while the eggplant continues to cook. When the eggplant is fully charred and soft in the center, remove it from the oven and set aside to cool.

5. When the peppers are cool enough to handle, slip the charred skins off. Discard the charred skins. Seed the peppers and place them in a food processor.

6. Add the garlic to the food processor and pulse until the vegetables are coarsely chopped. Add the rest of the olive oil, the vinegar, and remaining ½ teaspoon of salt and process to a smooth purée.

7. Transfer the vegetable mixture to a medium saucepan and bring to a simmer over medium-high heat. Lower the heat to medium-low and let simmer, stirring occasionally, for 30 minutes. Remove from the heat and cool to room temperature. Serve at room temperature.

★ TIP: Ajvar can be stored in an airtight container in the refrigerator for up to two weeks. Bring it to room temperature before serving.

PER SERVING: CALORIES: 144; TOTAL FAT: 11G; SATURATED FAT: 2G; CARBS: 12G; PROTEIN: 2G; SODIUM: 471MG; FIBER: 5G

GREECE

SPANIKOPITA TRIANGLES
WITH SPINACH AND FETA

Makes 25 to 30 triangles   Prep time: 20 minutes   Cook time: 30 minutes

VEGETARIAN   *Crisp triangles of flaky phyllo dough filled with savory feta and spinach are always a hit. Phyllo dough—a flour-based pastry that is stretched into tissue-thin sheets—has been made in the Mediterranean since at least the 13th century. While making it at home requires far more effort than most home cooks can muster, good quality, machine-made phyllo dough can be purchased frozen in most supermarkets. Thaw it in the refrigerator overnight before using.*

1 (10-ounce) package frozen spinach, thawed and drained

½ cup olive oil, divided

1 garlic clove, minced

1 teaspoon minced fresh rosemary

2 cups (about 8 ounces) crumbled feta cheese

1 tablespoon freshly squeezed lemon juice

½ teaspoon freshly ground black pepper

1 egg, beaten

10 phyllo sheets, thawed if frozen

1. Preheat the oven to 350°F.

2. Squeeze the thawed spinach to remove as much of the water as possible. Chop.

3. In a large skillet over medium-high heat, heat 1 tablespoon olive oil and cook the garlic in it, stirring, for about 2 minutes, until it begins to brown. Stir in the spinach and rosemary and cook for 2 minutes more. Transfer the cooked spinach to a large bowl and add the feta, lemon juice, pepper, and egg. Stir to mix well. Set the mixture aside and let cool.

4. Place the remaining 7 tablespoons of olive oil in a small dish. Unroll the phyllo sheets on a clean work surface. Cut the sheets lengthwise into 3-inch-wide strips (you should get three 14-inch-by-3-inch strips from each sheet). Arrange two strips on the work surface perpendicular to your body (cover the remaining strips with plastic wrap and then a damp dish towel to keep them from drying out.) Brush the strips lightly all over with olive oil. »

5. Place about a tablespoon of filling in the bottom (closest to you) corner of each strip and fold the phyllo over the filling to form a triangle. Fold over again to form another triangle, the way you would fold a flag. Continue folding until you have a neat triangular packet. Repeat with the remaining phyllo and filling. Place each finished packet, seem side down, on a large baking sheet. Brush the tops of the triangles with the remaining olive oil.

6. Bake in the preheated oven for about 25 minutes, until the phyllo is crisp and golden brown. Transfer the packets to a wire rack to cool slightly. Serve warm or at room temperature.

PER TRIANGLE: CALORIES: 96; TOTAL FAT: 7G; SATURATED FAT: 2G; CARBS: 7G; PROTEIN: 3G; SODIUM: 83MG; FIBER: 1G

LEBANON

CLASSIC HUMMUS
WITH TAHINI

Makes about 2 cups   Prep time: 5 minutes   Cook time: None

VEGETARIAN | DAIRY-FREE | GLUTEN-FREE | QUICK & EASY   *Hummus has become popular around the world, and the variations on the theme are endless. This is a classic version—with chickpeas, tahini, garlic, and lemon—similar to what you'll find in Lebanon. Serve it with warm whole-wheat pita bread for dipping.*

2 cups drained canned chickpeas,
    liquid reserved
½ cup tahini
¼ cup olive oil, plus more for garnish
2 cloves garlic, peeled, or to taste
Juice of 1 lemon, plus more as needed
1 tablespoon ground cumin
Salt
Freshly ground black pepper
1 teaspoon paprika, for garnish
2 tablespoons chopped flat-leaf parsley,
    for garnish
4 whole-wheat pita bread or flatbread
    rounds, warmed

1. In a food processor, combine the chickpeas, tahini, oil, garlic, lemon juice, and cumin. Season with salt and pepper, and process until puréed. With the food processor running, add the reserved chickpea liquid until the mixture is smooth and reaches the desired consistency.

2. Spoon the hummus into a serving bowl, drizzle with a bit of olive oil, and sprinkle with the paprika and parsley.

3. Serve immediately, with warmed pita bread or flatbread, or cover and refrigerate for up to 2 days. Bring to room temperature before serving.

PER ¼ CUP SERVING: CALORIES: 309; TOTAL FAT: 16G; SATURATED FAT: 3G; CARBS: 36G; PROTEIN: 9G; SODIUM: 341MG; FIBER: 7G

GREECE

CHARRED EGGPLANT DIP
WITH FETA AND MINT

Makes about 1½ cups   Prep time: 5 minutes   Cook time: 20 minutes

VEGETARIAN | GLUTEN-FREE | QUICK & EASY   *This is a Greek version of* babaganoush, *the eggplant dip common in Lebanon and Syria. Here, it is made without tahini, getting its intense flavor instead from smoky charred eggplant, tangy feta cheese, lemon juice, and fresh mint. Serve with toasted pita triangles or slices of crusty bread.*

1 medium eggplant (about 1 pound)
2 tablespoons lemon juice
¼ cup olive oil
½ cup crumbled feta cheese
½ cup finely diced red onion
3 tablespoons chopped fresh mint leaves
1 tablespoon finely chopped flat-
  leaf parsley
¼ teaspoon cayenne pepper
¾ teaspoon salt

1. Preheat the broiler to high.

2. Line a baking sheet with aluminum foil.

3. Put the whole eggplant on the prepared baking sheet and poke it in several places with the tines of a fork. Cook under the broiler, turning about every 5 minutes, until the eggplant is charred on all sides and very soft in the center, about 15 to 20 minutes total. Remove from the oven and set aside until cool enough to handle.

4. When the eggplant is cool enough to handle, cut it in half lengthwise and scoop out the flesh, discarding the charred skin.

5. Add the lemon juice and olive oil and mash to a chunky purée with a fork. Add the cheese, onion, mint, parsley, cayenne, and salt.

6. Serve at room temperature.

★ TIP: The eggplant dip can be made a day or two in advance and stored in the refrigerator. Bring it to room temperature before serving.

PER ½ CUP SERVING: CALORIES: 71; TOTAL FAT: 6G; SATURATED FAT: 2G; CARBS: 3G; PROTEIN: 2G; SODIUM: 237MG; FIBER: 2G

PORTUGAL

PORTUGUESE CRAB SPREAD

Serves 4   Prep time: 5 minutes   Cook time: None

GLUTEN-FREE | QUICK & EASY   *In Portugal's seaside towns, stuffed crab—a crab shell stuffed with crab salad—is a common sight. Serve this with slices of crusty whole-wheat bread or crackers.*

1 pound fresh crab meat

2 hard-boiled eggs, chopped

1 stalk celery, finely diced

1 tablespoon finely chopped
   flat-leaf parsley

⅓ cup mayonnaise

¼ cup cream

1 tablespoon mustard

2 tablespoons port or sherry

½ teaspoon cayenne pepper

1 teaspoon salt

½ teaspoon freshly ground black pepper

1. In a medium bowl, combine the crab, eggs, celery, and parsley, and toss to mix.

2. In a small bowl, stir together the mayonnaise, cream, mustard, port or sherry, cayenne, salt, and pepper.

3. Add the mayonnaise mixture to the crab mixture and gently fold them together until well combined. Cover and refrigerate until ready to serve.

4. Serve chilled.

PER SERVING: CALORIES: 263; TOTAL FAT: 12G; SATURATED FAT: 2G; CARBS: 9G; PROTEIN: 18G; SODIUM: 1,468MG; FIBER: 1G

GREECE

BULGUR-STUFFED GRAPE LEAVES
(DOLMA)

Makes about 25   Prep time: 60 minutes   Cook time: 1 hour

VEGETARIAN | DAIRY-FREE *Stuffed vegetables are common throughout the Mediterranean, and* dolma *is a Turkish word that refers to brined vine leaves stuffed with grains (usually rice) or meat. This vegetarian version is filled with a lemony mixture of cracked bulgur wheat, the same whole grain that is used to make tabbouleh, making this like a cross between the two dishes.*

¾ cup whole-grain quick-cooking bulgur

1 cup chopped scallions

1 cup chopped plum tomatoes

¼ cup chopped fresh dill, plus
  2 tablespoons, divided

¼ cup chopped fresh mint, plus
  2 tablespoons, divided

¼ cup olive oil, plus 2 tablespoons,
  divided

1½ teaspoons lemon juice, plus
  2 tablespoons, divided

¾ teaspoon salt

½ teaspoon freshly ground black pepper

½ teaspoon ground cumin

1 (7- or 8-ounce) jar brined grape leaves
  (about 28 leaves), drained, stems
  trimmed if needed

Fresh dill sprigs (for garnish)

Fresh mint sprigs (for garnish)

1. In a large bowl, mix the bulgur, scallions, tomatoes, ¼ cup dill, ¼ cup mint, ¼ cup of the olive oil, 1½ teaspoons lemon juice, salt, pepper, and cumin and toss to mix well. Let sit at room temperature for 30 to 60 minutes.

2. Cover the bottom of a stockpot completely with flattened grape leaves.

3. Spread a grape leaf open on your work surface, with the vein-side down. Put about 1 tablespoon of the bulgur mixture in the center of the leaf. Fold the sides of the leaves over the filling and then roll up like a tiny burrito. As you finish each filled grape leaf, place it in the leaf-lined pot, seam side down. The filled grape leaves should fit closely together, filling the bottom of the pot and then layering the stuffed leaves as necessary. Repeat until all of the leaves have been filled. »

4. Add water to the pot to cover the stuffed leaves by about an inch. Add the remaining 2 tablespoons lemon juice and 2 tablespoons olive oil to the water. Place a round pan or heat-safe dish on top of the stuffed leaves to keep them from floating. Bring the liquid to a simmer over medium heat, then reduce the heat to very low, cover, and simmer for about 45 to 55 minutes, until the bulgur is tender.

5. Remove the pot from the heat and let cool to room temperature before carefully removing the stuffed leaves. Arrange the stuffed leaves on a serving platter, cover, and chill until ready to serve. Serve chilled, garnished with dill and mint sprigs.

PER PIECE: CALORIES: 30; TOTAL FAT: 2G; SATURATED FAT: 0G; CARBS: 3G; PROTEIN: 1G; SODIUM: 149MG; FIBER: 1G

ROASTED PEPPER BRUSCHETTA
WITH CAPERS AND BASIL

Serves 6 to 8   Prep time: 10 minutes   Cook time: 15 minutes

VEGETARIAN | DAIRY-FREE | QUICK & EASY   *Traditionally,* bruschetta *refers to toasted bread rounds topped with garlic, olive oil, vinegary tomatoes, and fresh basil. In this version, multi-colored roasted bell peppers are substituted for the tomatoes and the dressing is perked up with capers and a touch of Dijon mustard.*

2 red bell peppers

2 yellow bell peppers

2 orange bell peppers

2 tablespoons olive oil, plus ¼ cup

¾ teaspoon salt, divided

½ teaspoon freshly ground
    black pepper, divided

3 tablespoons red wine vinegar

1 teaspoon Dijon mustard

1 clove garlic, minced

2 tablespoons capers, drained

¼ cup chopped fresh basil leaves, divided

1 whole-wheat baguette or other crusty
    bread, thinly sliced

1. Preheat the broiler to high and line a large baking sheet with aluminum foil.

2. Brush the peppers all over with 2 tablespoons of the olive oil and sprinkle with ½ teaspoon of the salt and ¼ teaspoon of the pepper.

3. Broil the peppers, turning every 3 minutes or so, until the skin is charred on all sides. Place them in a bowl, cover with plastic wrap, and let steam for 10 minutes. Slip the skins off and discard them. Seed and dice the peppers.

4. In a large bowl, whisk together the vinegar, mustard, garlic, the remaining ¼ teaspoon salt, and the remaining ¼ teaspoon of pepper. Still whisking, slowly add the remaining ¼ cup oil in a thin stream until the dressing is emulsified. Stir in the capers, 2 tablespoons of the basil, and the diced peppers.

5. Toast the bread slices and then spoon the pepper mixture over them, drizzling with extra dressing. Garnish with the remaining basil and serve immediately.

PER SERVING: CALORIES: 243; TOTAL FAT: 6G; SATURATED FAT: 1G; CARBS: 39G; PROTEIN: 8G; SODIUM: 755MG; FIBER: 4G

SOUTHERN ITALY

FLATBREAD WITH RICOTTA
AND ORANGE-RAISIN RELISH

Serves 4 to 6   Prep time: 5 minutes   Cook time: 8 minutes

VEGETARIAN | QUICK & EASY   *Flatbread is like a very thin-crusted pizza. You can use store-bought, prebaked flatbread crust, or substitute Indian* naan *or Middle Eastern* lavosh. *Here it gets a topping of creamy ricotta cheese and a sweet-tart raisin and orange relish that gives it a distinctively Southern Italian flavor. Peppery arugula adds a bright, fresh counterpoint.*

¾ cup golden raisins, roughly chopped
1 shallot, finely diced
1 tablespoon olive oil
1 tablespoon red wine vinegar
1 tablespoon honey
1 tablespoon chopped flat-leaf parsley
1 tablespoon fresh orange zest strips
Pinch of salt
1 oval prebaked whole-wheat flatbread,
   such as naan or pocketless pita
8 ounces whole-milk ricotta cheese
½ cup baby arugula

1. Preheat the oven to 450°F.

2. In a small bowl, stir together the raisins, shallot, olive oil, vinegar, honey, parsley, orange zest, and salt.

3. Place the flatbread on a large baking sheet and toast in the preheated oven until the edges are lightly browned, about 8 minutes.

4. Spoon the ricotta cheese onto the flatbread, spreading with the back of the spoon. Scatter the arugula over the cheese. Cut the flatbread into triangles and top each piece with a dollop of the relish. Serve immediately.

PER SERVING: CALORIES: 195; TOTAL FAT: 9G; SATURATED FAT: 4G; CARBS: 25G; PROTEIN: 6G; SODIUM: 135MG; FIBER: 1G

CYPRUS

GRILLED HALLOUMI WITH WATERMELON,
CHERRY TOMATOES, OLIVES, AND HERB OIL

Serves 4   Prep time: 5 minutes   Cook time: 5 minutes

VEGETARIAN | GLUTEN-FREE | QUICK & EASY   Halloumi *is a distinctive Cypriot cheese made from a combination of sheep's and goat's milk. It holds its shape well when heated, and it is commonly grilled or fried. Here the hot grilled cheese and blistered cherry tomatoes are combined with cool, crisp cucumber and garnished with salty olives and an aromatic herb-infused oil.*

½ cup coarsely chopped fresh basil

3 tablespoons coarsely chopped
    fresh mint leaves, plus thinly sliced
    mint for garnish

1 clove garlic, coarsely chopped

½ cup olive oil, plus more for brushing

½ teaspoon salt, plus a pinch

½ teaspoon freshly ground black pepper,
    plus a pinch

¾ pound cherry tomatoes

8 ounces Halloumi cheese, cut crosswise
    into 8 slices

2 cups thinly sliced watermelon,
    rind removed

¼ cup sliced, pitted Kalamata olives

1. Heat a grill or grill pan to high.

2. In a food processor or blender, combine the basil, chopped mint, and garlic and pulse to chop. While the machine is running, add the olive oil in a thin stream. Strain the oil through a fine-meshed sieve and discard the solids. Stir in ½ teaspoon of salt and ½ teaspoon of pepper.

3. Brush the grill rack with olive oil. Drizzle 2 tablespoons of the herb oil over the tomatoes and cheese and season them with pinches of salt and pepper. Place the tomatoes on the grill and cook, turning occasionally, until their skins become blistered and begin to burst, about 4 minutes. Place the cheese on the grill and cook until grill marks appear and the cheese begins to get melty, about 1 minute per side.

4. Arrange the watermelon on a serving platter. Arrange the grilled cheese and tomatoes on top of the melon. Drizzle the herb oil over the top and garnish with the olives and sliced mint. Serve immediately.

PER SERVING: CALORIES: 535; TOTAL FAT: 50G; SATURATED FAT: 17G; CARBS: 12G; PROTEIN: 14G; SODIUM: 663MG; FIBER: 2G

SOUTHERN ITALY

PEA AND ARUGULA CROSTINI
WITH PECORINO ROMANO

Serves 6 to 8   Prep time: 10 minutes   Cook time: 15 minutes

VEGETARIAN, QUICK & EASY   *Pecorino Romano, a hard, salty sheep's milk cheese, is made primarily in Sardinia. It's often paired with fresh fava beans, but peas—which take well to the freezer and are easier to prepare than fresh favas—make a fine substitute. Fresh, peppery, baby arugula lends a high note and a bit of fresh crunch.*

1½ cups fresh or frozen peas

1 loaf crusty whole-wheat bread, cut into thin slices

3 tablespoons olive oil, divided

1 small garlic clove, finely mined or pressed

Juice of ½ lemon

½ teaspoon salt

¼ teaspoon freshly ground black pepper

1 cup (packed) baby arugula

¼ cup thinly shaved Pecorino Romano

1. Preheat the oven to 350°F.

2. Fill a small saucepan with about ½ inch of water. Bring to a boil over medium-high heat. Add the peas and cook for 3 to 5 minutes, until tender. Drain and rinse with cold water.

3. Arrange the bread slices on a large baking sheet and brush the tops with 2 tablespoons olive oil. Bake in the preheated oven for about 8 minutes, until golden brown.

4. Meanwhile, in a medium bowl, mash the peas gently with the back of a fork. They should be smashed but not mashed into a paste. Add the remaining 1 tablespoon olive oil, lemon juice, garlic, salt, and pepper and stir to mix.

5. Spoon the pea mixture onto the toasted bread slices and top with the arugula and cheese. Serve immediately.

PER SERVING: CALORIES: 301; TOTAL FAT: 13G; SATURATED FAT: 5G; CARBS: 32G; PROTEIN: 14G; SODIUM: 833MG; FIBER: 6G

SPAIN

SHRIMP AND CHICKPEA FRITTERS

Serves 6   Prep time: 5 minutes, plus 10 minutes for batter to rest   Cook time: 10 minutes

DAIRY-FREE | QUICK & EASY   *These fritters are somewhat indulgent, since they are fried in olive oil, but a small serving makes a great starter or tapas plate, and any damage is easily moderated by an accompanying meal that is loaded with vegetables and lean protein. Chickpea flour, which you can find in health food stores and the specialty food aisles of most supermarkets, gives these fritters a distinctive earthy flavor.*

2 tablespoons olive oil, plus ¼ cup, divided

½ small yellow onion, finely chopped

12 ounces raw medium shrimp, peeled, deveined, and finely chopped

¼ cup chickpea flour

2 tablespoon all-purpose flour

2 tablespoons roughly chopped parsley

1 teaspoon baking powder

½ teaspoon hot or sweet paprika

¾ teaspoon salt, plus additional to sprinkle over finished dish

½ lemon

1. Heat 2 tablespoons of the olive oil in a large skillet over medium-high heat. Add the onion and cook, stirring frequently, until softened, about 5 minutes. Using a slotted spoon, transfer the cooked onions to a medium bowl. Add the shrimp, chickpea flour, all-purpose flour, parsley, baking powder, paprika, and salt and mix well. Let sit for 10 minutes.

2. Heat the remaining ¼ cup olive oil in the same skillet set over medium-high heat. When the oil is very hot, add the batter, about 2 tablespoons at a time. Cook for about 2 minutes, until the bottom turns golden and the edges are crisp. Flip over and cook for another minute or two until the second side is golden and crisp. Drain on paper towels. Serve hot, with lemon squeezed over the top. Season with salt just before serving.

★ TIP: Make sure the oil is very hot before adding the batter, and don't crowd the pan. Too many fritters will lower the temperature of the oil. Making sure the oil is very hot will prevent the fritters from becoming greasy.

PER SERVING: CALORIES: 148; TOTAL FAT: 6G; SATURATED FAT: 1G; CARBS: 9G; PROTEIN: 15G; SODIUM: 435MG; FIBER: 3G

SPAIN

SPANISH HOME FRIES
WITH SPICY TOMATO SAUCE
(PATATAS BRAVAS)

Serves 6   Prep time: 5 minutes   Cook time: 1 hour

VEGETARIAN | DAIRY-FREE | GLUTEN-FREE   *This ubiquitous Spanish tapa usually involves frying potatoes in lots of oil, but here they are tossed in olive oil and roasted in the oven until crisp. Just like the traditional version, they are served with a spicy tomato sauce.*

4 russet potatoes, peeled, cut into large dice

¼ cup olive oil plus 1 tablespoon, divided

½ cup crushed tomatoes

1½ teaspoons red wine

1 teaspoon hot smoked paprika

1 serrano chile, seeded and chopped

½ teaspoon salt

¼ teaspoon freshly ground black pepper

1. Preheat the oven to 425°F.

2. Toss the potatoes with ¼ cup of olive oil and spread on a large baking sheet. Season with salt and pepper and roast in the preheated oven for about 50 to 60 minutes, turning once in the middle, until the potatoes are golden brown and crisp.

3. Meanwhile, make the sauce by combining the tomatoes, the remaining 1 tablespoon olive oil, wine, paprika, chile, salt, and pepper in a food processor or blender and process until smooth.

4. Serve the potatoes hot with the sauce on the side for dipping or spooned over the top.

PER SERVING: CALORIES: 201; TOTAL FAT: 11G; SATURATED FAT: 2G; CARBS: 25G; PROTEIN: 3G; SODIUM: 243MG; FIBER: 4G

6

SANDWICHES AND WRAPS

SPAIN

ROASTED VEGETABLE BOCADILLO
WITH ROMESCO SAUCE

Serves 4   Prep time: 10 minutes   Cook time: 20 minutes

VEGETARIAN | QUICK & EASY   *Bocadillos are small, Spanish-style sandwiches with simple fillings like thinly sliced serrano ham and manchego cheese. As with the American sandwich, in Spain you'll see versions of the bocadillo that range from a quick, humble, and relatively unremarkable snack to creative culinary masterpieces served in the hippest tapas bars. This vegetarian bocadillo includes the classic Spanish romesco sauce, made of roasted red peppers, almonds, garlic, and sherry vinegar.*

2 small yellow squash, sliced lengthwise

2 small zucchini, sliced lengthwise

1 medium red onion, thinly sliced

4 large button mushrooms, sliced

2 tablespoons olive oil

1 teaspoon salt, divided

½ teaspoon freshly ground black pepper, divided

2 roasted red peppers from a jar, drained

2 tablespoons blanched almonds

1 tablespoon sherry vinegar

1 small clove garlic

4 crusty multigrain rolls

4 ounces goat cheese, at room temperature

1 tablespoon chopped fresh basil

★ TIP: In Spain, you'll mostly see bocadillos made on crusty rolls similar in shape to American submarine sandwich rolls, only a bit smaller and with a crustier exterior. Feel free to use any type of small sandwich roll or a baguette cut into sandwich-length pieces.

1. Preheat the oven to 400°F.

2. In a medium bowl, toss the yellow squash, zucchini, onion, and mushrooms with the olive oil, ½ teaspoon salt, and ¼ teaspoon pepper. Spread on a large baking sheet. Roast the vegetables in the oven for about 20 minutes, until softened.

3. Meanwhile, in a food processor, combine the roasted peppers, almonds, vinegar, garlic, the remaining ½ teaspoon salt, and the remaining ¼ teaspoon pepper and process until smooth.

4. Split the rolls and spread ¼ of the goat cheese on the bottom of each. Place the roasted vegetables on top of the cheese, dividing equally. Top with chopped basil. Spread the top halves of the rolls with the roasted red pepper sauce and serve immediately.

PER SERVING: CALORIES: 394; TOTAL FAT: 20G; SATURATED FAT: 8G; CARBS: 37G; PROTEIN: 21G; SODIUM: 954MG; FIBER: 8G

GREECE

GRILLED EGGPLANT
AND CHOPPED GREEK SALAD WRAPS

Serves 4   Prep time: 10 minutes, plus 30 minutes resting time   Cook time: 20 minutes

VEGETARIAN   *Chopped vegetables and feta cheese are marinated in oil and balsamic vinegar, which infuses them with tangy flavor. Grilling gives the eggplant a succulent texture and a hint of smoky flavor.*

15 small tomatoes, such as cherry or
    grape tomatoes, halved
10 pitted Kalamata olives, chopped
1 medium red onion, halved and
    thinly sliced
¾ cup crumbled feta cheese (about
    4 ounces)
2 tablespoons balsamic vinegar
1 tablespoon chopped fresh parsley
1 clove garlic, minced
2 tablespoons olive oil, plus 2 teaspoons,
    divided
¾ teaspoon salt, divided
1 medium cucumber, peeled, halved
    lengthwise, seeded, and diced
1 large eggplant, sliced ½-inch thick
½ teaspoon freshly ground
    black pepper
4 whole-wheat sandwich wraps or
    whole-wheat flour tortillas

1. In a medium bowl, toss together the tomatoes, olives, onion, cheese, vinegar, parsley, garlic, 2 teaspoons olive oil, and ¼ teaspoon of salt. Let sit at room temperature for 20 minutes. Add the cucumber, toss to combine, and let sit another 10 minutes.

2. While the salad is resting, grill the eggplant. Heat a grill or grill pan to high heat. Brush the remaining 2 tablespoons olive oil onto both sides of the eggplant slices. Grill for about 8 to 10 minutes per side, until grill marks appear and the eggplant is tender and cooked through. Transfer to a plate and season with the remaining ½ teaspoon of salt and the pepper.

3. Heat the wraps in a large, dry skillet over medium heat just until warm and soft, about 1 minute on each side. Place 2 or 3 eggplant slices down the center of each wrap. Spoon some of the salad mixture on top of the eggplant, using a slotted spoon so that any excess liquid is drained off. Fold in the sides of the wrap and roll up like a burrito. Serve immediately.

PER SERVING: CALORIES: 445; TOTAL FAT: 20G; SATURATED FAT: 6G; CARBS: 58G; PROTEIN: 14G; SODIUM: 1,259MG; FIBER: 13G

LEBANON

FALAFEL WRAPS
WITH TAHINI SAUCE

Serves 8   Prep time: 15 minutes, plus 24 hours to soak beans   Cook time: 25 minutes

VEGETARIAN | DAIRY-FREE   *Falafel is made throughout the Middle East—in Egypt, Turkey, Israel, Syria, and Lebanon—using either fava beans or chickpeas and flavored with garlic, onion, and parsley. Most versions are deep fried, but these are baked in the oven, making the dish considerably lighter.*

1¾ cups dried chickpeas
¼ cup olive oil, divided
2 cloves garlic
1 small yellow or white onion, quartered
1 tablespoon ground cumin
½ teaspoon cayenne pepper
1 cup chopped flat-leaf parsley, plus
　　more for garnish
1 teaspoon salt
½ teaspoon freshly ground black pepper
½ teaspoon baking soda
1 tablespoon lemon juice
8 whole-wheat wraps, warmed
1 small head lettuce leaves, such as
　　butter or little gem
2 large tomatoes, diced
1 small red onion, halved and
　　thinly sliced
¾ cup Tahini Sauce (page 239)

★ TIP: Using dried, soaked chickpeas is a must as you won't get the right consistency with canned or precooked chickpeas.

1. In a large bowl, cover the chickpeas with about 3 or 4 inches of water and let soak for 24 hours, adding more water if needed. Drain.

2. Preheat the oven to 375°F.

3. Brush a large, rimmed baking sheet with 2 tablespoons olive oil.

4. In a food processor, combine the soaked chickpeas with the garlic, onion, cumin, cayenne, parsley, salt, pepper, baking soda, and lemon juice and process until everything is coarsely chopped and well mixed, but do not purée.

5. Form the mixture into about twenty 1½-balls. Flatten them to make patties. Place them on the baking sheet and brush with the remaining 2 tablespoons olive oil. Bake for 15 minutes then flip and bake for another 10 to 15 minutes until they are golden brown and crisp.

6. To make the wraps, place 2 or 3 patties in the center of each wrap. Add a lettuce leaf or two, some of the diced tomato, and some of the sliced onion. Drizzle with Tahini Sauce and garnish with parsley. Serve immediately.

PER SERVING: CALORIES: 416; TOTAL FAT: 22G; SATURATED FAT: 3G; CARBS: 47G; PROTEIN: 14G; SODIUM: 716MG; FIBER: 12G

CYPRUS

HALLOUMI, RED ONIONS,
AND TOMATOES ON CRUSTY BREAD

Serves 4   Prep time: 5 minutes   Cook time: 8 minutes

VEGETARIAN | QUICK & EASY   *On Cyprus, halloumi cheese rules supreme, and in this simple sandwich it gets all the attention, paired with ripe tomato, crisp red onion, and a sprinkling of fresh oregano. Ham or sliced pork loin is often added to the traditional Cypriot cheese and veggie sandwich, but this vegetarian version hardly needs anything else.*

2 tablespoons butter, at room temperature

4 seeded sandwich rolls, split

8 ounces halloumi cheese, sliced

1 large tomato, sliced

1 small red onion, sliced

¼ cup fresh oregano leaves

1 tablespoon olive oil

1. Spread the butter on the cut side of the bottom half of each roll. Top with a layer of cheese, a layer of tomato slices, a layer of sliced onion, and several oregano leaves. Place the top half of the roll on top. Repeat with the remaining rolls and fillings.

2. To grill the sandwich, heat a skillet or grill pan over high heat and brush with oil.

3. Place the sandwiches in the hot pan and place another heavy pan, such as a cast-iron skillet, on top to weigh them down. Cook for about 3 to 4 minutes, until crisp and golden on the bottom, and then flip over and repeat on the second side, cooking for an additional 3 to 4 minutes until golden and crisp. Slice each sandwich in half and serve hot.

PER SERVING: CALORIES: 526; TOTAL FAT: 31G; SATURATED FAT: 17G; CARBS: 44G; PROTEIN: 21G; SODIUM: 707MG; FIBER: 4G

TURKEY AND PROVOLONE PANINI
WITH ROASTED PEPPERS AND ONIONS

Serves 4   Prep time: 15 minutes   Cook time: 1 hour, 5 minutes

Provolone is a semi-hard cheese that was originally produced in Southern Italy. It is traditionally made with either cow or buffalo milk, or a combination, and it has a firm texture and a mild flavor. Sometimes provolone is smoked, which gives it a more complex flavor. For this panini, you can use either regular aged provolone or smoked provolone.

For the peppers and onions
2 red bell pepper, seeded and quartered
2 red onions, peeled and quartered
2 tablespoons olive oil
½ teaspoon salt
½ teaspoon freshly ground black pepper

For the panini
2 tablespoons olive oil
8 slices whole-wheat bread
8 ounces thinly sliced provolone cheese
8 ounces sliced roasted turkey or
    chicken breast

★ TIP: If you're short on time, you can buy jarred roasted red peppers at your local supermarket.

1. Preheat the oven to 375°F.

2. To roast the peppers and onions, toss them together with the olive oil, salt, and pepper on a large, rimmed baking sheet. Spread them out in a single layer and then bake in the preheated oven for 45 to 60 minutes, turning occasionally, until they are tender and beginning to brown. Remove the peppers and onions from the oven and let them cool for a few minutes until they are cool enough to handle. Skin the peppers and thinly slice them. Thinly slice the onions.

3. Preheat a skillet or grill pan over medium-high heat. »

4. To make the panini, brush one side of each of the 8 slices of bread with olive oil. Place 4 of the bread slices, oiled side down, on your work surface. Top each with ¼ of the cheese and ¼ of the turkey, and top with some of the roasted peppers and onions. Place the remaining 4 bread slices on top of the sandwiches, oiled side up.

5. Place the sandwiches in the skillet or grill pan (you may have to cook them in two batches), cover the pan, and cook until the bottoms have golden brown grill marks and the cheese is beginning to melt, about 2 minutes. Turn the sandwiches over and cook, covered, until the second side is golden brown and the cheese is melted, another 2 minutes or so. Cut each sandwich in half and serve immediately.

PER SERVING: CALORIES: 562; TOTAL FAT: 33G; SATURATED FAT: 12G; CARBS: 38G; PROTEIN: 31G; SODIUM: 1,737MG; FIBER: 6.5G

SOUTHERN ITALY

TAPENADE, TOMATO, AND AGED PROVOLONE PANINI

Serves 4   Prep time: 5 minutes   Cook time: 8 minutes

VEGETARIAN | QUICK & EASY   *Provolone cheese originated in the region of Calabria in Southern Italy and remains a favorite ingredient there. Here it is paired with rich olive tapenade and fresh summer tomatoes for a flavorful vegetarian grilled sandwich.*

½ cup Green Olive Tapenade with Harissa (page 251)
8 slices crusty whole-wheat bread
8 slices fresh, ripe tomato
8 fresh basil leaves
4 ounces aged provolone cheese, thinly sliced
Olive oil, for brushing

1. Spread the tapenade on 4 of the bread slices. Top each with 2 tomato slices and 2 basil leaves. Divide the cheese evenly among the sandwiches. Place the remaining bread slices on top of the sandwiches.

2. To make the panini, heat a skillet or grill pan over high heat and brush with the oil.

3. Place the sandwiches in the hot pan and place another heavy pan, such as a cast-iron skillet, on top to weigh them down. Cook for about 3 to 4 minutes, until crisp and golden on the bottom, and then flip over and repeat on the second side, cooking for an additional 3 to 4 minutes or so until golden and crisp. Slice each sandwich in half and serve hot.

★ TIP: For a creamier, gooier sandwich, substitute fresh mozzarella di bufala for the provolone.

PER SERVING: CALORIES: 352; TOTAL FAT: 21G; SATURATED FAT: 7G; CARBS: 26G; PROTEIN: 15G; SODIUM: 626MG; FIBER: 5G

HERBED FOCACCIA PANINI
WITH ANCHOVIES AND BURRATA

Serves 4   Prep time: 5 minutes   Cook time: 8 minutes

QUICK & EASY   *Burrata is a fresh, un-aged cheese from the Southern Italian region of Apulia that is made from the leftovers of the mozzarella-making process. To make this delicacy, mozzarella is formed into a pouch, which is filled with a combination of heavy cream and mozzarella scraps and then cinched up with a knot. The result is a super-creamy, yet mildly flavored cheese. If you can't find burrata, substitute fresh* mozzarella di bufala.

8 ounces burrata cheese, chilled and sliced

1 pound whole-wheat herbed focaccia, cut crosswise into 4 rectangles and split horizontally

1 can anchovy fillets packed in oil, drained

8 slices tomato, sliced

2 cups arugula

1 tablespoon olive oil

1. Divide the cheese evenly among the bottom halves of the focaccia rectangles. Top each with 3 or 4 anchovy fillets, 2 slices of tomato, and ½ cup arugula. Place the top halves of the focaccia on top of the sandwiches.

2. To make the panini, heat a skillet or grill pan over high heat and brush with the olive oil.

3. Place the sandwiches in the hot pan and place another heavy pan, such as a cast-iron skillet, on top to weigh them down. Cook for about 3 to 4 minutes, until crisp and golden on the bottom, and then flip over and repeat on the second side, cooking for an additional 3 to 4 minutes until golden and crisp. Slice each sandwich in half and serve hot.

PER SERVING: CALORIES: 596; TOTAL FAT: 30G; SATURATED FAT: 10G; CARBS: 58G; PROTEIN: 27G; SODIUM: 626MG; FIBER: 5G

SOUTHERN ITALY

SAUTÉED MUSHROOM, ONION, AND PECORINO ROMANO PANINI

Serves 4   Prep time: 10 minutes   Cook time: 20 minutes

VEGETARIAN | QUICK & EASY   *In Italy, what we think of as a boring grilled cheese sandwich is elevated to gourmet levels. This version includes sautéed mushrooms and onions and tangy Pecorino Romano cheese. Pecorino Romano is a hard, salty, sheep's milk cheese made in the far south of Italy.*

3 tablespoons olive oil, divided

1 small onion, diced

10 ounces button or cremini mushrooms, sliced

½ teaspoon salt

¼ teaspoon freshly ground black pepper

4 crusty Italian sandwich rolls

4 ounces freshly grated Pecorino Romano

★ TIP: A panini maker is the perfect way to cook these sandwiches, but if you don't have one, a grill pan or skillet will work perfectly. Just heat up the pan, place the sandwich in the center, and weigh it down with a second heavy skillet as it cooks.

1. Heat 1 tablespoon of the olive oil in a skillet over medium-high heat. Add the onion and cook, stirring, until it begins to soften, about 3 minutes. Add the mushrooms, season with salt and pepper, and cook, stirring, until they soften and the liquid they release evaporates, about 7 minutes.

2. To make the panini, heat a skillet or grill pan over high heat and brush with 1 tablespoon olive oil. Brush the inside of the rolls with the remaining 1 tablespoon olive oil. Divide the mushroom mixture evenly among the rolls and top each with ¼ of the grated cheese.

3. Place the sandwiches in the hot pan and place another heavy pan, such as a cast-iron skillet, on top to weigh them down. Cook for about 3 to 4 minutes, until crisp and golden on the bottom, and then flip over and repeat on the second side, cooking for an additional 3 to 4 minutes until golden and crisp. Slice each sandwich in half and serve hot.

PER SERVING: CALORIES: 468; TOTAL FAT: 21G; SATURATED FAT: 9G; CARBS: 52G; PROTEIN: 19G; SODIUM: 1,333MG; FIBER: 3G

GREECE

CHICKEN SAUSAGE-STUFFED
PITA SANDWICHES

Serves 4   Prep time: 5 minutes   Cook time: 10 minutes

QUICK & EASY   *Most supermarkets sell a dazzling array of chicken sausages. For these Greek-style pita sandwiches, choose ones with Greek-inspired ingredients—feta cheese, olives, roasted peppers, or pine nuts.*

4 (8-inch) pocket pita rounds
4 chicken sausages
1 large tomato, diced
½ small white onion, halved and
   thinly sliced
½ cup plain Greek yogurt or
   Tzatziki Sauce (page 241)
2 tablespoons flat-leaf parsley leaves,
   for garnish

1. Preheat the oven to 450°F.

2. Wrap the pita breads in aluminum foil and heat in the oven for about 10 minutes.

3. Meanwhile, sear the chicken sausages in a skillet over medium-high heat or on a grill, about 5 minutes per side. Remove from the heat and let rest for 5 minutes. Slice each sausage in half crosswise.

4. Remove the warm pita breads from the oven and halve each crosswise. Stuff each half with one sausage half and some diced tomato and sliced onion. Add a dollop of yogurt or Tzatziki Sauce and garnish with parsley leaves. Serve immediately.

PER SERVING: CALORIES: 269; TOTAL FAT: 5G; SATURATED FAT: 2G; CARBS: 40G; PROTEIN: 14G; SODIUM: 496MG; FIBER: 3G

GREECE

CHICKEN GYROS
WITH TZATZIKI AND GARLIC-HERB OIL

Serves 4   Prep time: 10 minutes   Cook time: 10 minutes

QUICK & EASY   *One bite of these chicken gyros—Greek sandwiches made on soft flatbread with garlicky Tzatziki Sauce—will transport you to the Greek islands. And the best part? Since they call for already cooked chicken, they're a great choice for busy weekday meals . . . or any time you have leftover chicken in the fridge.*

Tzatziki Sauce (page 241)
1 medium cucumber, diced
1 pint grape tomatoes, quartered
1 small red onion, diced
⅓ cup chopped flat-leaf parsley
¼ cup chopped fresh mint
½ head iceberg lettuce, thinly sliced
½ teaspoon lemon juice
½ teaspoon salt, divided
½ teaspoon freshly ground
    black pepper, divided
¼ cup olive oil
1 teaspoon dried oregano
2 garlic cloves, minced
4 (8-inch) pocketless pita rounds or
    naan, preferably whole-wheat
½ roast chicken, skin discarded, meat
    shredded (about 2¼ cups)

1. Preheat the broiler.

2. To make the chopped salad, in a medium bowl, combine the diced cucumber with the tomatoes, onion, parsley, mint, lettuce, lemon juice, ¼ teaspoon salt, and ¼ teaspoon pepper.

3. To make the garlic-herb oil, heat the olive oil, oregano, garlic, the remaining ¼ teaspoon salt, and the remaining ¼ teaspoon pepper in a small saucepan over medium-high heat, stirring, for about 2 minutes, until the garlic is aromatic. Toss 3 tablespoons of the garlic-herb oil with the chicken in a medium bowl.

4. Place the bread rounds on a baking sheet and brush the tops with the remaining garlic-herb oil. Cover with aluminum foil and heat under the broiler for about 4 minutes. Remove the foil and continue to broil until the bread begins to brown in spots, about 2 more minutes.

5. Dollop some of the Tzatziki Sauce on each bread round. Top with ¼ of the chicken and a handful of the chopped salad. Serve immediately.

PER SERVING: CALORIES: 446; TOTAL FAT: 18G; SATURATED FAT: 2G;
CARBS: 46G; PROTEIN: 31G; SODIUM: 731MG; FIBER: 8G

SPAIN

PEAR, MANCHEGO, AND
SPANISH CHORIZO BOCADILLO

Serves 4   Prep time: 5 minutes   Cook time: None

QUICK & EASY   *This simple bocadillo is a dressed-up version of the meat-and-cheese sandwiches you'll find in many cafés in Spain. With a spread of quince paste (membrillo) or fig jam and slices of sweet, juicy pear, it's like a swanky cheese plate on a roll.*

4 crusty whole-wheat bread rolls
¼ cup fig jam or quince paste
1 ripe pear, thinly sliced
4 ounces manchego cheese, thinly sliced
4 ounces Spanish chorizo, thinly sliced

Split the rolls and spread 1 tablespoon of the fig jam or quince paste on the inside of each. Top with the pear slices, cheese, and chorizo. Serve immediately.

PER SERVING: CALORIES: 284; TOTAL FAT: 6G; SATURATED FAT: 2G; CARBS: 47G; PROTEIN: 15G; SODIUM: 444MG; FIBER: 5G

SPAIN

BOCADILLO
WITH HERBED TUNA AND PIQUILLO PEPPERS

Serves 4   Prep time: 5 minutes, plus 15 minutes to cool   Cook time: 20 minutes

DAIRY-FREE   *Bocadillo are Spanish-style sandwiches served on rolls or a crusty baguette. They're usually pretty simple with basic fillings like meat and cheese, eggs, or grilled vegetables. If you can't find piquillo peppers, substitute jarred roasted red peppers instead.*

2 tablespoons olive oil, plus more
  for brushing

1 medium onion, finely chopped

2 leeks, white and tender green parts
  only, finely chopped

1 teaspoon chopped thyme

½ teaspoon dried marjoram

½ teaspoon salt

¼ teaspoon freshly ground
  black pepper

3 tablespoons sherry vinegar

1 carrot, finely diced

2 (8-ounce) jars Spanish tuna in
  olive oil

4 crusty whole-wheat sandwich
  rolls, split

1 ripe tomato, grated on the large holes
  of a box grater

4 piquillo peppers, cut into thin strips

1. Heat 2 tablespoons olive oil in a medium skillet over medium heat. Add the onion, leeks, thyme, marjoram, salt, and pepper. Stir frequently until the onions are softened, about 10 minutes. Stir in the vinegar and carrot and cook until the liquid has evaporated, 5 minutes. Transfer the mixture to a bowl and let cool to room temperature or refrigerate for 15 minutes or so.

2. In a medium bowl, combine the tuna, along with its oil, with the onion mixture, breaking the tuna chunks up with a fork.

3. Brush the rolls lightly with oil and toast under the broiler until lightly browned, about 2 minutes. Spoon the tomato pulp onto the bottom half of each roll, dividing equally and spreading it with the back of the spoon. Divide the tuna mixture among the rolls and top with the piquillo pepper slices. Serve immediately.

★ TIP: For this recipe, look for jars of tuna in olive oil imported from Spain in specialty markets or online. If you do use regular American tuna, be sure to use the kind in olive oil, not water.

PER SERVING: CALORIES: 412; TOTAL FAT: 23G; SATURATED FAT: 3G; CARBS: 26G; PROTEIN: 31G; SODIUM: 948MG; FIBER: 3G

MOROCCAN LAMB WRAP
WITH HARISSA

Serves 4   Prep time: 10 minutes, plus 1 hour to marinate   Cook time: 10 minutes

DAIRY-FREE   *The lamb in these wraps gets smoky flavor from the grill, and* harissa—*a North African hot red chile paste—provides a spicy kick. You can buy harissa in specialty markets, online, or in the international foods aisle of many supermarkets.*

1 clove garlic, minced

2 teaspoons ground cumin

2 teaspoons chopped fresh thyme

¼ cup olive oil, divided

1 lamb leg steak, about 12 ounces

4 (8-inch) pocketless pita rounds or naan, preferably whole-wheat

1 medium eggplant, sliced ½-inch thick

1 medium zucchini, sliced lengthwise into 4 slices

1 bell pepper (any color), roasted and skinned

6 to 8 Kalamata olives, sliced

Juice of 1 lemon

2 to 4 tablespoons harissa

2 cups arugula

1. In a large bowl, combine the garlic, cumin, thyme, and 1 tablespoon of the olive oil. Add the lamb, turn to coat, cover, refrigerate, and marinate for at least an hour.

2. Preheat the oven to 400°F.

3. Heat a grill or grill pan to high heat. Remove the lamb from the marinade and grill for about 4 minutes per side, until medium-rare. Transfer to a plate and let rest for about 10 minutes before slicing thinly across the grain.

4. While the meat is resting, wrap the bread rounds in aluminum foil and heat in the oven for about 10 minutes.

5. Meanwhile, brush the eggplant and zucchini slices with the remaining olive oil and grill until tender, about 3 minutes. Dice them and the bell pepper. Toss in a large bowl with the olives and lemon juice.

6. Spread some of the harissa onto each warm flatbread round and top each evenly with roasted vegetables, a few slices of lamb, and a handful of the arugula.

7. Roll up the wraps, cut each in half crosswise, and serve immediately.

PER SERVING: CALORIES: 553; TOTAL FAT: 24G; SATURATED FAT: 5G; CARBS: 53G; PROTEIN: 33G; SODIUM: 531MG; FIBER: 11G

7

PIZZA AND PASTA

TOMATO, OLIVE, CAPER, AND ANCHOVY PIZZA

Serves 4   Prep time: 10 minutes   Cook time: 12 minutes

DAIRY-FREE | QUICK & EASY   *The pizza we know and love today—topped with tomato sauce, cheese, and other toppings—originated in Napoli, Italy. The original version—pizza marinara—was made by fishermens' wives* (marinare). *It had a thin crust and a rich tomato sauce, but no cheese. Instead, olives, capers, and anchovies were—and are—often used as toppings.*

¼ cup olive oil, divided
1 cup tomato sauce
¼ cup tomato paste
1 clove garlic
1½ teaspoons dried oregano
Salt (optional)
1 pound Whole-Wheat Pizza Dough
     (page 248 or store-bought), thawed
     if frozen, at room temperature
All-purpose flour, as needed
4 medium yellow onions, halved through
     the root and thinly sliced crosswise
1 can anchovy fillets, rinsed and
     patted dry
2 tablespoons capers, rinsed
15 Kalamata or Niçoise olives, halved if
     large or left whole

1. Preheat the oven to 450°F.

2. Brush 2 large baking sheets or pizza stones with 1 tablespoon each of olive oil.

3. In a food processor, combine the tomato sauce, tomato paste, garlic, and oregano. Taste and add salt if needed.

4. Halve the pizza dough and flatten it on a lightly floured board. Using your hands or a rolling pin, press each half out into a rough oval, about 10 inches long by 5 inches wide. Place the flattened dough on the prepared baking sheets.

5. Brush each round of dough with 1 tablespoon of olive oil. Spread half of the sauce over each. Top with half of the onions, half of the anchovies, half of the capers, and half of the olives.

6. Repeat with the second half of the pizza dough and the remaining ingredients.

7. Bake in the preheated oven for 10 to 12 minutes, until the crust is golden brown.

8. Let the pizzas rest for 5 minutes after removing from the oven, then cut into wedges and serve.

★ TIP: Most supermarkets these days carry good raw pizza dough in both regular and whole-wheat versions. If this isn't an option, you can always make your own using the recipe on page 248.

PER SERVING: CALORIES: 539; TOTAL FAT: 20G; SATURATED FAT: 7G; CARBS: 67G; PROTEIN: 24G; SODIUM: 2,319MG; FIBER: 13G

CROATIA

CROATIAN DOUBLE-CRUST PIZZA
WITH GREENS AND GARLIC

Serves 4   Prep time: 15 minutes, plus 30 minutes resting time   Cook time: 20 minutes

VEGETARIAN   *Believe it or not, Croatians say they are the true inventors of pizza. They claim this traditional double-crusted tart, filled with garlicky greens and called* soparnik, *is the original pizza. The crust is more like a pastry crust made with olive oil than the yeasted dough found in other parts of Europe.*

4½ cups all-purpose flour

1¼ teaspoons salt, divided

1½ cups olive oil, plus 3 tablespoons, divided

1 cup warm water

1 pound Swiss chard or kale, tough center ribs removed, leaves julienned

¼ small head of green cabbage, thinly sliced

¼ teaspoon freshly ground black pepper

4 cloves garlic, minced

1. In a medium bowl, combine the flour and 1 teaspoon salt. Add 1½ cups olive oil and the warm water and stir with a fork until the mixture comes together and forms a ball. Wrap the ball in plastic wrap and refrigerate for at least 30 minutes.

2. While the dough is chilling, in a large bowl, toss together the greens, cabbage, 2 tablespoons olive oil, the remaining ¼ teaspoon salt, and the pepper.

3. Preheat the oven to 400°F.

4. Halve the dough and place the halves on two sheets of lightly floured parchment paper. Roll or pat the dough out into two ¼-inch-thick, 11-inch-diameter rounds.

5. Spread the greens mixture over one of the dough rounds, leaving about an inch clear around the edge. Place the second dough round over the greens and fold the edges together to seal the two rounds together. Bake in the preheated oven until the crust is golden brown, about 20 minutes.

6. While the pizza is in the oven, combine 1 tablespoon of olive oil with the garlic. When the pizza is done, remove it from the oven and immediately brush the garlic-oil mixture over the crust. Cut into wedges and serve hot.

★ TIP: To make this dish even more nutritious, substitute whole-wheat flour for half of the all-purpose flour in the crust.

PER SERVING: CALORIES: 670; TOTAL FAT: 45G; SATURATED FAT: 6G; CARBS: 62G; PROTEIN: 10G; SODIUM: 504MG; FIBER: 5G

SOUTHERN ITALY

PENNE WITH TUNA
AND GREEN OLIVES

Serves 4   Prep time: 5 minutes   Cook time: 5 minutes

QUICK & EASY   *Canned tuna packed in olive oil, especially the high quality stuff imported from Europe, is a great ingredient to have in the pantry for quick meals. In fact, everything in this dish comes from the panty other than the fresh parsley. Whatever you do, don't drain off the olive oil that the tuna is packed it. It is loaded with flavor and serves as the main sauce for this dish.*

2 tablespoons olive oil

3 garlic cloves, minced

½ cup green olives

½ teaspoon salt

¼ teaspoon freshly ground black pepper

2 (6-ounce) cans tuna in olive oil (don't drain off the oil)

½ teaspoon wine vinegar

12 ounces penne pasta, cooked according to package directions

2 tablespoons chopped flat-leaf parsley

1. Heat the olive oil in a medium skillet over medium heat. Add the garlic and cook, stirring, 2 to 3 minutes, just until the garlic begins to brown. Add the olives, salt, pepper, and the tuna along with its oil. Cook, stirring, for a minute or two to heat the ingredients through. Remove from the heat and stir in the vinegar.

2. Add the cooked pasta to the skillet and toss to combine the pasta with the sauce. Serve immediately, garnished with the parsley.

PER SERVING: CALORIES: 511; TOTAL FAT: 22G; SATURATED FAT: 3G; CARBS: 52G; PROTEIN: 31G; SODIUM: 826MG; FIBER: 1G

GREECE

FLATBREAD PIZZA
WITH ROASTED CHERRY TOMATOES, ARTICHOKES, AND FETA

Serves 4   Prep time: 5 minutes   Cook time: 20 minutes

VEGETARIAN | QUICK & EASY   *While we think of pizza as an Italian specialty, you'll find versions of it all over the Mediterranean. This one includes Greek flavors of roasted tomatoes, artichoke hearts, feta, and fresh oregano, all piled on Middle Eastern–style flatbreads. However, if you want a more traditional pizza crust, feel free to use homemade or store-bought dough instead.*

1½ pounds cherry or grape tomatoes, halved

3 tablespoons olive oil, divided

½ teaspoon salt

½ teaspoon freshly ground black pepper

4 Middle Eastern–style flatbread rounds

1 can artichoke hearts, rinsed, well drained, and cut into thin wedges

8 ounces (about 1 cup) crumbled feta cheese

¼ cup chopped fresh Greek oregano

1. Preheat the oven to 500°F.

2. In a medium bowl, toss the tomatoes with 1 tablespoon olive oil, the salt, and the pepper. Spread out on a large baking sheet. Roast in the preheated oven until the tomato skins begin to blister and crack, about 10 to 12 minutes. Remove the tomatoes from the oven and reduce the heat to 450°F.

3. Place the flatbreads on a large baking sheet (or two baking sheets if necessary) and brush the tops with the remaining 2 tablespoons of olive oil. Top with the artichoke hearts, roasted tomatoes, and cheese, dividing equally.

4. Bake the flatbreads in the oven for about 8 to 10 minutes, until the edges are lightly browned and the cheese is melted. Sprinkle the oregano over the top and serve immediately.

PER SERVING: CALORIES: 318; TOTAL FAT: 24G; SATURATED FAT: 10G; CARBOHYDRATES: 20G; PROTEIN: 12G; SODIUM: 999MG; FIBER: 8G

GRILLED PIZZA
WITH CHERRY TOMATOES, PINE NUTS, AND BASIL OIL

Serves 4   Prep time: 10 minutes   Cook time: 10 minutes

VEGETARIAN | QUICK & EASY   *Thin-crust pizzas are a specialty of Southern Italian cuisine, especially in Naples and Sicily. Since most of us aren't lucky enough to have access to a wood-fired pizza oven, this version is grilled to get a similarly smoky and crisp crust.*

For the basil oil
1 cup (packed) fresh basil leaves, plus more for garnish
½ cup extra-virgin olive oil
1 small garlic clove
Salt

For the pizzas
1 pound whole-wheat pizza dough (page 248 or store-bought), thawed if frozen, at room temperature
¼ cup pine nuts
6 ounces Pecorino Romano, thinly sliced
1 pint cherry tomatoes, halved

1. To make the basil oil, in a food processor combine the basil, olive oil, garlic, and salt and pulse until the mixture is well combined and smooth.

2. Heat a grill to medium. To make the pizzas, brush a large baking sheet with some of the basil oil (the baking sheet will help you transport the pizzas from kitchen to grill). Halve the pizza dough and press or roll into two 10-inch rounds or ovals. Place the rounds on the prepared baking sheet and brush them with the remaining basil oil.

3. Place the dough rounds on the grill and cook until they begin to brown on the bottom, about 3 minutes. Transfer them back to the baking sheet, placing them browned-side up.

4. Distribute the pine nuts, cheese, and the tomatoes over the 2 dough rounds, dividing equally. Season with salt and pepper. Return the pizzas to the grill and cook until the crust is firm and cooked through and the cheese has melted, about 5 minutes. Transfer to a cutting board and garnish with additional basil leaves.

PER SERVING: CALORIES: 722; TOTAL FAT: 44G; SATURATED FAT: 19G; SODIUM: 1,507MG; CARBS: 54G; FIBER: 10G; PROTEIN: 25G

PINE NUT AND CURRANT COUSCOUS
WITH BUTTERNUT SQUASH

Serves 4   Prep time: 10 minutes   Cook time: 50 minutes

VEGETARIAN | DAIRY-FREE   *Made from durum wheat, couscous is a popular pasta commonly served in North Africa with stewed vegetables, beans, or meat. This vegetarian couscous dish is loaded with Moroccan flavor, including cinnamon, coriander, cumin, and red peppers.*

3 tablespoons olive oil

1 medium onion, chopped

3 cloves garlic, minced

6 canned plum tomatoes, crushed

1 cinnamon stick

1 teaspoon ground coriander

1 teaspoon ground cumin

1 teaspoon salt, divided

¼ teaspoon red pepper flakes

1½ pounds diced butternut squash

1 (16-ounce) can chickpeas,
    drained and rinsed

4½ cups vegetable broth, divided

1-inch strip lemon zest

½ cup currants

4 cups (about 5 ounces)
    chopped spinach

Juice of ½ lemon

¼ teaspoon pepper

1 cup whole-wheat couscous

¼ cup toasted pine nuts

1. Heat the olive oil in a medium saucepan set over medium heat. Add the onion and cook, stirring frequently, until softened and lightly browned, about 10 minutes. Stir in the garlic, tomatoes, cinnamon stick, coriander, cumin, ½ teaspoon of the salt, and the red pepper flakes and cook for about 3 minutes more, until the tomatoes begin to break down. Stir in the butternut squash, chickpeas, 3 cups broth, lemon zest, and currants and bring to a simmer.

2. Partially cover the pan and cook for about 25 minutes, until the squash is tender. Add the spinach and cook, stirring, for 2 or 3 more minutes, until the spinach is wilted. Stir in the lemon juice.

3. While the vegetables are cooking, prepare the couscous. Combine the remaining 1½ cups broth, the remaining ½ teaspoon of salt, and the pepper in a small saucepan and bring to a boil. Remove the pan from the heat and stir in the couscous. Cover immediately and let sit for about 5 minutes, until the liquid has been fully absorbed. Fluff with a fork.

4. Spoon the couscous into serving bowls, top with the vegetable and chickpea mixture, and sprinkle some of the pine nuts over the top of each bowl. Serve immediately.

★ TIP: A whole, raw butternut squash can be difficult to peel. Many supermarkets carry peeled and diced butternut squash in the fresh produce aisle or in the freezer section. Either is fine for this recipe. If you prefer to use a whole squash, purchase one that weighs about 2 pounds and microwave it on high for about 5 minutes to make it easier to peel.

PER SERVING: CALORIES: 920; TOTAL FAT: 26G; SATURATED FAT: 3G; CARBS: 141G; PROTEIN: 40G; SODIUM: 1,532MG; FIBER: 30G

WHOLE-WHEAT SPAGHETTI
À LA PUTTANESCA

Serves 6   Prep time: 5 minutes   Cook time: 20 minutes

DAIRY-FREE | QUICK & EASY   *The name of this spicy, aromatic sauce translates to "in the style of the whore," supposedly named for the ladies of the night in its native city of Napoli. Two explanations compete for where the name came from—it was either a quick meal that the ladies could make for themselves on short breaks between clients, or its intense, appetizing aroma served to lure would-be clients in. But who cares? With lots of garlic, tomatoes, olives, capers, red pepper flakes, and anchovies, it's an intensely flavorful sauce that turns whole-wheat spaghetti into a sexy meal.*

1 pound dried whole-wheat spaghetti
⅓ cup olive oil
5 garlic cloves, minced or pressed
4 anchovy fillets, chopped
½ teaspoon red pepper flakes
1 teaspoon salt
½ teaspoon freshly ground black pepper
1 (28-ounce) can tomato purée
1 pint cherry tomatoes, halved
½ cup pitted green olives, halved
2 tablespoons drained capers
¾ cup coarsely chopped basil

1. Cook the pasta according to the package instructions.

2. Meanwhile, heat the oil in a large skillet over medium-high heat. Add the garlic, anchovies, red pepper flakes, salt, and pepper. Cook, stirring frequently, until the garlic just begins to turn golden brown, 2 to 3 minutes. Add the tomato purée, olives, cherry tomatoes, and capers and let the mixture simmer, reducing the heat if necessary, and stirring occasionally, until the pasta is done, about 10 minutes.

3. Drain the pasta in a colander and then add it to the sauce, tossing with tongs until the pasta is well coated. Serve hot, garnished with the basil.

PER SERVING: CALORIES: 464; TOTAL FAT: 17G; SATURATED FAT: 2G; CARBS: 70G; PROTEIN: 12G; SODIUM: 707MG; FIBER: 12G

SOUTHERN ITALY

SPAGHETTI WITH FRESH MINT PESTO
AND RICOTTA SALATA

Serves 4   Prep time: 5 minutes   Cook time: 15 minutes

VEGETARIAN | QUICK & EASY   Ricotta salata *is nothing like the fresh, creamy ricotta cheese you're probably familiar with. This Sicilian cheese is made from sheep's milk and is aged for a minimum of 90 days. It has a dry, firm texture, similar to Pecorino Romano, and a sharp, salty flavor. It is ideal for grating over salads, shaving over pasta dishes, or adding to fresh herb pesto recipes like this one.*

1 pound spaghetti

¼ cup slivered almonds

2 cups packed fresh mint leaves, plus more for garnish

3 medium garlic cloves

1 tablespoon lemon juice and ½ teaspoon lemon zest from 1 lemon

⅓ cup olive oil

¼ teaspoon freshly ground black pepper

½ cup freshly grated ricotta salata, plus more for garnish

1. Set a large pot of salted water over high heat to boil for the pasta.

2. In a food processor, combine the almonds, mint leaves, garlic, lemon juice and zest, olive oil, and pepper and pulse to a smooth paste. Add the cheese and pulse to combine.

3. When the water is boiling, add the pasta and cook according to the package instructions. Drain the pasta and return it to the pot. Add the pesto to the pasta and toss until the pasta is well coated. Serve hot, garnished with additional mint leaves and cheese, if desired.

PER SERVING: CALORIES: 619; TOTAL FAT: 31G; SATURATED FAT: 8G; CARBS: 70G; PROTEIN: 21G; SODIUM: 113MG; FIBER: 4G

SPAIN

WHOLE-WHEAT CAPELLINI
WITH SARDINES, OLIVES, AND MANCHEGO

Serves 4   Prep time: 5 minutes   Cook time: 15 minutes

QUICK & EASY   *This is a quick, simple, and delicious pasta dish that can be whipped up from ingredients in your pantry. Using Spanish manchego cheese gives it a Spanish flair, but you could substitute any hard, dry grating cheese such as Parmesan or Pecorino Romano.*

1 (7-ounce) jar Spanish sardines in olive oil, chopped (reserve the oil)

1 medium onion, diced

4 cloves garlic, minced

2 medium tomatoes, sliced

1 pound whole-wheat capellini pasta, cooked according to package instructions

1 cup pitted, chopped cured black olives, such as Kalamata

3 ounces freshly grated manchego cheese

1. Heat the olive oil from the sardines in a large skillet over medium-high heat. Add the onion and garlic and cook, stirring frequently, until softened, about 5 minutes. Add the tomatoes and sardines and cook, stirring, 2 minutes more.

2. Add the cooked and drained pasta to the skillet with the sauce and toss to combine.

3. Stir in the olives and serve immediately, topped with the grated cheese.

★ TIP: Always cook pasta in generously salted water—about 2 tablespoons of salt per gallon of water. This salt flavors the pasta, which means you may not need to add any additional salt to the sauce, especially if you are using other salty ingredients like olives, sardines, or anchovies.

PER SERVING: CALORIES: 307; TOTAL FAT: 11G; SATURATED FAT: 2G; CARBS: 38G; PROTEIN: 8G; SODIUM: 433MG; FIBER: 6G

SPAIN

SPANISH ORZO
WITH SHRIMP, CHORIZO, AND PEAS

Serves 4   Prep time: 5 minutes   Cook time: 20 minutes

DAIRY-FREE | QUICK & EASY   *Similar in flavor to Spain's beloved paella, thanks to the combination of saffron, Spanish chorizo sausage, and seafood, this dish is simple to make using quick-cooking rice-shaped orzo pasta. Feel free to substitute other seafood for the shrimp, such as squid, scallops, clams, or mussels, or use a combination.*

12 ounces whole-wheat orzo

1 large pinch saffron threads, divided

4 ounces chorizo, diced

12 ounces peeled and deveined shrimp

2 roasted red peppers, from a jar, drained and sliced

1 cup fresh or frozen (thawed) peas

2 tablespoons chopped flat-leaf parsley

1. Cook the orzo according to the package instructions, adding half of the saffron to the water.

2. While the pasta is cooking, heat a large skillet over medium-high heat. Add the chorizo and cook, stirring frequently, until the sausage becomes slightly crisp and renders some of its fat, about 5 minutes. Drain some of the rendered fat if there is too much (there should be a tablespoon or two left). Stir in the remaining saffron, shrimp, peppers, and peas and cook, stirring, until the shrimp are fully opaque, about 2 to 3 minutes.

3. When the pasta is done, reserve about ½ cup of the cooking water and then drain the pasta in a colander. Add the pasta back to the cooking pot and stir in the chorizo and shrimp mixture. Add a bit of the reserved pasta cooking water and heat through over medium heat.

4. Just before serving, stir in ¾ of the parsley. Serve hot, garnished with the remaining parsley.

PER SERVING: CALORIES: 552; TOTAL FAT: 14G; SATURATED FAT: 4G; CARBS: 77G; PROTEIN: 37G; SODIUM: 160MG; FIBER: 6G

MOROCCO

MOROCCAN LAMB FLATBREAD
WITH PINE NUTS, MINT, AND RAS AL HANOUT

Serves 4   Prep time: 10 minutes   Cook time: 20 minutes

QUICK & EASY   Ras al hanout *is a North African spice blend that features prominently in Moroccan cooking. A pungent mix of warm spices—usually including cardamom, clove, cinnamon, coriander, cumin, paprika, mace, nutmeg, peppercorn, and turmeric—it is particularly suited for rich, meaty lamb. You can find ras al hanout in the spice rack of many supermarkets, in specialty markets, or online.*

1⅓ cups plain Greek yogurt
Juice of 1½ lemons, divided
1¼ teaspoons salt, divided
1 pound ground lamb
1 medium red onion, diced
1 clove garlic, minced
1 tablespoon ras al hanout
¼ cup chopped fresh mint leaves
Freshly ground black pepper
4 Middle Eastern-style flatbread rounds
2 tablespoons toasted pine nuts
16 cherry tomatoes, halved
2 tablespoons chopped cilantro

★ TIP: Ras al hanout makes a great spice rub for meat, chicken, or fish. Or blend it in a food processor with softened butter to make a compound butter that is delicious when spread on warm flatbread or drizzled over grilled vegetables.

1. Preheat the oven to 450°F.

2. In a small bowl, stir together the yogurt, the juice of ½ lemon, and ¼ teaspoon salt.

3. Heat a large skillet over medium-high heat. Add the lamb and cook, stirring frequently, until browned, about 5 minutes. Drain any excess rendered fat from the pan and then stir in the onion and garlic and cook, stirring, until softened, about 3 minutes more. Stir in the ras al hanout, mint, the remaining teaspoon of salt, and pepper.

4. Place the flatbread rounds on a baking sheet (or two if necessary) and top with the lamb mixture, pine nuts, and tomatoes, dividing equally. Bake in the preheated oven until the crust is golden brown and the tomatoes have softened, about 10 minutes. Scatter the cilantro over the flatbreads and squeeze the remaining lemon juice over them. Cut into wedges and serve dolloped with the yogurt sauce.

PER SERVING: CALORIES: 517; TOTAL FAT: 20G; SATURATED FAT: 7G; CARBS: 45G; PROTEIN: 50G; SODIUM: 1,111MG; FIBER: 16G

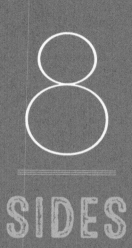

SIDES

SICILIAN-STYLE ROASTED CAULIFLOWER
WITH CAPERS, CURRANTS, AND CRISPY BREADCRUMBS

Serves 4   Prep time: 10 minutes   Cook time: 55 minutes

VEGETARIAN | DAIRY-FREE   *In Sicily, sweet, plump raisins are often combined with briny capers and salty anchovies. Here the distinctive flavor combination tops golden, caramelized cauliflower and is crowned with crunchy garlic breadcrumbs.*

1 large head of cauliflower (2 pounds), cut into 2-inch florets

6 tablespoons olive oil, divided

1 teaspoon salt

½ teaspoon freshly ground black pepper

3 garlic cloves, thinly sliced

2 tablespoons salt-packed capers, soaked, rinsed, and patted dry

¾ cup fresh whole-wheat breadcrumbs

½ cup chicken broth

1 teaspoon anchovy paste

⅓ cup golden raisins

1 tablespoon white wine vinegar

2 tablespoons chopped flat-leaf parsley

1. Preheat the oven to 425°F.

2. In a medium bowl, toss the cauliflower florets with 3 tablespoons olive oil, and the salt and pepper. Spread the cauliflower out in a single layer on a large, rimmed baking sheet and roast in the preheated oven, stirring occasionally, for about 45 minutes, until the cauliflower is golden brown and crispy at the edges.

3. While the cauliflower is roasting, put the remaining 3 tablespoons of olive oil in a small saucepan and heat over medium-low heat. Add the garlic and cook, stirring, for about 5 minutes, until the garlic begins to turn golden. Stir in the capers and cook for 3 minutes more. Add the breadcrumbs, stir to mix well, and cook until the breadcrumbs turn golden brown and are crisp. Use a slotted spoon to transfer the breadcrumbs to a bowl or plate.

4. In the same saucepan, stir together the broth and anchovy paste and bring to a boil over medium-high heat. Stir in the raisins and vinegar and cook, stirring occasionally, for 5 minutes, until the liquid has mostly been absorbed.

5. When the cauliflower is done, transfer it to a large serving bowl. Add the raisin mixture and toss to mix. Top with the breadcrumbs and serve immediately, garnished with parsley.

★ TIP: The individual parts of this recipe can be made ahead and assembled before serving. Roast the cauliflower up to 4 hours ahead and let stand at room temperature until ready to assemble. The breadcrumbs and raisin mixtures can be prepared 2 hours ahead and kept at room temperature. Reheat the cauliflower and raisins before assembling the dish.

PER SERVING: CALORIES: 366; TOTAL FAT: 24G; SATURATED FAT: 3G; CARBS: 37G; PROTEIN: 9G; SODIUM: 1,102MG; FIBER: 7G

MOROCCO

HONEY AND SPICE
GLAZED CARROTS

Serves 4   Prep time: 5 minutes   Cook time: 5 minutes

VEGETARIAN | DAIRY-FREE | GLUTEN-FREE | QUICK & EASY   *In this simple dish, quick-cooked carrots are dressed in a mixture of warm spices, honey, olive oil, vinegar, and fresh herbs. It makes an easy and delicious side that's perfect alongside any sort of grilled or roasted meat or fish. It can also be served at room temperature, making it a great choice for a potluck or picnic.*

4 large carrots, peeled and sliced on the diagonal into ½-inch-thick rounds

1 teaspoon ground cinnamon

1 teaspoon ground ginger

3 tablespoons olive oil

½ cup honey

1 tablespoon red wine vinegar

1 tablespoon chopped flat-leaf parsley

1 tablespoon chopped cilantro

2 tablespoons toasted pine nuts

1. Bring a large saucepan of lightly salted water to a boil and add the carrots. Cover and cook for about 5 minutes, until the carrots are just tender. Drain in a colander, then transfer to a medium bowl.

2. Add the cinnamon, ginger, olive oil, honey, and vinegar and toss to combine well. Add the parsley and cilantro and toss again to incorporate. Garnish with the pine nuts. Serve immediately or let cool to room temperature.

PER SERVING: CALORIES: 281; TOTAL FAT: 14G; SATURATED FAT: 2G; CARBS: 43G; PROTEIN: 1G; SODIUM: 42MG; FIBER: 2G

SOUTHERN ITALY

ROASTED FENNEL
WITH PARMESAN

Serves 4   Prep time: 5 minutes   Cook time: 30 minutes

VEGETARIAN | GLUTEN-FREE   *Fresh fennel, which grows abundantly in the Mediterranean, is an often overlooked vegetable here in the United States. It is a versatile vegetable with a light licorice flavor and a crisp bite when eaten raw. When sautéed or roasted, it becomes beautifully caramelized and sweet, which is delightful in this dish, paired with toasted Parmesan cheese.*

2 fennel bulbs (about 2 pounds), cored and cut into 8 wedges each (reserve fronds for garnish)

¼ cup olive oil

Salt

Freshly ground black pepper

1¼ teaspoons red pepper flakes

½ cup freshly grated Parmesean cheese

1. Preheat the oven to 350°F.

2. Arrange the fennel wedges on a large, rimmed baking sheet and drizzle the oil over the top.

3. Sprinkle each wedge with a pinch each of salt, black pepper, and red pepper flakes. Sprinkle the cheese over the top.

4. Bake in the preheated oven for about 30 minutes, until the fennel is tender and the cheese is golden brown. Remove from the oven and let cool in the oil until just warm. Using a slotted metal spatula, transfer the fennel to plates and garnish with the reserved fennel fronds.

PER SERVING: CALORIES: 237; TOTAL FAT: 19G; SATURATED FAT: 6G; CARBS: 10G; PROTEIN: 11G; SODIUM: 363MG; FIBER: 4G

SOUTHERN ITALY

ROASTED ASPARAGUS AND FINGERLING POTATOES
WITH THYME

Serves 4   Prep time: 5 minutes   Cook time: 20 minutes

VEGETARIAN | GLUTEN-FREE | QUICK & EASY   *Roasting asparagus concentrates its natural sweetness, and roasting thinly sliced fingerling potatoes to a golden brown makes them slightly crisp on the outside and creamy in the middle. The two together are divine.*

1 pound asparagus, trimmed

1 pound fingerling potatoes, cut into thin rounds

2 scallions, thinly sliced

3 tablespoons olive oil

¾ teaspoon salt

¼ teaspoon freshly ground black pepper

1 tablespoon fresh thyme leaves

1. Preheat the oven to 450°F.

2. In a large baking dish, combine the asparagus, potatoes, and scallions and toss to mix. Add the olive oil, salt, and pepper and toss again to coat all of the vegetables in the oil. Spread the vegetables out in as thin a layer as possible and roast in the preheated oven, stirring once, until the vegetables are tender and nicely browned, about 20 minutes. Just before serving, sprinkle with the thyme leaves. Serve hot.

★ TIP: Look for thin asparagus spears for this recipe, since they'll cook more quickly than fatter spears.

PER SERVING: CALORIES: 197; TOTAL FAT: 11G; SATURATED FAT: 2G; CARBS: 24G; PROTEIN: 5G; SODIUM: 449MG; FIBER: 5G

SPAIN

BAKED TOMATOES
WITH SPICED AMARANTH STUFFING

Serves 6   Prep time: 10 minutes   Cook time: 50 minutes

VEGETARIAN | DAIRY-FREE | GLUTEN-FREE   *Amaranth is a gluten-free grain that, like buckwheat and quinoa, is high in plant protein. When cooked, it takes on a creamy porridge-like consistency similar to grits or polenta. It takes well to both sweet and savory seasonings, and both are used in this Spanish-style stuffed tomato recipe.*

1 tablespoon olive oil
1 small onion, diced
1 clove garlic, minced
1 cup amaranth
1 cup vegetable broth or water
1 cup diced tomatoes, drained
¼ cup chopped fresh parsley
½ teaspoon ground cinnamon
½ cup golden raisins
½ cup toasted pine nuts
¾ teaspoon salt
½ teaspoon freshly ground black pepper
6 large ripe tomatoes

1. Preheat the oven to 375°F.

2. Heat the olive oil over medium heat in a medium saucepan. Add the onion and garlic and cook, stirring frequently, until the onion is softened, about 5 minutes. Stir in the amaranth and then the broth or water and bring to a boil over high heat. Lower the heat to low, cover, and cook, stirring occasionally, for about 20 minutes, until the amaranth is tender and the liquid has been absorbed.

3. Remove the pan from the heat and stir in the diced tomatoes, parsley, cinnamon, raisins, pine nuts, salt, and pepper.

4. Cut a slice off the bottom of each tomato to make a flat bottom for it to sit on. Scoop out the seeds and core of the tomato to make a shell for filling. Arrange the hollowed-out tomatoes in a baking dish.

5. Fill the tomatoes with the amaranth mixture and bake in the preheated oven for about 25 minutes, until the tomatoes have softened, but still hold their shape. Serve hot.

PER SERVING: CALORIES: 306; TOTAL FAT: 13G; SATURATED FAT: 2G; CARBS: 43G; PROTEIN: 10G; SODIUM: 439MG; FIBER: 7G

MOROCCO

COUSCOUS-STUFFED EGGPLANTS

Serves 4   Prep time: 10 minutes   Cook time: 45 minutes

VEGETARIAN | DAIRY-FREE   *Eggplant is common in many Mediterranean cuisines. In North Africa, it is often stuffed with a flavorful couscous mixture. Serve this filling side dish alongside grilled meats or fish. If you like, garnish it with a dollop of Tzatziki Sauce (page 241).*

2 medium eggplants
   (about 8 ounces each)
1 tablespoon olive oil
⅓ cup whole-wheat couscous
3 tablespoons diced dried apricots
4 scallions, thinly sliced
1 large tomato, seeded and diced
2 tablespoons chopped fresh mint leaves
1 tablespoon chopped, toasted pine nuts
1 tablespoon lemon juice
½ teaspoon salt
¼ teaspoon freshly ground black pepper

1. Preheat the oven to 400°F.

2. Halve the eggplants lengthwise and score the cut sides with a knife, cutting all the way through the flesh but being careful not to cut through the skin. Brush the cut sides with the olive oil and place the eggplant halves, cut-side up, on a large, rimmed baking sheet. Roast in the preheated oven for about 20 to 30 minutes, until the flesh is softened.

3. While the eggplant is roasting, place the couscous in a small saucepan or heat-safe bowl and cover with boiling water. Cover and let stand until the couscous is tender and has absorbed the water, about 10 minutes.

4. When the eggplants are soft, remove them from the oven (don't turn the oven off) and scoop the flesh into a large bowl, leaving a bit of eggplant inside the skin so that the skin holds its shape. Be cautious not to break the skin. Chop or mash the eggplant flesh and add the couscous, dried apricots, scallions, tomato, mint, pine nuts, lemon juice, salt, and pepper and stir to mix well.

5. Spoon the couscous mixture into the eggplant skins and return them to the baking sheet. Bake in the oven for another 15 minutes or so, until heated through. Serve hot.

PER SERVING: CALORIES: 146; TOTAL FAT: 5G; SATURATED FAT: 1G; CARBS: 22G; PROTEIN: 4G; SODIUM: 471MG; FIBER: 6G

SAUTÉED FAVA BEANS
WITH OLIVE OIL, GARLIC, AND CHILES

Serves 4   Prep time: 10 minutes   Cook time: 7 minutes

VEGETARIAN | DAIRY-FREE | GLUTEN-FREE | QUICK & EASY   *Fava beans, also called broad beans, grow throughout the Mediterranean where they are cooked fresh as in this recipe or dried and stewed like other dried beans. Cooking with fresh favas is slightly fussy since they have to be removed from their pods, then boiled, and then the individual beans must have their tough outer skin removed, but the tender, bright green legumes are totally worth it.*

3½ pounds fresh fava beans, shelled (4 cups)
2 tablespoons olive oil
2 cloves garlic, minced
2 teaspoons fresh lemon juice
1 teaspoon finely grated lemon zest
½ teaspoon crushed red pepper flakes
½ teaspoon salt
¼ teaspoon freshly ground black pepper

1. Bring a medium saucepan of lightly salted water to a boil. Add the shelled favas and cook for 3 to 4 minutes, until tender. Drain the favas and immediately place them in an ice water bath to stop their cooking. When cool, peel the tough outer skin off the beans.

2. Heat the olive oil in a large skillet over medium-high heat. Add the garlic and cook, stirring, until it is aromatic but not browned, about 30 seconds. Add the beans and cook, stirring, until heated through, about 2 minutes. Stir in the lemon juice, lemon zest, red pepper flakes, salt, and pepper and remove from the heat. Serve immediately.

PER SERVING: CALORIES: 576; TOTAL FAT: 9G; SATURATED FAT: 1G; CARBS: 88G; PROTEIN: 39G; SODIUM: 311MG; FIBER: 38G

SOUTHERN ITALY

WHITE BEANS
WITH TOMATOES, KALE, AND PANCETTA

Serves 4   Prep time: 5 minutes   Cook time: 20 minutes

GLUTEN-FREE | QUICK & EASY   *White cannellini beans are popular throughout Italy, where they are often stewed with vegetables and sausage or cured meats. A bit of pancetta—Italian-style cured, unsmoked pork belly, similar to bacon—adds lots of flavor. You can substitute regular bacon if that is what you have on hand, or leave it out altogether for a vegetarian version.*

1 tablespoon olive oil

4 ounces pancetta, diced

1 pound kale, tough center ribs removed, leaves julienned

1 medium onion, diced

2 cloves garlic, thinly sliced

2 dried hot red chiles

¾ teaspoon salt

1 teaspoon finely chopped rosemary

1 teaspoon finely chopped sage

1 (15-ounce) can diced tomatoes with juice

1 (19-ounce) can cannellini beans, drained and rinsed

Freshly ground black pepper

1. Heat the olive oil in a large skillet over medium-high heat. Add the pancetta and cook, stirring frequently, until the fat begins to render, about 3 minutes. Reduce the heat to medium, add the kale, onion, garlic, chiles, and salt, and cook, stirring frequently, until the onion is softened and beginning to brown, about 7 minutes. Stir in the rosemary and sage and then the tomatoes along with their juice. Bring to a simmer.

2. Stir in the beans to the skillet and cook, stirring occasionally, until the sauce begins to thicken, about 7 more minutes. Taste and add pepper if needed. Serve hot.

★ TIP: To julienne the kale, roll the leaves up into long cigars and slice them crosswise into thin ribbons.

PER SERVING: CALORIES: 722; TOTAL FAT: 17G; SATURATED FAT: 5G; CARBS: 101G; PROTEIN: 47G; SODIUM: 1,181MG; FIBER: 37G

SPAIN

ZUCCHINI FRITTERS
WITH MANCHEGO AND SMOKED PAPRIKA YOGURT

Serves 4 to 6   Prep time: 10 minutes, plus 20 minutes to drain zucchini   Cook time: 10 minutes

VEGETARIAN   *Vegetable fritters are popular throughout the Mediterranean. These get distinctive Spanish flavor from manchego cheese and smoked paprika. Using creamy Greek yogurt for the sauce instead of the more traditional aioli or mayonnaise lightens the dish without sacrificing flavor.*

6 small zucchini, grated on the large holes of a box grater

1¼ teaspoons salt, divided

1 cup plain Greek yogurt

2 teaspoons smoked paprika

Juice of ½ lemon

4 ounces manchego cheese, grated

¼ cup finely chopped fresh parsley

4 scallions, thinly sliced

3 eggs, beaten

½ cup all-purpose flour

¼ teaspoon freshly ground black pepper

Neutral-flavored oil (such as grapeseed, safflower, or sunflower seed) for frying

★ TIP: This is a versatile recipe that can be easily modified based on what you have on hand. Use yellow squash in place of zucchini, use Parmesan or feta in place of the manchego, substitute mint or oregano for the parsley, or serve with a garlic aioli instead of the smoked paprika yogurt.

1. Put the grated zucchini in a colander. Sprinkle 1 teaspoon of salt over the top and then toss to combine. Let sit over the sink for at least 20 minutes to drain. Transfer the zucchini to a clean dishtowel and squeeze out as much of the water as you can.

2. Meanwhile, make the yogurt sauce. In a small bowl, stir together the yogurt, smoked paprika, lemon juice, and the remaining ¼ teaspoon of salt.

3. In a large bowl, combine the zucchini, cheese, parsley, scallions, eggs, flour, and pepper and stir to mix.

4. Fill a large saucepan with ½ inch of oil and heat over medium-high heat. When the oil is very hot, drop the batter in by rounded tablespoons, cooking 4 or 5 fritters at a time, flattening each dollop with the back of the spoon. Cook until golden on the bottom, about 2 minutes, then flip and cook on the second side until golden, about 2 minutes more. Transfer the cooked fritters to a plate lined with paper towels to drain and repeat until all of the batter has been cooked.

PER SERVING: CALORIES: 237; TOTAL FAT: 14G; SATURATED FAT: 2G; CARBS: 18G; PROTEIN: 11G; SODIUM: 655MG; FIBER: 3G

GREECE

MASHED POTATOES
WITH GREEK YOGURT, SCALLIONS, AND DILL

Serves 4   Prep time: 5 minutes   Cook time: 20 minutes

VEGETARIAN | GLUTEN-FREE | QUICK & EASY   *Mashed potatoes aren't common in Greece, but these get Greek flavor from fresh dill and scallions and richness from Greek yogurt and olive oil instead of cream or butter. Serve this dish alongside roasted meats for a lighter version of the all-American classic.*

1½ teaspoons salt, plus additional if needed, divided

2 pounds potatoes, cut into 1-inch dice

½ cup plain Greek yogurt

½ cup milk, plus additional if needed

2 teaspoons olive oil

2 scallions, thinly sliced

1 tablespoon chopped fresh dill

1. Fill a medium saucepan with water and add 1 teaspoon of salt. Add the potatoes and cook for about 15 to 20 minutes, until they are fork-tender.

2. Drain the potatoes and return them to the pot. Add the yogurt, milk, the remaining ½ teaspoon of salt, the olive oil, and the scallions. Mash to the desired consistency using a potato masher.

3. Add additional salt or milk if needed and serve immediately, garnished with the dill.

PER SERVING: CALORIES: 224; TOTAL FAT: 5G; SATURATED FAT: 2G; CARBS: 40G; PROTEIN: 6G; SODIUM: 922MG; FIBER: 6G

GREECE

RICE PILAF
WITH SPINACH AND MINT

Serves 4 to 6   Prep time: 10 minutes   Cook time: 30 minutes

VEGETARIAN | DAIRY-FREE | GLUTEN-FREE   *Rice is a popular side dish in Greece, where it is often cooked in pilafs with vegetables and seasonings. This version, loaded with nutritious spinach and flavored with fresh mint, is a perfect accompaniment to any type of grilled or roasted meat or vegetable.*

½ cup olive oil
1 large onion, diced
2 pounds fresh spinach, chopped
2 tablespoons chopped fresh mint leaves
2½ cups water
2 tablespoons tomato paste
1 teaspoon salt
½ teaspoon freshly ground black pepper
1 cup uncooked long-grain white rice

1. Heat the olive oil in a medium saucepan over medium heat. Add the onion and cook, stirring frequently, until softened, about 5 minutes. Add the spinach and mint and cook 3 to 5 minutes more, until the spinach is wilted.

2. Stir in the water, tomato paste, salt, and pepper and bring to a boil. Stir in the rice, cover, reduce the heat to low, and simmer for about 20 minutes, until the rice is tender and the water has been absorbed. Serve hot.

★ TIP: Always keep a few packages of spinach in your freezer for those times when fresh spinach is out of season or you simply need to save time. For this recipe, you can swap 4 (10-ounce) packages of frozen chopped spinach instead of the fresh spinach; just thaw it out and squeeze out as much moisture as you can.

PER SERVING: CALORIES: 368; TOTAL FAT: 21G; SATURATED FAT: 3G; CARBS: 41G; PROTEIN: 9G; SODIUM: 622MG; FIBER: 6G

WARM ASPARAGUS, PEA, AND FAVA BEAN SALAD

Serves 4   Prep time: 10 minutes   Cook time: 10 minutes

GLUTEN-FREE | QUICK & EASY   *Fava beans, peas, and asparagus are used frequently in Mediterranean cooking. Since they all come up in the spring, they make a delightful salad for an Easter lunch or any springtime meal. Pecorino is a distinctly southern Italian cheese and it adds the perfect sharp bite to balance the sweetness of the vegetables.*

3 tablespoons olive oil

1 tablespoon freshly squeezed lemon juice

½ teaspoon salt

½ teaspoon freshly ground black pepper

2 cups fresh fava beans (from about 2 pounds pods) or frozen fava beans, thawed

1 cup fresh or frozen (thawed) peas

2 bunches asparagus, trimmed

4 slices bacon, cooked and crumbled

3 tablespoons fresh mint leaves

1 to 2 ounces Pecorino cheese, shaved thin

1. In a medium bowl, whisk together the olive oil, lemon juice, salt, and pepper.

2. To prepare fresh fava beans and peas, bring a large pan of salted water to a boil, add the favas, and cook for 1 minute. Add the peas and cook for another 3 minutes. Transfer the cooked favas and peas using a slotted spoon to a colander to drain (reserve the cooking water). If you are using frozen favas and peas, bring them to room temperature. Add the favas and peas to the bowl with the olive oil mixture.

3. Bring the reserved water in the saucepan back to a boil, add the asparagus, and cook for about 4 minutes, until just tender. Transfer the asparagus to a colander to drain using, cut the spears into 2-inch lengths, and then add them to the bowl with the favas, peas, and dressing. Toss to coat the vegetables well.

4. Top the salad with the bacon, mint leaves, and cheese and serve immediately.

PER SERVING: CALORIES: 497; TOTAL FAT: 20G; SATURATED FAT: 6G; CARBS: 52G; PROTEIN: 31G; SODIUM: 848MG; FIBER: 22G

9

VEGETARIAN

GREECE

EGGPLANTS STUFFED WITH WALNUTS AND FETA

Serves 6   Prep time: 10 minutes, plus 30 minutes to drain eggplant   Cook time: 55 minutes

VEGETARIAN   *In the Mediterranean, eggplant is often diced and either sautéed or roasted along with other vegetables, or broiled or grilled and puréed into a spread. Here, halved eggplants are hollowed out and filled with a stuffing studded with tomatoes, feta cheese, and walnuts.*

3 medium eggplants, halved lengthwise

2 teaspoons salt, divided

¼ cup olive oil, plus 2 tablespoons, divided

2 medium onions, diced

1½ pints cherry or grape tomatoes, halved

¾ cup roughly chopped walnut pieces

2¼ teaspoons ground cinnamon

1½ teaspoons dried oregano

½ teaspoon freshly ground black pepper

¼ cup whole-wheat breadcrumbs

⅔ cup (about 3 ounces) crumbled feta cheese

1. Scoop out the flesh of the eggplants, leaving a ½-inch thick border of flesh in the skins. Dice the flesh that you removed and place it in a colander set over the sink. Sprinkle 1½ teaspoons of salt over the diced eggplant and inside the eggplant shells and let stand for 30 minutes. Rinse the shells and the pieces and pat dry with paper towels.

2. Heat ¼ cup of olive oil in a large skillet over medium heat. Add the eggplant shells, skin-side down, and cook for about 4 minutes, until browned and softened. Turn over and cook on the cut side until golden brown and soft, about 4 minutes more. Transfer to a plate lined with paper towel to drain.

3. Drain off all but about 1 to 2 tablespoons of the oil in the skillet and heat over medium-high heat. Add the onions and cook, stirring, until beginning to soften, about 3 minutes. Add the diced eggplant, tomatoes, walnuts, cinnamon, oregano, ¼ cup water, the remaining ½ teaspoon of salt, and the pepper. Cook, stirring occasionally, until the vegetables are golden brown and softened, about 8 minutes.

4. Preheat the broiler to high.

5. In a small bowl, toss together the breadcrumbs and 1 tablespoon olive oil.

6. Arrange the eggplant shells cut-side up on a large, rimmed baking sheet. Brush each shell with about ½ teaspoon of olive oil. Cook under the broiler until tender and just starting to turn golden brown, about 5 minutes. Remove the eggplants from the broiler and reduce the heat of the oven to 375°F.

7. Spoon the sautéed vegetable mixture into the eggplant shells, dividing equally. Sprinkle the breadcrumbs over the tops of the filled eggplants, dividing equally. Sprinkle the cheese on top, again dividing equally. Bake in the oven until the filling and shells are heated through and the topping is nicely browned and crisp, about 35 minutes.

★ TIP: Sprinkling salt over the eggplant and letting it sit before cooking pulls out excess liquid and also eliminates any bitter flavor. You can omit this step if you wish to limit sodium.

PER SERVING: CALORIES: 274; TOTAL FAT: 15G; SATURATED FAT: 4G; CARBS: 34G; PROTEIN: 7G; SODIUM: 973MG; FIBER: 13G

CYPRUS

MARINATED VEGGIE KABOBS
WITH HALLOUMI AND FLATBREAD

Serves 4   Prep time: 10 minutes, plus 20 minutes to marinate   Cook time: 12 minutes

VEGETARIAN | QUICK & EASY   *The distinctively salty Cypriot cheese* halloumi *makes this simple grilled veggie kabob dish into a satisfying, yet light, meal. Using summer vegetables like tomatoes, peppers, and zucchini makes this a great dish for grilling outside on a hot summer day. If you prefer, you can cook the skewers under the broiler or on a grill pan on the stove.*

Juice of 1 lemon

¼ cup chopped fresh mint leaves

3 tablespoons olive oil, plus more for
oiling the grill

¾ teaspoon salt

½ teaspoon freshly ground black pepper

8 ounces halloumi cheese, cut into
1½-inch dice

1 large orange bell pepper, cut into
1½-inch squares

1 large red bell pepper, cut into 1½-inch
squares

2 medium zucchini, shaved lengthwise
into strips

1 pint cherry tomatoes

4 whole-wheat flatbread rounds

1. In a large bowl, combine the lemon juice, mint, 3 tablespoons olive oil, salt, and pepper and stir to mix. Add the cheese, peppers, zucchini strips, and tomatoes, and toss to coat. Let marinate for 20 minutes.

2. Meanwhile, soak 8 bamboo skewers in water. Preheat the grill to high and brush the grate lightly with oil.

3. Thread the cheese and vegetables onto the skewers, dividing equally and alternating ingredients so that you have some of each vegetable and the cheese on each skewer. The zucchini strips can be folded and skewered through the center holding them in ribbon shape.

4. Grill the skewers on the hot grill, turning every few minutes, until the vegetables are softened and the cheese and vegetables begin to brown in places, about 12 minutes total.

5. Meanwhile, heat the flatbreads on the grill. Serve the kabobs and flatbread immediately.

PER SERVING: CALORIES: 514; TOTAL FAT: 31G; SATURATED FAT: 14G; CARBS: 42G; PROTEIN: 21G; SODIUM: 1,195MG; FIBER: 8G

SOUTHERN ITALY

FAVA BEAN PURÉE
WITH CHICORY

Serves 4   Prep time: 5 minutes, plus overnight soaking time for the beans   Cook time: 2 hours, 10 minutes

VEGETARIAN   *This is a classic dish from the Puglia region of Southern Italy—the heel of the boot, as it were. It uses dried fava beans and fresh chicory (also known as endive), which is slightly bitter and crisp when raw, but becomes sweet and tender when sautéed.*

½ pound dried fava beans, soaked in water overnight and drained
1 pound chicory leaves
¼ cup olive oil
1 small onion, chopped
1 clove garlic, minced
Salt

1. In a saucepan, cover the fava beans by at least an inch of water and bring to a boil over medium-high heat. Reduce the heat to low, cover, and simmer until very tender, about 2 hours. Check the pot from time to time to make sure there is enough water and add more as needed.

2. Drain off any excess water and then mash the beans with a potato masher.

3. While the beans are cooking, bring a large pot of salted water to a boil. Add the chicory and cook for about 3 minutes, until tender. Drain.

4. In a medium skillet, heat the olive oil over medium-high heat. Add the onion and a pinch of salt and cook, stirring frequently, until softened and beginning to brown, about 5 minutes. Add the garlic and cook, stirring, for another minute. Transfer half of the onion mixture, along with the oil, to the bowl with the mashed beans and stir to mix. Taste and add salt as needed.

5. Serve the purée topped with some of the remaining onions and oil, with the chicory leaves on the side.

PER SERVING: CALORIES: 336; TOTAL FAT: 14G; SATURATED FAT: 2G; CARBS: 40G; PROTEIN: 17G; SODIUM: 59MG; FIBER: 19G

MOROCCO

SPICED CHICKPEAS
WITH PRESERVED LEMONS

Serves 4   Prep time: 10 minutes   Cook time: 30 minutes

VEGETARIAN | DAIRY-FREE | GLUTEN-FREE   *In North African cuisine, lemons are often preserved in salt and lemon juice along with other flavorings and used to add deep flavor to stews and sauces. Preserved lemons are easy to make (see page 246) and will keep for months in your refrigerator. You can also buy them at specialty markets or online.*

2 tablespoons olive oil

1 medium onion, diced

4 medium carrots, cut into thin rounds

2 cloves garlic, minced

1 teaspoon salt

1 teaspoon Aleppo pepper

½ teaspoon ground cumin

½ teaspoon ground coriander

¼ teaspoon allspice

¼ teaspoon ground cinnamon

2 (15-ounce) cans chickpeas, drained and rinsed

1 Preserved Lemons with Moroccan Spices (page 246), rinsed and finely chopped

3 dried dates, pitted and chopped

2 cups (about 5 ounces) baby kale or baby chard, chopped

2 tablespoons lemon juice

1. Heat the olive oil in a stockpot over medium-high heat. Add the onion and cook, stirring frequently, until it is soft and beginning to brown, about 8 minutes. Add the carrots, garlic, salt, Aleppo pepper, cumin, coriander, allspice, and cinnamon and cook, stirring, for 1 minute more. Add the chickpeas, preserved lemon, and 3 cups of water and bring to a simmer.

2. Reduce the heat to medium-low and let simmer for 5 minutes. Stir in the dates and cook 10 minutes more. Add the kale and cook, stirring, until the leaves are wilted, about 2 minutes more. Stir in the lemon juice just before serving. Serve hot.

PER SERVING: CALORIES: 915; TOTAL FAT: 20G; SATURATED FAT: 2G; CARBS: 149G; PROTEIN: 43G; SODIUM: 694MG; FIBER: 41G

GREECE

BAKED GIGANTE BEANS
WITH TOMATOES AND HERBS

Serves 6   Prep time: 10 minutes, plus overnight to soak the beans   Cook time: 3 hours

VEGETARIAN | DAIRY-FREE | GLUTEN-FREE   *Giant white beans* (gigantes) *baked in an herb-studded tomato sauce is a classic Greek dish called* plaki gigantes. *It is often garnished with crumbled feta cheese and served with crusty bread for dipping and scooping as a vegetarian entrée or as part of a mezze* (appetizer) *platter.*

1 pound dried gigante beans, soaked in
    water overnight
¾ cup olive oil
2 medium onions, diced
2 stalks celery, diced
6 cloves garlic, minced
1 (15-ounce) can crushed tomatoes
¾ cup chopped fresh parsley
⅓ cup chopped fresh mint leaves
1 tablespoon crushed, dried oregano
1 tablespoon salt
2 teaspoons freshly ground black pepper

★ TIP: Gigante beans are large, white beans that can be found in specialty markets or online. If you can't find them, substitute any large, white bean such as large limas, flageolets, or butter beans.

1. In a stockpot, cover the beans by 5 inches of water and bring to a boil over high heat. Reduce the heat to low and simmer until the beans are just tender, about 45 minutes. Drain the beans, reserving 2 cups of the cooking liquid.

2. Preheat the oven to 350°F.

3. Heat the olive oil in a large skillet over medium-high heat. Add the onions and celery and cook, stirring frequently, until softened, about 5 minutes. Add the garlic and cook, stirring, 2 minutes more. Stir in the tomatoes, the reserved bean cooking water, parsley, mint, dried oregano, salt, and pepper and bring to a boil. Reduce the heat if necessary and simmer for 10 minutes.

4. Spread the beans out in an even layer in a 9-by-13-inch baking dish. Spoon the sauce over the top. Bake in the preheated oven, stirring about every 30 minutes and adding additional water if needed, for 2 hours.

5. Remove from the oven and let rest for about 15 minutes before serving. Serve hot.

PER SERVING: CALORIES: 527; TOTAL FAT: 26G; SATURATED FAT: 4G; CARBS: 58G; PROTEIN: 19G; SODIUM: 1,311MG; FIBER: 20G

ROOT VEGETABLE SOUP
WITH GARLIC AIOLI

Serves 4   Prep time: 10 minutes   Cook time 25 minutes

VEGETARIAN | DAIRY-FREE | GLUTEN-FREE | QUICK & EASY   *This vegetable hot pot is deceptively simple. The ingredients are humble and accessible, but the finished dish is far more than the sum of its parts. The vegetables become meltingly tender, the broth takes on the vegetables' earthy flavors, and the garlicky aioli dissolves into the soup as you eat, giving the soup even more flavor and richness.*

For the soup
8 cups vegetable broth
½ teaspoon salt
1 medium leek, cut into thick rounds
1 pound carrots, peeled and diced
1 pound potatoes, peeled and diced
1 pound turnips, peeled and cut into
    1-inch cubes
1 red bell pepper, cut into strips
2 tablespoons fresh oregano

For the aioli
5 garlic cloves, minced
¼ teaspoon salt
⅔ cup olive oil
1 drop lemon juice

1. Bring the broth and salt to a boil and add the vegetables one at a time, letting the water return to a boil after each addition. Add the carrots first, then the leeks, potatoes, turnips, and finally the red bell peppers. Let the vegetables cook for about 3 minutes after adding the green beans and bringing to a boil. The process will take about 20 minutes in total.

2. Meanwhile, make the aioli. In a mortar and pestle, grind the garlic to a paste with the salt. Using a whisk and whisking constantly, add the olive oil in a thin stream. Continue whisking until the mixture thickens to the consistency of mayonnaise. Add the lemon juice.

3. Serve the vegetables in the broth, dolloped with the aioli and garnished with the fresh oregano.

★ TIP: You can make the aioli in a small food processor. Grind the garlic and salt together and then add the oil in a thin stream with the processor running.

PER SERVING: CALORIES: 559; TOTAL FAT: 37G; SATURATED FAT: 6G; SODIUM: 2,130MG; CARBS: 46G; FIBER: 10G; PROTEIN: 15G

PROVENÇAL RATATOUILLE
WITH HERBED BREADCRUMBS AND GOAT CHEESE

Serves 4   Prep time: 10 minutes   Cook time: 1 hour and 5 minutes

VEGETARIAN   *Ratatouille is a stewed vegetable dish that originated in Southern France, in the region of Provence. There are many methods for making ratatouille, but the end result is usually a casserole of summer vegetables—tomatoes, eggplant, zucchini, bell peppers—flavored with onions, garlic, and fresh herbs. This version is topped with tangy goat cheese and crisp, herbed breadcrumbs. Serve it over pasta or polenta, if you like, or with hunks of crusty bread.*

6 tablespoons olive oil, divided

2 medium onions, diced

2 cloves garlic, minced

2 medium eggplants, halved lengthwise and cut into ¾-inch thick half rounds

3 medium zucchini, halved lengthwise and cut into ¾-inch thick half rounds

2 red bell peppers, seeded and cut into 1½-inch pieces

1 green bell pepper, seeded and cut into 1½-inch pieces

1 (14-ounce) can diced tomatoes, drained

1 teaspoon salt

½ teaspoon freshly ground black pepper

8 ounces fresh breadcrumbs

1 tablespoon chopped fresh parsley

1 tablespoon chopped fresh basil

1 tablespoon chopped fresh chives

6 ounces soft, fresh goat cheese

1. Preheat the oven to 375°F.

2. Heat 5 tablespoons of the olive oil in a large skillet over medium heat. Add the onions and garlic and cook, stirring frequently, until the onions are soft and beginning to turn golden, about 8 minutes. Add the eggplant, zucchini, and bell peppers and cook, turning the vegetables occasionally, for another 10 minutes. Stir in the tomatoes, salt, and pepper and let simmer for 15 minutes.

3. While the vegetables are simmering, stir together the breadcrumbs, the remaining tablespoon of olive oil, the parsley, basil, and chives.

4. Transfer the vegetable mixture to a large baking dish, spreading it out into an even layer. Crumble the goat cheese over the top, then sprinkle the breadcrumb mixture evenly over the top. Bake in the preheated oven for about 30 minutes, until the topping is golden brown and crisp. Serve hot.

PER SERVING: CALORIES: 701; TOTAL FAT: 37G; SATURATED FAT: 10G; CARBS: 77G; PROTEIN: 23G; SODIUM: 1,185MG; FIBER: 18G

MOROCCAN RED LENTIL AND PUMPKIN STEW

Serves 4   Prep time: 10 minutes   Cook time: 30 minutes

VEGETARIAN | DAIRY-FREE | GLUTEN-FREE   *Red lentils are full of protein and fiber, and they cook quickly, making this an easy one-pot vegetarian meal. Serve it with a dollop of Greek yogurt or a dab of spicy harissa, if you like, plus whole-wheat flatbread for dipping and scooping.*

2 tablespoons olive oil

1 teaspoon ground cumin

1 teaspoon ground turmeric

1 tablespoon curry powder

1 large onion, diced

1 teaspoon salt

2 tablespoons minced fresh ginger

4 cloves garlic, minced

1 pound pumpkin, peeled, seeded, and cut into 1-inch dice

1 red bell pepper, seeded and diced

1½ cups red lentils, rinsed

6 cups vegetable broth

¼ cup chopped cilantro, for garnish

1. Heat the olive oil in a stockpot over medium heat. Add the cumin, turmeric, and curry powder and cook, stirring, for 1 minute, until fragrant. Add the onion and salt and cook, stirring frequently, until softened, about 5 minutes. Add the ginger and garlic and cook, stirring frequently, for 2 more minutes. Stir in the pumpkin and bell pepper, and then the lentils and broth and bring to a boil.

2. Reduce the heat to low and simmer, uncovered, for about 20 minutes, until the lentils are very tender. Serve hot, garnished with cilantro.

PER SERVING: CALORIES: 458; TOTAL FAT: 11G; SATURATED FAT: 2G; CARBS: 64G; PROTEIN: 29G; SODIUM: 1,743MG; FIBER: 28G

EGGS POACHED IN MOROCCAN TOMATO SAUCE

Serves 4   Prep time: 10 minutes   Cook time: 35 minutes

VEGETARIAN | DAIRY-FREE | GLUTEN-FREE   *In Mediterranean cuisine, eggs are seen as a quick and healthy protein that's perfect to serve for dinner. In this classic North African dish, they are poached in a spicy tomato sauce.* Ras al hanout *is a North African spice blend that can be found in the spice rack of many supermarkets, in specialty markets, or online.*

1 tablespoon olive oil
1 medium yellow onion, diced
2 red bell peppers, seeded and diced
1¾ teaspoons sweet paprika
1 teaspoon ras al hanout
½ teaspoon cayenne pepper
1 teaspoon salt
¼ cup tomato paste
1 (28-ounce) can diced
   tomatoes, drained
8 eggs
¼ cup chopped cilantro

1. Heat the olive oil in a skillet over medium-high heat. Add the onion and bell peppers and cook, stirring frequently, until softened, about 5 minutes. Stir in the paprika, ras al hanout, cayenne, salt, and tomato paste and cook, stirring occasionally, for 5 minutes.

2. Stir in the diced tomatoes, reduce the heat to medium-low, and simmer for about 15 minutes, until the tomatoes break down and the sauce thickens.

3. Make 8 wells in the sauce and drop one egg into each. Cover the pan and cook for about 10 minutes, until the whites are fully set, but the yolks are still runny.

4. Spoon the sauce and eggs into serving bowls and serve hot, garnished with cilantro.

★ TIP: To avoid breaking the yolks when you add the eggs to the pan, crack each into a separate ramekin and gently tip it into the sauce before cracking the next egg.

PER SERVING: CALORIES: 238; TOTAL FAT: 13G; SATURATED FAT: 3G; CARBS: 18G; PROTEIN: 15G; SODIUM: 735MG; FIBER: 5G

GREECE

GREEK FRITTATA
WITH TOMATO-OLIVE SALAD

Serves 4 to 6   Prep time: 10 minutes   Cook time: 25 minutes

VEGETARIAN | QUICK & EASY   *Though frittatas are technically Italian, this version, studded with feta cheese and scallions and served with a tomato and olive salad—is distinctly Greek in flavor. It makes a wonderful light meal and since the frittata can be served either warm or at room temperature, it can easily be made ahead.*

For the frittata

2 tablespoons olive oil

6 scallions, thinly sliced

4 cups (about 5 ounces) baby spinach leaves

8 eggs

¼ cup whole-wheat breadcrumbs, divided

1 cup (about 3 ounces) crumbled feta cheese

¾ teaspoon salt

¼ teaspoon freshly ground black pepper

For the tomato-olive salad

2 tablespoons olive oil

1 tablespoon lemon juice

¼ teaspoon dried oregano

½ teaspoon salt

¼ teaspoon freshly ground black pepper

1 pint cherry, grape, or other small tomatoes, halved

3 pepperoncini, stemmed and chopped

½ cup coarsely chopped pitted Kalamata olives

1. Preheat the oven to 450°F.

2. Heat the olive oil in an oven-safe skillet set over medium-high heat. Add the scallions and spinach and cook, stirring frequently, for about 4 minutes, until the spinach wilts.

3. In a medium bowl, whisk together the eggs, 2 tablespoons breadcrumbs, cheese, ¾ cup water, salt, and pepper. Pour the egg mixture into the skillet with the spinach and onions and stir to mix. Sprinkle the remaining 2 tablespoons of breadcrumbs evenly over the top. Bake the frittata in the preheated oven for about 20 minutes, until the egg is set and the top is lightly browned.

4. While the frittata is cooking, make the salad. In a medium bowl, whisk together the olive oil, lemon juice, oregano, salt, and pepper. Add the tomatoes, pepperoncini, and olives and toss to mix well.

5. Invert the frittata onto a serving platter and slice it into wedges. Serve warm or at room temperature with the tomato-olive salad.

PER SERVING: CALORIES: 341; TOTAL FAT: 27G; SATURATED FAT: 8G; CARBS: 12G; PROTEIN: 15G; SODIUM: 1,379MG; FIBER: 2G

SPAIN

SWEET POTATO
SPANISH TORTILLA

Serves 4   Prep time: 10 minutes   Cook time: 20 minutes

VEGETARIAN | GLUTEN-FREE | QUICK & EASY   *Spanish tortilla is Spain's version of the frittata with the addition of potatoes. This version uses sweet potatoes for a boost of color and nutrition.*

½ cup bottled roasted red bell peppers (about 3 ounces), drained and rinsed

1 tablespoon dry-roasted almonds, coarsely chopped

2 tablespoons olive oil, divided

¾ teaspoon salt, divided

⅛ teaspoon cayenne pepper

2 cloves garlic, minced

8 ounces sweet potatoes, cut into thin (about ¼-inch) slices

2 tablespoons milk

½ teaspoon freshly ground black pepper

6 eggs

2 egg whites

2 cups baby spinach leaves

1. Preheat the broiler to high. To make the sauce, in a food processor, combine the roasted peppers, almonds, 1 tablespoon olive oil, ¼ teaspoon of salt, cayenne, and garlic and pulse to a smooth purée.

2. Put the sweet potatoes in a skillet with 1 cup of water and bring to a boil over medium-high heat. Reduce the heat to low, cover, and simmer until the potatoes are tender, about 4 minutes. Drain the potatoes.

3. In a medium bowl, whisk together the milk, the remaining ½ teaspoon of salt, pepper, eggs, and egg whites.

4. Heat the remaining 1 tablespoon of olive oil in a medium, oven-safe skillet over medium-high heat. Add the potatoes and cook, flipping occasionally, until they begin to brown, about 5 minutes. Add the spinach and cook, stirring, until it wilts, about 1 minute. Add the egg mixture, reduce the heat to medium-low, cover, and cook, shaking the pan once in a while, for 4 minutes.

5. Transfer the skillet to the broiler to finish cooking. Broil until the center is fully set and the top is golden brown, about 5 minutes. Serve warm or at room temperature, drizzled with the sauce.

PER SERVING: CALORIES: 259; TOTAL FAT: 15G; SATURATED FAT: 3G; CARBS: 20G; PROTEIN: 12G; SODIUM: 613MG; FIBER: 3G

SPAIN

VEGETARIAN PAELLA
WITH GREEN BEANS AND CHICKPEAS

Serves 4   Prep time: 10 minutes   Cook time: 35 minutes

VEGETARIAN | DAIRY-FREE | GLUTEN-FREE   *Paella is a classic Spanish dish in which saffron-scented rice is cooked with vegetables and topped with seafood, sausage, or other meats. This vegetarian version is made with green beans and chickpeas instead of meat, but with the rich flavors of saffron, onion, garlic, and tomatoes, you'll hardly notice the difference.*

Pinch of saffron (about 8 threads)
3 cups vegetable broth
1 tablespoon olive oil
1 large yellow onion, diced
4 cloves garlic, thinly sliced
1 red bell pepper, diced
¾ cup crushed tomatoes, fresh
   or canned
2 tablespoons tomato paste
1½ teaspoons hot paprika
1 teaspoon salt
½ teaspoon freshly ground black pepper
1½ cups green beans, trimmed
   and halved
1 (15-ounce) can chickpeas, drained
   and rinsed
1 cup short-grain white rice
1 lemon, cut into wedges, for serving

⭐ TIP: In Spain, paella is made with short-grain white rice. You can substitute any short-grain or medium-grain white rice, but don't use long-grain rice, as it won't soak up the flavors the way the shorter grains will.

1. In a small bowl, mix the saffron threads with 3 tablespoons of warm water.

2. In a medium saucepan, bring the broth to a simmer over medium-high heat. Reduce the heat to low and let the broth simmer.

3. In a large cast-iron skillet, heat the olive oil over medium-high heat. Add the onion and cook, stirring frequently, until softened, about 5 minutes. Add the garlic and bell pepper and cook for about 7 minutes more, until the pepper is softened. Stir in the tomatoes, tomato paste, paprika, the saffron-water mixture, and the salt and pepper.

4. Add the green beans, chickpeas, and rice. Add the warm broth and bring the mixture to a boil over medium-high heat. Reduce the heat to low and let simmer, uncovered, until the rice is cooked and the liquid has evaporated, about 20 minutes. Serve hot, garnished with lemon wedges.

PER SERVING: CALORIES: 709; TOTAL FAT: 12G; SATURATED FAT: 2G; CARBS: 121G; PROTEIN: 33G; SODIUM: 1,248MG; FIBER: 22G

TURKEY

TURKISH RED LENTIL AND BULGUR
KOFTE

Serves 4   Prep time: 10 minutes   Cook time: 45 minutes

VEGETARIAN | DAIRY-FREE   Kofte *are Turkish-style meatballs that are usually grilled. This vegetarian version combines red lentils and bulgur and is flavored with parsley, scallions, and lemon. Serve it with lettuce leaves or flatbread for wrapping and Tzatziki Sauce (page 241), if you like.*

⅓ cup olive oil, plus 2 tablespoons, divided, plus more for brushing
1 cup red lentils
½ cup bulgur
1 teaspoon salt
1 medium onion, finely diced
2 tablespoons tomato paste
1 teaspoon ground cumin
¼ cup finely chopped flat-leaf parsley
3 scallions, thinly sliced
Juice of ½ lemon

1. Preheat the oven to 400°F.

2. Brush a large, rimmed baking sheet with olive oil.

3. In a medium saucepan, combine the lentils with 2 cups water and bring to a boil. Reduce the heat to low and cook, stirring occasionally, for about 15 minutes, until the lentils are tender and have soaked up most of the liquid. Remove from the heat, stir in the bulgur and salt, cover, and let sit for 15 minutes or so, until the bulgur is tender.

4. Meanwhile, heat ⅓ cup olive oil in a medium skillet over medium-high heat. Add the onion and cook, stirring frequently, until softened, about 5 minutes. Stir in the tomato paste and cook for 2 minutes more. Remove from the heat and stir in the cumin.

5. Add the cooked onion mixture to the lentil-bulgur mixture and stir to combine. Add the parsley, scallions, and lemon juice and stir to mix well.

6. Shape the mixture into walnut-sized balls and place them on the prepared baking sheet. Brush the balls with the remaining 2 tablespoons of olive oil and bake for 15 to 20 minutes, until golden brown. Serve hot.

PER SERVING: CALORIES: 460; TOTAL FAT: 25G; SATURATED FAT: 4G; CARBS: 48G; PROTEIN: 16G; SODIUM: 604MG; FIBER: 19G

WHOLE-WHEAT RIGATONI
WITH ARTICHOKES, OLIVES, AND ORANGE ZEST

Serves 4   Prep time: 10 minutes   Cook time: 15 minutes

VEGETARIAN | QUICK & EASY   *Pairing sweet fruit with vegetables and other savory ingredients like olives is common in many Mediterranean cuisines, particularly North African and Southern Italian. Here, earthy artichokes and salty olives are perked up with the brightness of orange zest and tossed with toothsome whole-wheat pasta.*

1 pound whole-wheat rigatoni

2 tablespoons butter

6 tablespoons olive oil

2 cloves garlic, minced

2 tablespoons minced fresh rosemary

½ cup pitted and halved Kalamata olives, drained

6 artichoke hearts in oil, drained and quartered

⅓ cup dry white wine, plus 1 tablespoon

Finely grated zest of ½ orange

Salt

Freshly ground black pepper

¼ cup freshly grated Pecorino Romano

1. Cook the pasta according to the package instructions. Drain.

2. While the pasta is cooking, heat the butter and olive oil together in a large skillet over medium-high heat. When the butter is melted, stir in the garlic, rosemary, olives, and artichokes. Cook, stirring occasionally, for 3 minutes.

3. Stir in the wine and bring to a boil. Cook until the alcohol has evaporated, about 2 minutes.

4. Add the orange zest, salt, and pepper to season, and remove from the heat.

5. Add the cooked pasta to the vegetable mixture in the skillet and cook, tossing to mix well, over high heat for about 30 seconds, until the pasta is well coated with sauce and everything is heated through. Serve hot, garnished with cheese.

PER SERVING: CALORIES: 704; TOTAL FAT: 36G; SATURATED FAT: 11G; CARBS: 76G; PROTEIN: 19G; SODIUM: 495MG; FIBER: 15G

SWISS CHARD AND GOAT CHEESE CANNELLONI
WITH TOMATO SAUCE

Serves 4   Prep time: 15 minutes   Cook time: 35 minutes

VEGETARIAN   *As easy to make as lasagna, this stuffed pasta dish—filled with nutritious chard and tangy goat cheese and topped with a simple tomato sauce—makes an impressive vegetarian entrée.*

1 pound Swiss chard, tough center ribs removed, leaves julienned

¼ cup olive oil, plus 2 tablespoons, divided

1 medium onion, diced

6 ounces fresh goat cheese, crumbled

½ cup grated Pecorino Romano, divided

1¼ cups fresh whole-wheat breadcrumbs

½ teaspoon salt

¼ teaspoon freshly ground black pepper

2 cups tomato sauce

1 pound cannelloni sheets, cooked and cooled

½ cup plain dry whole-wheat breadcrumbs, as needed

1. Preheat the oven to 350°F.

2. Bring a large pot of salted water to a boil over high heat. Add the chard leaves, stirring to submerge them. Cook for 3 to 4 minutes, until tender. Remove the leaves from the water using a slotted spoon and immediately place them in an ice water bath. Let the leaves chill and then drain them in a colander for several minutes. Squeeze out any excess water and chop.

3. Meanwhile, heat ¼ cup olive oil in a medium saucepan set over medium heat. Add the onion and cook, stirring often, until softened, about 5 minutes. Stir in the chard, cover, reduce the heat to low, and cook for 2 minutes. Put the mixture in a large bowl and set aside to cool for about 10 minutes.

4. Add the goat cheese, ¼ cup of the Pecorino Romano, and the fresh breadcrumbs, salt, and pepper to the greens and stir to mix.

5. Brush a baking dish with a bit of olive oil and pour in the tomato sauce. Spread it over the bottom.

6. On a separate plate, fill the pasta by dividing the greens and cheese mixture between the cooked pasta sheets, then roll up the pasta around the filling into cylinders. Each stuffed pasta cylinder should be approximately 3 inches in diameter. Cut the stuffed pasta tubes into 4-inch lengths and arrange them in a single layer in the baking dish, seam-side down. Brush the cannelloni with the remaining 2 tablespoons of olive oil.

7. In a small bowl, combine the dry breadcrumbs and the remaining ¼ cup Pecorino Romano. Sprinkle the breadcrumb mixture evenly over the pasta tubes.

8. Bake, uncovered, for about 20 minutes, until very hot and beginning to brown on top. Serve hot.

PER SERVING: CALORIES: 727; TOTAL FAT: 35G; SATURATED FAT: 15G; CARBS: 76G; PROTEIN: 34G; SODIUM: 1,755MG; FIBER: 12G

SEAFOOD

CLAM CATAPLANA
WITH CHOURIÇO

Serves 4   Prep time: 5 minutes   Cook time: 25 minutes

DAIRY-FREE | GLUTEN-FREE | QUICK & EASY   Cataplana *is a classic Portuguese seafood dish—often made with a mixture of shellfish and sausage—that is cooked in a copper pan by the same name. If you don't have a cataplana, use a large, wide, heavy-bottomed saucepan with a tight-fitting lid.*

2 tablespoons olive oil

2 medium red onions, thinly sliced

2 cloves garlic, minced

1 large bulb fennel, cored and sliced

6 ounces Portuguese chouriço sausage (or linguiça or Spanish chorizo), diced

¼ teaspoon crushed red pepper flakes

1 pound chopped fresh tomatoes

4 pounds littleneck clams

½ cup dry white wine

2 tablespoons chopped flat-leaf parsley

1. Heat the olive oil in a cataplana or a large, heavy saucepan, over medium-high heat. Add the onions, garlic, and fennel, and cook, stirring frequently, until the vegetables are soft, about 5 minutes. Add the sausage and cook, stirring, until the sausage and vegetables begin to brown, about 5 minutes more. Stir in the red pepper flakes and tomatoes and cook, stirring occasionally, until the tomatoes begin to break down, about 5 more minutes.

2. Add the clams on top of the vegetables, add the wine, cover, and cook over medium-high heat for about 8 minutes, until most of the clams have opened (discard any that haven't opened).

3. Serve the clams in bowls, with the broth, vegetables, and sausage ladled over them. Garnish with parsley just before serving.

★ TIP: Clams should be alive when you buy them, with their shells firmly closed. To check if your clams are still living, give them a quick tap and watch for their shells to tighten.

PER SERVING: CALORIES: 500; TOTAL FAT: 20G; SATURATED FAT: 5G; CARBS: 66G; PROTEIN: 12G; SODIUM: 1,981MG; FIBER: 6G

GREECE

LEMON-OREGANO
GRILLED SHRIMP

Serves 6   Prep time: 10 minutes   Cook time: 6 minutes

DAIRY-FREE | GLUTEN-FREE | QUICK & EASY   *Lemon and oregano are the quintessential flavors of Greece. Stirred together in a garlicky olive oil infusion and drizzled over plump grilled shrimp, the combination will transport you straight to the Greek Isles.*

½ cup oregano leaves

1 clove garlic, minced

1 teaspoon finely grated lemon zest

3 tablespoons lemon juice

¾ teaspoon salt, plus more for seasoning shrimp

½ teaspoon freshly ground black pepper, plus more for seasoning shrimp

½ cup olive oil, plus 2 tablespoons, divided

2½ pounds large shrimp, peeled and deveined

1. In a small bowl, stir together the oregano, garlic, lemon zest, lemon juice, salt, and pepper. Whisk in ½ cup of olive oil until well combined.

2. Preheat the grill to high heat.

3. Place the shrimp in a large bowl and toss with the remaining 2 tablespoons of olive oil and a pinch or two of salt and pepper. Thread the shrimp onto skewers, 3 to 5 at a time depending on the size of the shrimp. Place the skewers on the grill and cook for 2 to 3 minutes per side, just until the shrimp are cooked through and just beginning to char. As the shrimp are cooked, transfer the skewers to a serving platter. Spoon the sauce over the skewers and serve immediately.

PER SERVING: CALORIES: 389; TOTAL FAT: 26G; SATURATED FAT: 4G; CARBS: 8G; PROTEIN: 36G; SODIUM: 530MG; FIBER: 3G

GARLIC PRAWNS
WITH TOMATOES AND BASIL

Serves 4   Prep time: 10 minutes   Cook time: 10 minutes

DAIRY-FREE | GLUTEN-FREE | QUICK & EASY   *Garlicky shrimp makes a quick, delicious, and healthy Mediterranean-style meal. The traditional Italian shrimp scampi is usually loaded with butter, but this version uses just a touch of olive oil. Plump shrimp are tossed in a quick sauce of garlic, basil, tomatoes, and white wine. Serve this dish on its own or over pasta, polenta, or alongside roasted potatoes.*

2 tablespoons olive oil

1¼ pounds shrimp, peeled and deveined

3 cloves garlic, minced

⅛ teaspoon crushed red pepper flakes

¾ cup dry white wine

1½ cups grape tomatoes

¼ cup finely chopped fresh basil, plus more for garnish

¾ teaspoon salt

½ teaspoon freshly ground black pepper

1. Heat the olive oil in a medium skillet over medium-high heat. Add the shrimp and cook about 1 minute on each side, until just cooked through. Transfer the shrimp to a plate, leaving the oil in the pan.

2. Add the garlic and red pepper flakes to the oil in the pan and cook, stirring, for 30 seconds. Stir in the wine and cook until it is reduced by about half. Add the tomatoes and cook, stirring, for 3 to 4 minutes more, until the tomatoes begin to break down. Stir in the basil, salt, pepper, and the reserved shrimp. Cook 1 to 2 minutes more, until heated through. Serve hot, garnished with the remaining basil.

PER SERVING: CALORIES: 282; TOTAL FAT: 10G; SATURATED FAT: 2G; CARBS: 7G; PROTEIN: 33G; SODIUM: 299MG; FIBER: 1G

STUFFED CALAMARI
IN TOMATO SAUCE

Serves 4 to 6   Prep time: 10 minutes   Cook time: 25 minutes

QUICK & EASY   *Stuffed squid in tomato sauce is a Sardinian specialty. This version is stuffed with a breadcrumb, onion, garlic, Pecorino, and raisin stuffing that is both savory and sweet.*

For the squid

½ cup olive oil, plus 3 tablespoons, divided

2 large onions, finely chopped

4 cloves garlic, finely chopped

1 cup grated Pecorino Romano, plus ¼ cup, divided

½ cup finely chopped flat-leaf parsley, plus ¼ cup, divided

6 cups breadcrumbs

1 cup raisins

12 large squid tubes, cleaned

12 toothpicks

For the tomato sauce

2 tablespoons olive oil

4 cloves garlic, finely chopped

2 (28-ounce) cans crushed tomatoes

½ cup finely chopped basil

1 teaspoon salt

1 teaspoon pepper

★ TIP: Buying already cleaned squid tubes will save you time, but doing it yourself won't take more than 5 minutes or so.

1. Preheat the oven to 350°F.

2. To make the filling for the squid, heat 2 tablespoons olive oil in a large skillet over medium-high heat. Add the onions and cook, stirring frequently, until softened, about 5 minutes. Transfer the onions to a large mixing bowl and add ½ cup of olive oil, garlic, 1 cup of cheese, ½ cup of parsley, breadcrumbs, and raisins and stir to mix.

3. Drizzle the remaining 1 tablespoon of olive oil in a baking dish large enough to hold the squid in a single layer. Stuff the filling into the squid tubes, dividing it equally. Use a toothpick to secure the open end of the squid. Lay the tubes in the baking dish. Bake in the preheated oven for 10 minutes.

4. While the squid is in the oven, make the tomato sauce. Heat the oil in a large skillet over medium-high heat. Add the garlic and stir for 30 seconds. Add the tomatoes, basil, salt, and pepper and simmer for 5 minutes.

5. Remove the baking dish from the oven, and spoon the tomato sauce over the top. Sprinkle the remaining ¼ cup of cheese and the remaining ¼ cup of parsley over the top. Bake for another 10 minutes or so, until the cheese is melted. Serve immediately.

PER SERVING: CALORIES: 1,304; TOTAL FAT: 49G; SATURATED FAT: 17G; CARBS: 150G; PROTEIN: 67G; SODIUM: 4,221MG; FIBER: 19G

SPAIN

SPANISH FISH STEW
WITH SAFFRON

Serves 4   Prep time: 10 minutes   Cook time: 10 minutes

DAIRY-FREE | QUICK & EASY   *Saffron gives this Spanish fish stew its distinctive flavor and a beautiful reddish hue. While saffron is expensive, you only need a pinch, and the unique taste is impossible to recreate with other herbs or spices. The broth is thickened with toasted bread, a technique common to Iberian (Portuguese and Spanish) cuisine.*

Pinch of saffron (about 8 threads)
¾ cup olive oil, divided
2 medium onions, diced
1 teaspoon salt, divided
1 tablespoon tomato paste
½ cup dry white wine
3 cups fish broth or bottled clam juice
2 cloves garlic, peeled and minced
3 slices toasted bread
2½ pounds cod or other meaty white fish
1 tablespoon finely chopped flat-leaf parsley

1. In a small bowl, combine the saffron threads with 2 tablespoons of warm water.

2. Heat ½ cup of olive oil in a large Dutch oven over medium-high heat. Add the onions and ½ teaspoon of salt and cook, stirring frequently, until softened, about 5 minutes. Add the tomato paste and cook, stirring, for 1 more minute. Add the wine and bring to a boil. Add the fish broth or clam juice and the soaked saffron and bring back to a boil. Reduce the heat to low and let simmer, uncovered, for 10 minutes.

3. Meanwhile, in a food processor, combine the garlic and bread and process until coarsely ground. Add the remaining ¼ cup of olive oil and ½ teaspoon of salt and pulse just to mix. Add the fish to the pot, cover, and cook for about 6 minutes, or until the fish is just cooked through. Stir in the sauce. Taste and adjust seasoning if needed. Ladle the stew into serving bowls and serve immediately, garnished with parsley.

PER SERVING: CALORIES: 779; TOTAL FAT: 41G; SATURATED FAT: 6G; CARBS: 31G; PROTEIN: 67G; SODIUM: 1,513MG; FIBER: 3G

GREECE

GRILLED SQUID
WITH YELLOW SPLIT PEA PURÉE

Serves 4   Prep time: 10 minutes   Cook time: 1 hour and 10 minutes

DAIRY-FREE | GLUTEN-FREE   *This yellow split pea purée is a classic Greek dish, often served as part of a mezze (appetizer) platter topped with raw onions, lemon juice and olive oil or stewed onions and capers. Topping it with grilled squid turns it into a satisfying entrée.*

6 tablespoons olive oil, divided

1 large red onion, finely diced

1½ cups yellow split peas

4 cups vegetable broth or water, plus more as needed

1½ pounds cleaned squid, bodies cut into ½-inch rings and tentacles left whole

1½ teaspoons salt, divided

½ teaspoon freshly ground pepper, plus more to taste

¼ cup lemon juice

¼ cup finely chopped flat-leaf parsley

1 lemon, cut into wedges

1. Heat 2 tablespoons of olive oil in a large saucepan set over medium heat. Add the onion and cook, stirring frequently, until softened, about 5 minutes. Stir in the split peas and then the broth or water. Raise the heat to high and bring to a boil.

2. Reduce the heat to low, cover, and cook, stirring every once in a while, for 45 to 60 minutes, adding additional broth or water if needed, until the peas are very tender and most of the liquid has been absorbed.

3. In a medium bowl, toss the squid with 1 tablespoon of oil, 1 teaspoon salt, and ½ teaspoon pepper.

4. When the peas are cooked, purée them in the pot using an immersion blender or in batches in a food processor or countertop blender. Add 1 tablespoon olive oil, lemon juice, and the remaining ½ teaspoon salt. Process to a creamy consistency and then transfer to a serving platter.

5. Brush the grill rack with olive oil and preheat the grill to medium-high heat.

6. Thread the squid (rings and tentacles) on skewers. Cook the squid on the grill for about 2 minutes per side. Take the squid off the skewers and arrange them on top of the split pea purée. Drizzle the remaining tablespoon of olive oil over the top, garnish with parsley, and serve immediately with the lemon wedges.

★ TIP: Buying already cleaned squid tubes will save you time, but doing it yourself won't take more than 5 minutes or so.

PER SERVING: CALORIES: 629; TOTAL FAT: 25G; SATURATED FAT: 4G; CARBS: 51G; PROTEIN: 49G; SODIUM: 1,653MG; FIBER: 20G

SPAIN

SHRIMP PAELLA

Serves 4   Prep time: 10 minutes   Cook time: 25 minutes

DAIRY-FREE | GLUTEN-FREE | QUICK & EASY   *Paella is the national dish of Spain. It usually consists of saffron-scented rice cooked with vegetables and topped with a mixture of seafood, sausage, and other meats. This simplified version includes shrimp and peas. A paella pan is the ideal cooking vessel, but a large cast-iron skillet is a fine substitute.*

2 tablespoons olive oil

1 medium onion, diced

1 red bell pepper, diced

3 cloves garlic, minced

Pinch of saffron (about 8 threads)

¼ teaspoon hot paprika

1 teaspoon salt

½ teaspoon freshly ground black pepper

3 cups chicken broth, divided

1 cup short-grain white rice

1 pound peeled and deveined
    large shrimp

1 cup frozen peas, thawed

1. Heat the oil in a wide, heavy skillet set over medium heat. Add the onion and bell pepper and cook, stirring frequently, until the vegetables are softened, about 6 minutes. Add the garlic, saffron, paprika, salt, and pepper and stir to mix. Stir in 2½ cups of broth, and the rice.

2. Bring the mixture to a boil, then lower the heat to low, cover, and simmer until the rice is nearly cooked through, about 12 minutes. Scatter the shrimp and peas over the rice and add the remaining ½ cup of broth. Place the lid back on the skillet and cook for about 5 minutes more, until the shrimp are just cooked through. Serve immediately.

★ TIP: In Spain, paella is made with short-grain white rice varieties such as bomba or Valencia. Use one of these if you can, but if they're not available, you can substitute any short-grain or medium-grain white rice. Don't use long-grain rice, however, as it won't soak up the flavors the way the shorter grains will.

PER SERVING: CALORIES: 409; TOTAL FAT: 10G; SATURATED FAT: 1G; CARBS: 51G; PROTEIN: 25G; SODIUM: 1,414MG; FIBER: 4G

SOUTHERN ITALY

SICILIAN BAKED COD
WITH HERBED BREADCRUMBS

Serves 4   Prep time: 5 minutes   Cook time: 25 minutes

DAIRY-FREE | QUICK & EASY   *This simple baked dish packs all of the intense flavors associated with Sardinian cooking: sweet red onion, bright fresh herbs, the tang of red wine vinegar, and the salty umami of anchovy paste. You can substitute any firm-fleshed white fish for the cod.*

2 tablespoons olive oil, divided

1 medium red onion, halved and cut into half circles

1 tablespoon red wine vinegar

¾ teaspoon salt, divided, plus more for seasoning

¼ teaspoon freshly ground black pepper, plus more for seasoning

½ teaspoon anchovy paste

3 tablespoons dried breadcrumbs

2 tablespoons chopped flat-leaf parsley

2 tablespoons chopped fresh mint leaves

2 tablespoons chopped fresh basil leaves

4 (6-ounce) cod fillets

½ cup dry white wine

1. Preheat the oven to 400°F.

2. Heat 1 tablespoon of olive oil in a medium skillet over medium-high heat. Add the onion and cook, stirring frequently, until softened, about 5 minutes. Add the vinegar and season with the salt and pepper. Cook for about 30 seconds more. Spread the onions into an even layer in a baking dish large enough to hold the fish in a single layer.

3. Heat the remaining 1 tablespoon of olive oil in the same skillet over low heat. Add the anchovy paste and cook, stirring, for about 1 minute. Add the breadcrumbs and toss to coat them in oil. Remove the breadcrumbs to a bowl and let them cool a bit. Add the parsley, mint, and basil, ¼ teaspoon of salt, and a pinch of pepper.

4. Arrange the fish fillets on top of the onions and season with the remaining ½ teaspoon of salt and ¼ teaspoon of pepper. Sprinkle the breadcrumbs equally over the fillets. Pour the wine into the dish.

5. Bake, adding a little more wine or water if necessary until cooked through, about 10 to 15 minutes, depending on the thickness of the fish fillets. Serve hot.

PER SERVING: CALORIES: 299; TOTAL FAT: 10G; SATURATED FAT: 1G; CARBS: 8G; PROTEIN: 40G; SODIUM: 652MG; FIBER: 1G

SPAIN

BRAISED MONKFISH
WITH SHERRY AND ALMONDS

Serves 4　Prep time: 10 minutes　Cook time: 25 minutes

DAIRY-FREE | GLUTEN-FREE | QUICK & EASY　*In this recipe, monkfish is braised in a distinctly Spanish sauce made of red bell peppers, almonds, garlic, and sherry. If you like, you can substitute any meaty white fish for the monkfish, such as cod or halibut.*

2 tablespoons olive oil

1 medium onion, diced

2 red bell peppers, diced

1½ teaspoons salt

½ teaspoon freshly ground black pepper

3 cloves garlic, minced

⅓ cup dry sherry

1 cup bottled clam juice

¼ cup blanched slivered almonds

4 monkfish fillets, about 6 ounces each

2 tablespoons chopped flat-leaf parsley

1.　Heat the olive oil in a large saucepan over medium heat. Add the onion, peppers, salt, and pepper and cook, stirring frequently, for about 5 minutes, until the vegetables are softened. Add the garlic and sherry and cook for 1 more minute. Stir in the clam juice and bring to a simmer. Reduce the heat to low, cover, and simmer for 10 minutes.

2.　Transfer the onion mixture to a food processor or blender and process to a smooth purée. Add the almonds and pulse until they are finely ground. Pour the sauce back into the saucepan and return to a simmer over medium heat.

3.　Add the fish to the sauce, cover the pan, and simmer for 10 to 12 minutes, until the fish is just cooked through. Slice the fish into ¼-inch thick slices and serve immediately, garnished with parsley.

PER SERVING: CALORIES: 337; TOTAL FAT: 14G; SATURATED FAT: 1G; CARBS: 15G; PROTEIN: 34G; SODIUM: 1,135MG; FIBER: 3G

SOUTHERN
ITALY

SOUTHERN ITALIAN SEAFOOD STEW
IN TOMATO BROTH

Serves 6   Prep time: 15 minutes   Cook time: 1 hour and 20 minutes

DAIRY-FREE | GLUTEN-FREE   *Seafood stew is made in virtually all of the coastal regions in Italy, but in the south, it almost always includes calamari, prawns, and mussels and is cooked in a broth flavored with tomatoes and shellfish. It often has a kick of spice, as well. Serve it with bread for dipping.*

½ cup olive oil
1 fennel bulb, cored and finely chopped
2 stalks celery, finely chopped
1 medium onion, finely chopped
1 tablespoon dried oregano
½ teaspoon crushed red pepper flakes
1½ pounds cleaned squid, bodies cut
    into ½-inch rings, tentacles halved
2 cups dry white wine
One (28-ounce) can tomato purée
1 bay leaf
1 teaspoon salt
½ teaspoon freshly ground black pepper
1 cup bottled clam juice
1 pound whole head-on prawns
1½ pounds mussels, scrubbed
1 lemon, cut into wedges, for serving

1. In a large Dutch oven, heat the olive oil over medium-high heat. Add the fennel, celery, onion, oregano, and red pepper flakes and reduce the heat to medium. Cook, stirring occasionally, for about 15 minutes, until the vegetables soften. Stir in the squid, reduce the heat to low, and simmer for 15 minutes.

2. Add the wine to the pot, raise the heat to medium-high, and bring to a boil. Cook, stirring occasionally, until the wine has evaporated. Reduce the heat again to low and add the tomato purée, bay leaf, salt, and pepper. Cook gently, stirring every once in a while, for about 40 minutes, until the mixture becomes very thick.

3. Stir in 2 cups of water and the clam juice, raise the heat again to medium-high, and bring to a boil. »

4. Add the shrimp and mussels and cook, covered, for 5 minutes or so, until the shells of the mussels have opened and the prawns are pink and cooked through.

5. To serve, ladle the seafood and broth into bowls and garnish with the lemon wedges. Serve hot.

★ TIP: This recipe can be partially prepared ahead of time. Follow the recipe through step 2, then let it cool to room temperature, cover, and refrigerate overnight. Reheat the broth before continuing on to step 3 of the recipe.

PER SERVING: CALORIES: 599; TOTAL FAT: 21G; SATURATED FAT: 3G; SODIUM: 1,258MG; CARBS: 43G; FIBER: 7G; PROTEIN: 45G

MOROCCAN BRAISED HALIBUT
WITH CINNAMON AND CAPERS

Serves 4   Prep time: 5 minutes   Cook time: 20 minutes

DAIRY-FREE | GLUTEN-FREE | QUICK & EASY   *Cinnamon is frequently used in savory dishes in North African cuisine. Here, where it's paired with meaty halibut, briny capers, and tomatoes, it adds depth and earthiness. Serve this fish over rice or couscous if you like.*

¼ cup olive oil

¾ teaspoon ground cumin

1 (15-ounce) can diced tomatoes, drained

1½ tablespoons drained capers

½ teaspoon cinnamon

½ teaspoon salt, divided

½ teaspoon freshly ground
   black pepper, divided

4 halibut fillets, about 6 ounces each
   and 1-inch-thick

1. Heat the olive oil in a large skillet over medium heat. Add the cumin and cook, stirring, for 1 minute. Add the tomatoes, capers, cinnamon, ¼ teaspoon of salt, and ¼ teaspoon of pepper and cook for about 10 minutes, until the mixture is thickened.

2. Dry the fish well with paper towels and then season all over with the remaining ¼ teaspoon of salt and ¼ teaspoon of pepper. Add the fish to the sauce in the pan, cover, and simmer for 8 to 10 minutes, until the fish is cooked through. Serve immediately.

PER SERVING: CALORIES: 309; TOTAL FAT: 14G; SATURATED FAT: 2G; CARBS: 5G; PROTEIN: 40G; SODIUM: 525MG; FIBER: 2G

GREECE

PAN-ROASTED SWORDFISH
WITH OLIVES, TOMATOES, EGGPLANT, AND ZUCCHINI

Serves 4   Prep time: 5 minutes   Cook time: 15 minutes

DAIRY-FREE | GLUTEN-FREE | QUICK & EASY   *Swordfish has a firm, meaty texture and a mild flavor, making it easy to adapt to many different preparations. Here it is pan-roasted and topped with a flavorful medley of vegetables. Serve it with crusty bread, or a cooked grain to round out the meal.*

¼ cup olive oil, divided
2 garlic cloves, minced
1 small onion, thinly sliced
½ medium eggplant, diced
2 medium zucchini, diced
2 cups cherry tomatoes, halved
1 cup whole, pitted Kalamata olives
4 swordfish fillets, with skin, about 6 to 8 ounces each
Salt and freshly ground black pepper
2 tablespoons olive oil
¼ cup Green Olive Tapenade with Harissa (page 251) or store-bought tapenade

1. Preheat the oven to 375°F.

2. In a large skillet, heat 2 tablespoons of olive oil over medium-high heat. Add the garlic and onion and cook, stirring, until softened, about 5 minutes. Add the eggplant and cook, stirring occasionally, until it begins to soften, about 3 minutes. Add the zucchini and continue to cook, stirring occasionally, until the zucchini and eggplant are both softened and beginning to brown. Add the tomatoes and olives and cook, stirring occasionally, 1 to 2 minutes, just until the tomatoes begin to blister.

3. Meanwhile, pat the fish dry with paper towels. Season the fish on both sides with salt and pepper. Heat the remaining 2 tablespoons of olive oil over medium-high heat in a large oven-safe skillet. Place the fish in the skillet and cook for about 3 minutes, just until the bottom begins to turn golden and the edges of the fish become opaque. Turn the fish over carefully and then transfer the skillet to the oven and roast for about 3 minutes, until the fish is cooked through and just opaque in the center.

4. Serve the fish immediately, topped with the cooked vegetables and Green Olive Tapenade.

PER SERVING: CALORIES: 605; TOTAL FAT: 37G; SATURATED FAT: 6G; SODIUM: 738MG; CARBS: 16G; FIBER: 6G; PROTEIN: 54G

SAGE-STUFFED WHOLE TROUT
WITH ROASTED VEGETABLES

Serves 4   Prep time: 10 minutes   Cook time: 35 minutes

DAIRY-FREE | GLUTEN-FREE   *Roasting fish whole makes for a dramatic presentation. Stuffing it with herbs and cooking it atop a bed of roasted vegetables gives it loads of flavor. This recipe calls for sage, but you could substitute any herb you like, such as basil, thyme, or oregano.*

2 red bell peppers, seeded and cut into 1-inch-wide strips

1 (15-ounce) can artichoke hearts, drained and cut into quarters

1 large red onion, halved through the stem and cut into 1-inch-wide wedges

4 cloves garlic, halved

3 tablespoons olive oil, divided

1½ teaspoons salt, divided

¾ teaspoon freshly ground black pepper, divided

2 whole rainbow trout, cleaned with head on

3 cups sage leaves

Juice of ½ lemon

★ TIP: When buying fresh fish, avoid those with cloudy eyes and a fishy smell, and ask your fishmonger to peel back the gills so you can take a look. One clear indicator of freshness is gills that are deep red or almost purple in color.

1. Preheat the oven to 475°F.

2. In a large baking dish, toss the bell peppers, artichoke hearts, onion, and garlic with 2 tablespoons of the olive oil. Sprinkle with 1 teaspoon of salt and ½ teaspoon of pepper. Roast the vegetables in the preheated oven for 20 minutes. Reduce the heat to 375°F.

3. While the vegetables are roasting, prepare the fish. Brush the fish inside and out with the remaining 1 tablespoon of olive oil and season with the remaining ½ teaspoon of salt and ¼ teaspoon of pepper. Stuff each fish with half of the sage leaves.

4. Remove the vegetables from the oven and place the fish on top. Put back in the oven and bake at 375°F for about 15 minutes more, until the fish is cooked through. Remove from the oven, squeeze the lemon juice over the fish, and let rest for 5 minutes.

5. To serve, halve the fish. Spoon roasted vegetables onto 4 serving plates and serve half a fish alongside each, topped with some of the sage leaves.

PER SERVING: CALORIES: 527; TOTAL FAT: 26G; SATURATED FAT: 6G; CARBS: 34G; PROTEIN: 45G; SODIUM: 1,077MG; FIBER: 18G

LAYERED BACALHAU
AND POTATO CASSEROLE

Serves 6   Prep time: 15 minutes, plus 24 hours to soak the fish   Cook time: 1 hour and 15 minutes

DAIRY-FREE | GLUTEN-FREE   Bacalhau *is cod that has been preserved in salt. It originated as a way to preserve the plentiful fish before refrigeration, but it is still a cherished food to this day in the Mediterranean. Preserving the meaty fish adds flavor and dimension to it much the way the process of making prosciutto does for pork.*

2 pounds salt cod
6 tablespoons olive oil, plus extra for greasing and drizzling
4 medium waxy potatoes, sliced ¼-inch thick
½ teaspoon salt
2 large yellow onions, sliced
4 cloves garlic, minced
Pinch of nutmeg
White pepper

★ TIP: Make sure you plan ahead, since the salt cod must be soaked in several changes of water for 24 hours before cooking.

1. Rinse the salt cod and then place it in a large, non-reactive pot. Add cold water to cover and refrigerate for 24 hours, changing the water 2 or 3 times.

2. Preheat the oven to 400°F and brush a 9-by-13-inch baking dish and a large baking sheet generously with olive oil.

3. Put the potatoes in a saucepan and cover them with water. Add the salt. Bring the water to a boil, reduce the heat to low, and simmer until the potatoes are just tender, about 10 minutes. Drain.

4. Drain the soaking water from the fish, add more clean water to cover, and bring to a boil over medium-high heat. Reduce the heat to medium-low and simmer for about 10 minutes, until the fish is tender. Drain.

5. While the fish is simmering, heat 3 tablespoons of olive oil in a large skillet set over medium heat. Add the onions and cook, stirring frequently, for about 6 minutes, until they are just beginning to brown. Stir in the garlic and remove from the heat. »

6. Place the fish in a large bowl and flake it with a fork. Discard the skin and bones. Stir the onion mixture into the fish, along with the nutmeg, the remaining 3 tablespoons olive oil, and season with white pepper. Transfer the mixture to the prepared baking dish, packing it in in a tight, even layer. Top with the potato slices.

7. Place the prepared baking sheet over the baking dish and invert the baking dish but do not remove it. Bake in the preheated oven for about 30 minutes, then carefully remove the baking dish and continue to bake for another 10 to 15 minutes, until the fish is lightly browned. Serve hot, garnished with parsley.

PER SERVING: CALORIES: 417; TOTAL FAT: 16G; SATURATED FAT: 2G; CARBS: 30G; PROTEIN: 39G; SODIUM: 10G; FIBER: 4G

GREECE

GRILLED SALMON SOUVLAKI
WITH TZATZIKI

Serves 4   Prep time: 10 minutes   Cook time: 6 minutes

GLUTEN-FREE | QUICK & EASY   Souvlaki *is a Greek word that refers to chunks of marinated meat that are skewered and grilled, often along with vegetables. This version combines meaty salmon marinated in herbs, garlic, lemon juice, and vinegar with red bell peppers. It is served with a creamy Tzatziki Sauce (page 241). Offer grilled flatbread alongside for wrapping, or serve it over rice.*

6 tablespoons lemon juice

3 tablespoons olive oil

2 tablespoons balsamic vinegar

1 tablespoon smoked paprika

1 tablespoon fresh dill

1 tablespoon minced fresh oregano

2 cloves garlic, minced or grated

½ teaspoon salt

½ teaspoon freshly ground black pepper

1 pound fresh salmon, skin removed and diced into chunks

1 red bell pepper, cut into chunks

1 recipe Tzatziki Sauce (page 241)

1. Soak 8 bamboo skewers in water for 20 minutes.

2. In a medium bowl, whisk together the lemon juice, olive oil, vinegar, smoked paprika, dill, oregano, garlic, salt, and pepper. Add the salmon and toss to coat well.

3. Heat the grill to medium-high heat.

4. Thread the salmon and bell pepper chunks onto the prepared skewers, alternating them. Cook on the grill until the fish is cooked through, about 3 minutes per side. Remove the skewers from the grill and let rest for 5 minutes before serving.

5. Serve hot with the Tzatziki Sauce.

PER SERVING: CALORIES: 279; TOTAL FAT: 19G; SATURATED FAT: 4G; CARBS: 5G; PROTEIN: 23G; SODIUM: 368MG; FIBER: 2G

11

POULTRY

TURKEY

TURKISH CHICKEN KABOBS
WITH ALEPPO PEPPER AND YOGURT

Serves 4 to 6   Prep time: 10 minutes, plus 1 hour to marinate   Cook time: 12 minutes

GLUTEN-FREE   *Marinating the chicken in yogurt tenderizes the meat and keeps it super moist. The Aleppo pepper adds additional tang, a kick of heat, and a nice reddish hue. Serve this chicken with a crisp green salad for a light and satisfying meal on a warm evening.*

1½ tablespoons Aleppo pepper, plus additional for garnish

1 cup plain Greek yogurt

3 tablespoons olive oil, plus more for brushing

2 tablespoons red wine vinegar

2 tablespoons tomato paste

2 teaspoons salt

1 teaspoon freshly ground black pepper

6 cloves garlic, peeled and smashed

2 unpeeled lemons; 1 thinly sliced into rounds, 1 cut into wedges for serving

1¾ pounds skinless boneless chicken (thighs and/or breasts), cut into 1¼-inch cubes

1. In a large bowl, combine the Aleppo pepper with 1 tablespoon of warm water and let stand for about 5 minutes, until the mixture turns to a thick paste. Stir in the yogurt, olive oil, vinegar, tomato paste, salt, and pepper. Add the garlic and lemon slices along with the cubed chicken. Cover and refrigerate for at least 1 hour (or as long as overnight).

2. Soak 10 to 12 bamboo skewers in water for about 20 minutes.

3. Heat the grill to medium-high and brush with oil. Thread the marinated chicken onto the skewers (discard the marinade), dividing evenly among the skewers. Cook the skewers on the grill for about 10 to 12 minutes, turning occasionally, until the chicken is cooked through and nicely browned. Transfer the cooked chicken, on the skewers, onto a serving platter and serve with lemon wedges.

★ TIP: *Aleppo* is a Turkish or Syrian chile with a bit more heat than sweet paprika and a distinctive tangy flavor. You can buy it in specialty markets or online, or you can use a mixture of equal parts crushed red pepper flakes and sweet paprika in its place.

PER SERVING: CALORIES: 301; TOTAL FAT: 11G; SATURATED FAT: 2G; CARBS: 7G; PROTEIN: 44G; SODIUM: 1,035MG; FIBER: 1G

SOUTHERN ITALY

MINT PESTO CHICKEN

Serves 4 to 6   Prep time: 5 minutes, plus 1 hour to marinate   Cook time: 40 minutes

GLUTEN-FREE   *Mint Pesto (page 245) is a vibrant alternative to the traditional basil pesto. Here it is mixed with lemon juice to make a quick and flavorful marinade for chicken. Serve this with a fresh tomato salad and rice or pasta.*

¾ cup Mint Pesto (page 245)
6 tablespoons lemon juice
¾ teaspoon salt
6 bone-in, skinless chicken pieces
   (breast or thigh or a combination)

1. In a large bowl, combine the pesto, lemon juice, and salt. Add the chicken and stir to coat well. Cover and refrigerate for at least 1 hour (or as long as overnight).

2. Preheat the oven to 350°F.

3. Place the chicken on a large, rimmed baking sheet and pour the extra marinade over the top.

4. Bake in the preheated oven until the chicken is cooked through and browned on top, about 35 to 40 minutes. Serve hot.

★ TIP: This chicken dish is also delicious served at room temperature, making it a perfect choice for a picnic.

PER SERVING: CALORIES: 372; TOTAL FAT: 20G; SATURATED FAT: 4G; CARBS: 3G; PROTEIN: 43G; SODIUM: 666MG; FIBER: 1G

CHICKEN CACCIATORE
WITH WILD MUSHROOMS AND FRESH FENNEL

Serves 6 to 8   Prep time: 10 minutes   Cook time: 1 hour and 10 minutes

DAIRY-FREE | GLUTEN-FREE   *The word* cacciatore *means "hunter" in Italian and refers to a meat dish braised in a tomato-based sauce with other vegetables and herbs. Wild porcini mushrooms are used frequently in Southern Italian cuisine, both fresh and dried.*

½ ounce dried porcini mushrooms

1 cup boiling water

2 tablespoons olive oil

12 boneless, skinless chicken thighs (about 3 pounds), trimmed of fat

1 large green bell pepper, seeded and cut into rings

1 large onion, halved and thinly sliced

1 large fennel bulb, trimmed, halved, cored and thinly sliced

3 cloves garlic, minced

1 tablespoon minced fresh rosemary

2 teaspoons freshly grated orange zest

1 teaspoon fresh thyme leaves

3 tablespoons red wine vinegar

¾ cup dry white wine

2 tablespoons tomato paste

1 teaspoon salt

1. Preheat the oven to 350°F.

2. Soak the porcinis in the boiling water for about 20 minutes.

3. While the mushrooms are soaking, heat the olive oil in a large skillet over medium-high heat. Brown the chicken pieces on all sides, working in batches if needed. Transfer the chicken to a 9-by-13-inch baking dish as the pieces are browned.

4. Reduce the heat under the skillet to medium. Add the pepper, onion, and fennel and cook, stirring frequently, until softened, about 5 minutes. Stir in the garlic, rosemary, orange zest, and thyme and cook, stirring, for another 30 seconds. Add the vinegar and cook, stirring, 1 minute longer. Remove from the heat.

5. Remove the mushrooms from the water, reserving the soaking water, and chop them coarsely. Add the chopped mushrooms and the soaking water to the pan along with the wine, tomato paste, and salt.

6. Bring to a simmer over medium heat, then add the hot mixture to the baking dish, pouring it over the chicken legs. Cover with aluminum foil and bake in the preheated oven for 45 minutes. Remove from the oven and let it rest for 5 to 10 minutes before serving. Serve hot.

PER SERVING: CALORIES: 468; TOTAL FAT: 19G; SATURATED FAT: 5G; CARBS: 9G; PROTEIN: 58G; SODIUM: 527MG; FIBER: 3G

CHICKEN MEATBALLS
WITH FRESH BASIL AND PECORINO ROMANO

Serves 4   Prep time: 10 minutes   Cook time: 20 minutes

QUICK & EASY *Chicken meatballs are lighter than the traditional beef or beef-and-pork ones you usually see on Italian menus. The addition of herby fresh basil makes these a perfect choice for a light spring or summer meal. Serve the meatballs by themselves or with Southern Italian–Style Tomato Sauce (page 243) over pasta, if you like. They'd also make a great filling for a wrap, drizzled with Tzatziki Sauce (page 241).*

Olive oil, for brushing
1 pound ground chicken
1¼ cups whole-wheat breadcrumbs
2 ounces freshly grated
    Pecorino Romano
2 cloves garlic, minced
1 egg, lightly beaten
¼ cup chopped fresh basil
1 teaspoon salt
½ teaspoon freshly ground black pepper

1. Preheat the oven to 400°F.

2. Line a large rimmed baking sheet with parchment paper, and brush the parchment lightly with olive oil.

3. In a large bowl, combine the chicken, breadcrumbs, cheese, garlic, egg, basil, salt, and pepper and mix well.

4. Form the chicken mixture into 1½-inch balls. As they are formed, place the meatballs onto the prepared baking sheet. Once all the meatballs have been formed, brush them with olive oil.

5. Bake in the preheated oven for about 20 minutes, until the meatballs are cooked through and golden brown on top. Serve hot.

PER SERVING: CALORIES: 483; TOTAL FAT: 22G; SATURATED FAT: 8G; CARBS: 25G; PROTEIN: 42G; SODIUM: 1,220MG; FIBER: 2G

CHICKEN WITH ARTICHOKES

Serves 4   Prep time: 10 minutes, plus 30 minutes to marinate   Cook time: 20 minutes

DAIRY-FREE *Artichokes have been cultivated in Southern Italy since Roman times, and they are used in myriad ways in the region's cuisine. Artichokes have a deep, complex, earthy flavor and a tender, meaty texture. Here they are combined with a bit of lemon and garlic to flavor juicy pan-seared chicken breasts.*

1 cup chicken broth

2 tablespoons all-purpose flour

4 tablespoons olive oil, divided

1½ teaspoons grated lemon zest

2 tablespoons lemon juice, divided

3 cloves garlic, minced, divided

4 (6-ounce) skinless, boneless chicken breast halves

¼ teaspoon salt

¼ teaspoon freshly ground black pepper

2 shallots, thinly sliced

1 tablespoon chopped fresh rosemary

2 ounces pancetta, finely chopped

½ cup dry sherry

2 cups artichoke hearts, quartered frozen (thawed), or canned (drained and rinsed)

4 teaspoons chopped fresh flat-leaf parsley, divided

1. In a small bowl, whisk together the broth and flour.

2. In a medium bowl, mix 1 tablespoon of olive oil, the lemon zest, 4 teaspoons of lemon juice, and 1 clove of minced garlic. Add the chicken and turn to coat well. Marinate at room temperature for 30 minutes.

3. Drain the chicken from the marinade, discarding the marinade and sprinkle the salt and pepper evenly over the chicken pieces. Heat 2 tablespoons of olive oil in a large skillet over medium-high heat. Cook the chicken in the skillet for about 5 minutes per side, until browned and cooked through. Transfer the chicken breasts to a plate as they are finished cooking.

4. Lower the heat under the pan to medium, add the remaining 1 tablespoon of olive oil to the pan and the shallots, rosemary, and pancetta. Cook until the shallots are softened, about 3 minutes. Add the remaining 2 cloves of garlic and cook, stirring, for 30 seconds more.

5. Splash the sherry into the pan and cook, stirring, until it is mostly evaporated, about 4 minutes. Add the broth and flour mixture and bring almost to a boil. Stir in the artichoke hearts and cook until the sauce thickens, about 1 more minute. Stir the remaining 2 teaspoons of lemon juice and 2 teaspoons of parsley and return the chicken breasts to the pan. Let cook for a minute or two longer, until heated through. Serve hot, garnished with the remaining parsley.

PER SERVING: CALORIES: 498; TOTAL FAT: 27G; SATURATED FAT: 7G; CARBS: 15G; PROTEIN: 48G; SODIUM: 806MG; FIBER: 5G

GREECE

GREEK CHICKEN DRUMSTICKS
WITH ROASTED LEMON, FRESH OREGANO, AND FETA CHEESE

Serves 4   Prep time: 15 minutes   Cook time: 1 hour, 15 minutes

Roasting lemons both concentrates and mellows their tart-sweet flavor. Here they are paired with fresh oregano to flavor chicken that's quickly pan-seared and then finished in the oven. A topping of salty feta cheese and crunchy, garlicky bread crumbs is just the touch to take this dish from ordinary to extraordinary. Serve this dish with rice pilaf or garlicky sautéed vegetables on the side.

3 medium lemons, two cut into wedges and seeded and the third zested

¼ cup olive oil, plus 1 tablespoon, divided

1¼ teaspoons salt, divided

8 chicken drumsticks

½ teaspoon freshly ground black pepper

½ cup whole-wheat bread crumbs

1 garlic clove, minced

3 ounces feta cheese, cut into 8 slices

3 tablespoons chopped fresh oregano

1. Preheat the oven to 325°F and line a large, rimmed baking sheet with parchment paper.

2. Place the lemon wedges on the prepared baking sheet in a single layer and brush with 1 tablespoon olive oil and sprinkle with ¼ teaspoon salt. Roast the lemons in the preheated oven for about 20 minutes, until they begin to soften.

3. While the lemons are roasting, prepare the chicken. Sprinkle the remaining salt and the pepper over the drumsticks, seasoning them on all sides.

4. Heat 2 tablespoons of olive oil in a large skillet (large enough to fit all the chicken in a single layer, or do this step in 2 batches) set over medium-high heat. Add the drumsticks and cook for about 3 minutes on each side, until they are golden brown all over. »

5. Remove the lemons from the oven and add the chicken to the baking sheet. Return the pan to the oven and cook for 30 minutes.

6. Meanwhile, in a small bowl, stir together the breadcrumbs, the remaining 2 tablespoons of olive oil, garlic, and the lemon zest.

7. Top each drumstick with a slice of cheese and top the cheese with a mound of the breadcrumb mixture. Sprinkle the oregano over the top. Return the pan to the oven and bake for another 20 to 25 minutes, until the chicken is cooked through. Serve immediately.

PER SERVING: CALORIES: 404; TOTAL FAT: 24G; SATURATED FAT: 7G; SODIUM: 1,176MG; CARBS: 17G; FIBER: 4G; PROTEIN: 31G

GREECE

SPINACH AND FETA-STUFFED
CHICKEN BREASTS

Serves 4   Prep time: 15 minutes   Cook time: 45 minutes

Wrapping stuffed chicken breasts in crispy phyllo pastry makes this dish both visually impressive and delicious, but it takes a lot less effort than you might think. You could wvariety.

4 skinless, boneless chicken
   breast halves
1 tablespoon olive oil
5 ounces fresh spinach, chopped
½ teaspoon salt, plus a pinch
1 cup (about 4 ounces) crumbled
   feta cheese
2 tablespoons toasted pine nuts
1 teaspoon minced fresh thyme
2 teaspoons lemon juice
2 cloves garlic, minced
¼ teaspoon freshly ground black pepper
8 sheets frozen (thawed) phyllo dough
¼ cup butter, melted

1. Preheat the oven to 350°F.

2. Cover the chicken breasts with plastic wrap and pound with a mallet or rolling pin to flatten each to about ½-inch thickness.

3. Heat the olive oil in a large skillet over medium-high heat. Add the spinach and a pinch of salt and cook, stirring, for about 1 minute, until the spinach is wilted. Drain the spinach in a colander and then squeeze out any excess water.

4. In a medium bowl, stir together the spinach, cheese, pine nuts, thyme, lemon juice, and garlic. Spoon some of the spinach mixture onto the center of each flattened chicken breast half, dividing the mixture evenly between the chicken pieces. Roll the chicken around the filling. Sprinkle the remaining ½ teaspoon salt and the pepper over the chicken. »

5. Unfold 1 piece of phyllo dough and brush it all over with melted butter. Top it with a second phyllo sheet. Place 1 rolled-up chicken breast on the short side of the phyllo, fold in the sides of the phyllo over the chicken, and then roll up to completely wrap the chicken in the phyllo. Place the wrapped chicken on a rimmed baking sheet and brush with a bit more of the melted butter. Repeat with the remaining phyllo sheets, melted butter, and chicken pieces.

6. Bake in the preheated oven until the chicken is cooked through and the pastry is golden brown, about 35 to 40 minutes.

★ TIP: Thaw phyllo dough overnight in the refrigerator and then let it sit at room temperature for an hour or two before unrolling.

PER SERVING: CALORIES: 583; TOTAL FAT: 34G; SATURATED FAT: 16G; CARBS: 34G; PROTEIN: 37G; SODIUM: 1,134MG; FIBER: 2G

MOROCCO

CHERMOULA-MARINATED GRILLED CHICKEN BREASTS
WITH PARSLEY AND RADISH SALAD

Serves 4   Prep time: 10 minutes, plus 1 hour to marinate   Cook time: 50 minutes

DAIRY-FREE | GLUTEN-FREE   *Chermoula is an intensely flavorful mixture of fresh herbs, dried spices, lemon juice, and olive oil. It makes a great marinade for any type of meat or fish. Here it flavors mild white meat chicken. An herby and sharp parley and radish salad adds a fresh and refreshing counterpoint to the rich spiciness of the marinade. Serve with couscous if desired.*

For the chicken
4 skinless, boneless chicken
    breast halves
⅔ cup Moroccan Chermoula (page 250)

For the salad
10 medium or 12 small red radishes,
    stemmed and sliced into thin rounds
1 Persian cucumber, sliced into
    thin rounds
¼ red onion, thinly sliced
1 cup tightly packed flat-leaf
    parsley leaves
1 tablespoon lemon juice
¼ teaspoon salt
2 tablespoons olive oil
¼ teaspoon freshly ground black pepper
1 tablespoon toasted sesame seeds

1. Score each of the chicken breasts in 2 or 3 places to allow the marinade to really penetrate the meat deeply. Sprinkle each chicken breast with a small pinch of salt and pepper and then place it in a medium bowl with the chermoula. Toss to coat well, cover, and refrigerate for at least an hour (or as long as overnight).

2. Preheat the oven to 400°F.

3. Arrange the marinated chicken in a large baking, pour the remaining marinade over the chicken, and roast in the preheated oven for about 45 to 50 minutes, until the chicken is cooked through.

4. Just before serving, make the salad. Combine the radishes, cucumber, onion, and parsley in a medium bowl. Add the lemon juice, salt, and olive oil and toss to coat well. Garnish with the pepper and toasted sesame seeds and serve immediately, alongside the chicken.

PER SERVING: CALORIES: 426; TOTAL FAT: 30G; SATURATED FAT: 5G; CARBS: 7G; PROTEIN: 35G; SODIUM: 411MG; FIBER: 2G

SPAIN

BAKED CHICKEN
WITH OLIVES AND RAISINS

Serves 4 Prep time: 5 minutes, plus 1 hour to marinate Cook time: 50 minutes

DAIRY-FREE | GLUTEN-FREE *This Spanish-inspired chicken dish takes just minutes to toss together. The chicken is marinated in a mixture of herbs, vinegar, olives, and raisins and then the whole thing is baked in the oven. It makes an easy weeknight dinner for the family, but feels special enough for a dinner party.*

¼ cup olive oil

¼ cup red wine vinegar

2 teaspoons chopped fresh oregano

1 teaspoon salt

½ teaspoon garlic powder

¼ teaspoon freshly ground black pepper

3 bay leaves

½ cup golden raisins

¼ cup sliced or halved pitted green olives

4 boneless, skinless chicken breast halves

2 tablespoons honey

½ cup dry white wine

1. Whisk together the olive oil, vinegar, oregano, salt, garlic powder, black pepper, bay leaves, raisins, and olives in a medium bowl. Score each chicken breast in several places to allow the marinade to penetrate the meat deeply. Add the chicken to the bowl, toss to coat well, cover, and refrigerate for 1 hour (or as long as overnight).

2. Preheat the oven to 350°F.

3. Lift the chicken pieces out of the marinade, reserving the marinade, and arrange them in a single layer in a baking dish. Whisk the honey and wine into the reserved marinade and pour the mixture over the chicken. Bake in the preheated oven, basting the meat with the sauce occasionally, for about 45 to 50 minutes, until the chicken is cooked through. Serve immediately.

★ TIP: You can substitute other dried fruits—like diced dried apricots, figs, or prunes—for the raisins, if you like.

PER SERVING: CALORIES: 451; TOTAL FAT: 22G; SATURATED FAT: 4G; CARBS: 35G; PROTEIN: 34G; SODIUM: 757MG; FIBER: 1G

SPAIN

SAFFRON CHICKEN STEW
WITH SPANISH CHORIZO AND CHICKPEAS

Serves 4   Prep time: 10   Cook time: 20 minutes

DAIRY-FREE | QUICK & EASY   *Spanish chorizo is a pork sausage seasoned with smoked paprika and other spices. Here it adds depth of flavor to a simple tomato-based chicken stew. Chickpeas add textural interest as well as extra protein, fiber, and other nutrients.*

4 boneless, skinless chicken breast halves
1 teaspoon salt
½ teaspoon freshly ground black pepper
¼ cup all-purpose flour
3 tablespoons olive oil, divided
8 ounces Spanish chorizo, diced
3 cloves garlic, minced
1 (14-ounce) can tomato purée
2 teaspoons sherry vinegar
Pinch saffron threads
1 (15-ounce) can chickpeas, drained and rinsed
1 tablespoon minced fresh thyme

1. Sprinkle each piece of chicken with salt and pepper. Put the flour on a plate, and dredge each chicken breast, coating well.

2. Heat 2 tablespoons of olive oil in a large skillet set over medium-high heat. Add the chicken pieces and cook for about 3 minutes on each side, until golden brown. Transfer the browned chicken pieces to a plate.

3. Add the remaining 1 tablespoon of olive oil to the pan and then add the chorizo and garlic. Cook, stirring frequently, for about 2 minutes, until the chorizo starts to brown. Stir in the tomato purée, vinegar, saffron, chickpeas, and thyme. Bring to a boil. Return the browned chicken pieces to the pan, nestling them into the sauce. Reduce the heat to low, cover the skillet, and cook for about 10 minutes more, until the chicken is cooked through. Serve hot.

PER SERVING: CALORIES: 1,035; TOTAL FAT: 47G; SATURATED FAT: 13G; CARBS: 83G; PROTEIN: 70G; SODIUM: 1,431MG; FIBER: 22G

PORTUGAL

GRILLED WHOLE CHICKEN
WITH PIRI PIRI SAUCE

Serves 4   Prep time: 10 minutes, plus 4 hours to marinate   Cook time: 40 minutes

GLUTEN-FREE   *Piri Piri Sauce (page 244) is a hot pepper sauce invented by Portuguese settlers in Africa using African bird's eye chiles* (piri piri). *You can make your own Piri Piri Sauce, or you can buy it at specialty markets or online. You could also substitute another hot pepper sauce if you like.*

¼ cup chopped cilantro, plus
   3 tablespoons, divided

1 (2-inch) piece fresh ginger, peeled and
   thinly sliced

1 large shallot, quartered

5 cloves garlic, 3 left whole and
   2 minced

½ cup Piri Piri Sauce (page 244) or other
   hot pepper sauce, plus 2 tablespoons,
   divided

¼ cup olive oil, plus additional
   for brushing

¼ cup lemon juice, plus 2 tablespoons,
   divided

1 teaspoon salt

1 teaspoon freshly ground black pepper

1 (3½- to 4-pound) chicken, backbone
   removed, opened flat (spatchcocked)

1 large disposable aluminum baking pan
   (to catch drips)

3 tablespoons butter

1. Combine ¼ cup of cilantro, the ginger, shallot, and the 3 whole garlic cloves in a food processor and pulse to chop. Add ½ cup of Piri Piri Sauce, ¼ cup of olive oil, ¼ cup of lemon juice, the salt and pepper and process to a smooth purée.

2. Flatten the chicken and place it in a large baking dish. Pour half of the marinade over the chicken, spreading it to completely coat the chicken. Turn the chicken over and pour the remaining marinade over the chicken. Cover and refrigerate for at least 4 hours (or as long as overnight), turning once in a while.

3. Heat the grill to medium heat and place the disposable baking pan underneath.

4. To make the sauce, in a small saucepan, melt the butter. Add the remaining 3 tablespoons of cilantro and the 2 cloves minced garlic and cook for about 2 minutes, until the garlic begins to brown. Stir in the remaining 2 tablespoons of Piri Piri Sauce and the remaining 2 tablespoons of lemon juice. Reduce the heat to medium-low and let simmer for about 2 minutes. Remove from the heat (you may need to rewarm the sauce just before pouring it over the cooked chicken).

5. Remove the chicken from the marinade, discarding the marinade. Place the chicken, skin-side up, on the grill above the disposable pan. Close the grill and cook for about 40 minutes, turning the chicken a couple of times, until the skin is browned and the chicken is cooked through (it should reach 165°F on an instant-read thermometer). Cut the chicken into pieces using a large knife or poultry shears and place them on a serving platter. Pour the sauce mixture over the chicken pieces and serve immediately.

★ TIP: Ask your butcher to spatchcock the chicken for you or do it yourself by using poultry or kitchen shears to remove the backbone by cutting along both sides of it. Next, carefully cut out the bone running up the middle between the breasts so that the chicken will lay flat.

PER SERVING: CALORIES: 522; TOTAL FAT: 34G; SATURATED FAT: 10G; CARBS: 4G; PROTEIN: 40G; SODIUM: 757MG; FIBER: 1G

GREECE

SEARED DUCK BREAST
WITH ORANGE OUZO SAUCE

Serves 4   Prep time: 10 minutes   Cook time: 15 minutes

DAIRY-FREE | GLUTEN-FREE | QUICK & EASY   *Ouzo is an anise-flavored liqueur that is popular in both Greece and Cyprus. The anise flavor pairs beautifully with orange for a Greek spin on the classic French dish* Duck a l'Orange. *Duck breast is easy to cook—just be sure to cook it just to medium-rare or it will become tough.*

2 duck breast halves

1 teaspoon salt, plus a pinch

1 tablespoon olive oil

1 shallot, minced

1 Thai chile, or other small, hot chile, halved lengthwise

½ cup chopped fennel bulb, plus a handful of the minced fronds for garnish

¼ cup ouzo

1 cup chicken broth

Juice of one orange, about ½ cup

Freshly ground black pepper

1. Using a very sharp knife, score a cross-hatch pattern into the skin of each duck breast, cutting through the skin and the fat layer, but not into the meat. Sprinkle the salt evenly over them and let stand at room temperature for about 15 minutes.

2. Heat the olive oil in a large skillet over medium-high heat. Add the duck breasts, skin-side down, and cook over medium heat until the skin is nicely browned and a good amount of fat has been rendered, about 8 to 10 minutes. Turn the breasts over and cook until the meat is medium-rare, about 3 more minutes. Remove the breasts from the pan, tent with foil, and let rest for about 10 minutes.

3. While the duck is resting, make the sauce. In the same skillet over medium heat, cook the shallot, chile, and fennel bulb, until the vegetables begin to soften, about 3 minutes. Remove the pan from the heat and add the ouzo (be careful not to let it catch fire). Cook, scraping up any browned bits from the pan, until the liquid is reduced by half.

4. Add the broth and orange juice, along with a pinch of salt, and bring to a boil. Let the sauce boil until it is thick and syrupy, about 5 minutes more. Remove from the heat.

5. Slice the duck breast against the grain into ⅛-inch-thick slices. Arrange the slices onto 4 serving plates and drizzle the sauce over the top. Garnish with the chopped fennel fronds and serve immediately.

PER SERVING: CALORIES: 229; TOTAL FAT: 9G; SATURATED FAT: 1G; CARBS: 7G;
PROTEIN: 27G; SODIUM: 781MG; FIBER: 1G

MEAT

SOUTHERN ITALIAN BRAISED PORK RIBS
IN TOMATO SAUCE

Serves 6 to 8   Prep time: 15 minutes   Cook time: 3 hours

DAIRY-FREE | GLUTEN-FREE   *This braised meat dish is like a Southern Italian–style pulled pork. It is delicious on its own, but also makes a great thick, meaty sauce for pasta. If you don't have pancetta—Italian-style bacon—you can use regular bacon instead.*

½ cup dried porcini mushrooms
¼ cup olive oil
3 pounds country-style pork ribs, bone-in
¼ teaspoon salt, plus more to season
¼ pound pancetta, finely diced
1 large onion, minced in a food processor or finely chopped
2 stalks celery, minced in a food processor or chopped
1 medium carrot, shredded
2 tablespoons tomato paste
1 orange rind, cut in 3 strips
1 cup dry red wine
4 cups hot chicken broth
3 bay leaves
1 sprig fresh rosemary
Freshly ground black pepper

1. In a medium bowl, pour warm water over the dried porcini and let sit for about 20 minutes. Remove the mushrooms, reserving the soaking liquid, and chop them into small pieces.

2. In a stockpot, heat the olive oil over medium-high heat. Sear the ribs in the oil, browning them all over, for about 8 to 10 minutes. Transfer the browned ribs to a platter and sprinkle with ¼ teaspoon of salt.

3. In the same skillet, cook the pancetta over medium heat, until it begins to brown, about 2 minutes. Add the onions and cook, stirring, for about 2 minutes, until they begin to soften. Add the celery, carrot, and diced mushrooms. Cook, stirring frequently, until the vegetables soften and begin to brown. Stir in the tomato paste and cook, stirring, for 1 minute. Add the orange rind. Place the ribs back in the pan, along with any accumulated juices. Add the wine and bring to a boil. Cook, stirring occasionally, until the liquid is mostly evaporated, about 3 to 5 minutes. Add in the soaking water from the mushrooms and enough broth to cover the ribs, along with the bay leaves and rosemary. Bring to a boil.

4. Reduce the heat to medium-low, cover, and simmer for about 2 to 2½ hours, checking every 20 minutes or so and adding additional broth or water as needed to keep the ribs covered, until the meat is falling-off-the-bone tender.

5. Transfer the ribs to a platter. Discard the bay leaves, herb stems, and orange rind, as well as any bones or bone fragments that have ended up in the sauce. Pull the meat from the bones and shred. Stir the meat into the sauce, discarding the bones, and season with salt and pepper.

6. Serve the meat and sauce over pasta or rice, or alongside vegetables.

PER SERVING: CALORIES: 494; TOTAL FAT: 22G; SATURATED FAT: 6G; CARBS: 6G; PROTEIN: 60G; SODIUM: 1,019MG; FIBER: 1G

CYPRUS

SPICED BEEF
ON WHOLE-WHEAT FLATBREAD

Serves 4   Prep time: 10 minutes   Cook time: 15 minutes

QUICK & EASY   *Spiced meat is often formed into meatballs or used to top flatbreads in various parts of the Mediterranean. In Turkey, this dish would likely be made with lamb, while in Greece and Cyprus, beef is more common. If you like, you can cook the meat-topped flatbreads on the grill for a bit of smoky flavor.*

6 ounces lean ground beef

2 garlic cloves, minced

1 small onion, grated

3 tablespoons tomato paste

1 tablespoon minced flat-leaf parsley

½ teaspoon salt

¼ teaspoon cayenne pepper

¼ teaspoon ground cumin

¼ teaspoon sweet paprika

⅛ teaspoon ground cinnamon

4 whole-wheat flatbread rounds

½ cup plain Greek yogurt, for garnish

2 tablespoons cilantro leaves, for garnish

1 Persian cucumber, cut lengthwise into thin sheets

½ small red onion, thinly sliced

Lemon wedges, for serving

1. Preheat the oven to 475°F.

2. In medium skillet, brown the meat over medium-high heat, breaking up with a spatula, about 4 minutes. When the meat is browned, drain off the excess fat. Add the garlic and grated onion and cook, stirring, 1 minute. Add the tomato paste, parsley, salt, cayenne, cumin, paprika, and cinnamon and cook, stirring, for 1 more minute.

3. Place 2 flatbread rounds onto each of 2 large baking sheets and spoon the meat on top of them, dividing equally. Bake in the preheated oven, rotating the pans halfway through, for 6 to 8 minutes, until the edges of the flatbread are beginning to brown.

4. Remove from the oven and serve with a dollop of yogurt, a sprinkling of cilantro, a few strips of cucumber, and a few slices of red onion on top. Serve lemon wedges on the side for squeezing over the meat.

PER SERVING: CALORIES: 293; TOTAL FAT: 8G; SATURATED FAT: 2G; CARBS: 37G; PROTEIN: 21G; SODIUM: 793MG; FIBER: 5G

SOUTHERN ITALY

ROAST PORK TENDERLOIN
WITH TOMATOES, POTATOES, AND PESTO

Serves 4   Prep time: 10 minutes, plus 3 hours to brine   Cook time: 25 minutes

GLUTEN-FREE   *Brining is a simple process—essentially marinating meat in a salt-sugar-water solution—but it is the key to moist, tender, and flavorful pork tenderloin. This brine uses honey in place of the usual refined sugar. After a 3-hour brine, all the pork tenderloin needs is a rub of herbs and spices and a quick stint in a hot oven.*

For the Pork Tenderloin

3½ cups warm water

¼ cup plus ¾ teaspoon salt, divided

¼ cup plus 2 tablespoons honey, divided

¼ cup red wine vinegar

1 cup ice cubes

1 (1½-pound) pork tenderloin, trimmed

2 tablespoons balsamic vinegar

1 teaspoon freshly ground black pepper

2 garlic cloves, minced

¾ cup olive oil, divided

1 pound small new potatoes, halved or quartered if large

12 small tomatoes on the vine or 24 whole cherry tomatoes

For the Pesto

2 cups (packed) fresh basil leaves, plus more for garnish

⅓ cup pine nuts

3 garlic cloves

½ cup (about 2 ounces) freshly grated Parmesan cheese

1. In a large bowl, combine the water, ¼ cup salt, ¼ cup honey, and the red wine vinegar and stir until the salt and honey dissolve. Add the ice and stir to cool the water. Add the pork, cover, refrigerate for 3 hours, turning the pork over occasionally.

2. In a small bowl, combine the remaining 2 tablespoons of honey, balsamic vinegar, pepper, and the 2 minced garlic cloves and stir to mix well.

3. Preheat the oven to 450°F and brush a roasting pan with 1 tablespoon of olive oil.

4. Remove the pork from the brine (discard the brine) and pat very dry. Brush 1 tablespoon of olive oil all over the pork and then coat the pork evenly with the spice mixture. Place the pork in the prepared roasting pan.

5. In a medium bowl, toss the potatoes with 2 tablespoons olive oil and the remaining ¾ teaspoon salt. Arrange the potatoes around the pork roast in the roasting pan. Bake in the preheated oven for 10 minutes. Turn the pork over, stir the potatoes, add the tomatoes, scattering them around the roast, and roast for about

15 minutes more or until an instant-read thermometer inserted into the center of the pork roast registers 145°F and the potatoes are lightly browned and crisp.

6. While the pork and vegetables are roasting, make the pesto. In a food processor, combine the basil, pine nuts, and the remaining 3 garlic cloves and pulse several times to chop. Add the Parmesan cheese and pulse again until well combined. With the food processor running, add the remaining ½ cup olive oil in a slow, steady stream. Transfer to a small bowl, taste, and add salt and pepper as needed.

7. Transfer the pork to a cutting board, tent with aluminum foil, and let rest for 10 minutes. Slice the roast into ⅛-inch-thick pieces and serve immediately, drizzled with the pesto and with the roasted vegetables alongside.

★ TIP: This pork makes great sandwich meat. To cut it super thin, let it come to room temperature, then wrap and chill completely before slicing with a very sharp knife.

PER SERVING: CALORIES: 956; TOTAL FAT: 54G; SATURATED FAT: 10G; SODIUM: 2,019MG; CARBS: 67G; FIBER: 11G; PROTEIN: 60G

PORTUGAL

PORTUGUESE PORK
AND WHITE BEAN STEW

Serves 6   Prep time: 30 minutes, plus overnight to soak the beans   Cook time: 3 hours

DAIRY-FREE | GLUTEN-FREE   *This meat-and-bean stew is similar to the Brazilian* feijoada, *only it uses white beans instead of black. The ham hock and linguiça give the stew lots of meaty, smoky flavor, so don't be tempted to leave either one of them out. Serve this hearty stew with a crisp salad and crusty bread for dunking.*

2 tablespoons olive oil

1 pound pork shoulder, cut into large chunks

1 medium onion, diced

1 small ham hock

1½ teaspoons ground coriander

2 bay leaves

1 teaspoon salt

1 pound dried white beans, such as cannellini, soaked overnight

1 pound Portuguese linguiça sausage, left whole

1 large carrot, cut into rounds

6 cloves, peeled but left whole

1½ teaspoons tablespoon Piri Piri Sauce (page 244) or chile paste

¼ cup crushed tomatoes

¼ cup chopped flat-leaf parsley

1. Preheat the oven to 300°F.

2. In a large Dutch oven, heat the olive oil over medium-high heat. Add the pork shoulder and cook, turning every couple of minutes, until browned on all sides. Remove the meat from the pot and transfer to a plate or bowl.

3. Add the onion to the Dutch oven and cook, stirring frequently, until softened, about 5 minutes. Return the browned pork, along with any accumulated juices, to the pot and add the ham hock, coriander, bay leaves, and salt. Stir in the beans.

4. Add water to cover the pork by 1 inch. Bring just to a boil, cover, and transfer the pot to the preheated oven. Cook for about 90 minutes, until the beans are just tender.

5. Add the sausage, carrot, garlic cloves, Piri Piri Sauce, and tomatoes. Cover, return to the oven and cook for an additional 30 minutes or so, until the carrots are soft and the beans are very tender.

6. Remove the sausage from the pot, slice it into rounds, and add it back to the stew. Cover again and cook for another 10 minutes in the oven.

7. Let the stew rest in the pot, covered, for a few minutes before serving. Serve hot, garnished with parsley.

★ TIP: For this recipe, you can make your own Piri Piri Sauce (page 244), purchase it at specialty markets or online, or substitute any chile paste you like.

PER SERVING: CALORIES: 813; TOTAL FAT: 44G; SATURATED FAT: 14G; CARBS: 52G; PROTEIN: 52G; SODIUM: 1,036MG; FIBER: 13G

GREECE

GREEK LAMB MEATBALLS
WITH SALAD AND TZATZIKI

Serves 4   Prep time: 10 minutes   Cook time: 20 minutes

QUICK & EASY   *Lamb meatballs with fresh mint and other herbs are loaded with Greek flavor. Baking them in the oven instead of frying them in oil not only makes them healthier, but also significantly reduces the hands-on effort required.*

Olive oil, for brushing
¼ cup panko breadcrumbs
¼ cup milk
1¼ pounds ground lamb
1 teaspoon ground coriander
1 teaspoon ground cumin
1 clove garlic, minced
1 teaspoon dried oregano
1 tablespoon chopped fresh mint leaves
1 teaspoon salt
½ teaspoon freshly ground black pepper, plus more for garnish
¼ cup crumbled feta cheese
1 head butter lettuce, torn into pieces
1 large tomato, diced
1 cup mixed pitted olives
1 medium Persian cucumber, thinly sliced
Tzatziki Sauce (page 241)

1. Preheat the oven to 400°F.

2. Brush a large baking sheet with a little olive oil.

3. In a large bowl, combine the panko breadcrumbs and milk and let stand for 5 minutes. Add the lamb, coriander, cumin, garlic, oregano, mint, salt, and pepper, to the soaked breadcrumbs and mix well. Gently fold in the feta cheese, then form the mixture into 1½-inch balls. Arrange the meatballs in a single layer on the prepared baking sheet. Bake in the preheated oven for about 15 to 20 minutes, until cooked through and lightly browned.

4. While the meatballs are baking, make the salad. In a large bowl, toss together the lettuce, tomato, olives, and cucumber. Transfer to a serving platter. Just before serving, add the meatballs, drizzle with the Tzatziki Sauce, and garnish with pepper.

★ TIP: This meal comes together very quickly, especially if you make the salad and the Tzatziki Sauce while the meatballs bake.

PER SERVING: CALORIES: 434; TOTAL FAT: 20G; SATURATED FAT: 8G; CARBS: 17G; PROTEIN: 46G; SODIUM: 1,295MG; FIBER: 3G

MOROCCO

SPICED LAMB STEW
WITH FENNEL AND DATES

Serves 4   Prep time: 10 minutes   Cook time: 3 hours

DAIRY-FREE | GLUTEN-FREE   *Lamb cooked with spices, vegetables, and dried fruit is very Moroccan. The fennel in this dish nearly melts into the sauce and the lamb, too, becomes extremely tender. In Morocco, a meal like this would be cooked in a tagine—an earthenware dish with a tall, conical shaped lid—but a Dutch oven works just as well.*

2 tablespoons olive oil, divided

1 fennel bulb, trimmed, cored, and thinly sliced

1 red onion, thinly sliced

2 cloves garlic, thinly sliced

1½ pounds lamb shoulder, cut into 1½-inch cubes and dried with paper towels

1 teaspoon ground ginger

2 teaspoons ground cumin

2 teaspoons ground coriander

¼ teaspoon cayenne pepper

1 teaspoon salt

1 cup pitted chopped dates

2 cups water, divided

¼ cup chopped cilantro, for garnish

1. Heat 1 tablespoon of olive oil in a Dutch oven. Add the fennel, onion, and garlic and cook, stirring frequently, until softened and beginning to brown, about 7 minutes. Transfer the vegetables to a plate.

2. Add the remaining 1 tablespoon of olive oil to the pot and cook the lamb, turning every couple of minutes, until browned on all sides.

3. In a small bowl, combine the ginger, cumin, coriander, cayenne, and salt and mix well. Sprinkle the spice mixture over the meat in the pot and cook, stirring, for 1 minute.

4. Return the vegetables to the pot and add the dates and 1 cup of water. Reduce the heat to medium-low, cover, and cook, stirring occasionally and adding the remaining 1 cup of water as needed, for 2½ hours, until the lamb is very tender and the sauce has thickened. Serve immediately, garnished with cilantro.

★ TIP: Use a mandoline if you have one to slice the fennel very thinly.

PER SERVING: CALORIES: 539; TOTAL FAT: 20G; SATURATED FAT: 5G; CARBS: 52G; PROTEIN: 50G; SODIUM: 749MG; FIBER: 6G

MOROCCAN COUSCOUS
WITH LAMB, POMEGRANATE, AND PISTACHIOS

Serves 4   Prep time: 15 minutes   Cook time: 15 minutes

DAIRY-FREE | QUICK & EASY   *Couscous is Morocco's national dish. Some say the name is derived from the sound it makes as it cooks. Adding dried or fresh fruits, nuts, and warm spices like cinnamon is common, and it is often used as a bed for meat or vegetable stews or grilled or pan-seared meats.*

1 cup cilantro leaves

2 cloves garlic

1 tablespoon ground cumin

¼ teaspoon cayenne pepper

¼ cup lemon juice

1 teaspoon finely grated
lemon zest, divided

1½ teaspoons salt, divided

½ teaspoon freshly ground black pepper

2 tablespoons olive oil, plus 1 teaspoon,
divided

4 lamb loin chops (about 7 ounces
each), 1¼-inches thick, trimmed of
excess fat

1½ cups water

¼ teaspoon cinnamon

1 cup couscous

2 tablespoons chopped mint leaves

2 tablespoons chopped unsalted
pistachios

¼ cup pomegranate seeds, divided

¼ cup plus 2 tablespoons
pomegranate juice

1. Preheat the oven to 375°F.

2. Combine the cilantro, garlic, cumin, cayenne, lemon juice, ½ teaspoon of lemon zest, 1 teaspoon salt, the pepper, and 1 tablespoon of olive oil in a food processor and process to a smooth paste. Reserve 1 tablespoon of the paste and spread the rest all over the lamb chops. Let the chops stand for 10 minutes.

3. While the chops are marinating, bring the water to a boil in a small saucepan. Add the cinnamon, 1 tablespoon of olive oil, and the remaining ½ teaspoon of salt. Add the couscous, stir to mix, remove from the heat, cover, and let stand for 15 minutes, until the couscous is tender and the water has been absorbed.

4. In a large bowl, combine the couscous, mint, pistachios, half of the pomegranate seeds, and the remaining ½ teaspoon of lemon zest. Keep warm. »

5. While the couscous is steaming, heat the remaining teaspoon of olive oil in an oven-safe skillet. Scrape off the spice paste from the lamb chops and add them to the skillet. Cook until browned, about 2 to 3 minutes per side. Place the skillet in the preheated oven and cook for about 6 minutes more, until the chops are medium-rare. Remove the chops from the pan and pour off any excess fat from the pan.

6. Add the pomegranate juice to the hot skillet and set it over medium heat, along with the tablespoon of reserved spice paste. Cook, stirring and scraping up any browned bits from the pan, for about 2 minutes, until the liquid has been reduced to ¼ cup.

7. Spoon the couscous onto 4 serving plates. Place a lamb chop on top of each and spoon some of the sauce over the top. Garnish with the remaining pomegranate seeds and serve immediately.

PER SERVING: CALORIES: 718; TOTAL FAT: 27G; SATURATED FAT: 7G; CARBS: 47G; PROTEIN: 64G; SODIUM: 1,039MG; FIBER: 5G

SEARED STEAK
WITH FIG AND GARLIC SAUCE

Serves 4   Prep time: 10 minutes, plus 15 minutes to marinate   Cook time: 25 minutes

DAIRY-FREE | GLUTEN-FREE   *Flank steak is a lean cut of beef that is perfect for searing quickly in a hot pan. The pan collects any juices that run out while the steak cooks and they're later incorporated into the pan sauce. Serve this steak over couscous, bulgur, or polenta.*

For the steak

2 cloves garlic, minced

½ teaspoon freshly ground black pepper

¼ teaspoon cinnamon

¼ teaspoon ground ginger

¼ teaspoon allspice

Pinch of nutmeg

1 teaspoon salt

1 flank steak, about 1½ pounds, lightly scored in several spots with a sharp knife

⅓ cup dry red wine

For the sauce

2 tablespoons olive oil, divided

1 small onion, halved and thinly sliced

½ cup dry red wine

⅓ cup thinly sliced dried figs, stems removed

⅛ teaspoon cinnamon

⅛ teaspoon ground ginger

⅛ teaspoon allspice

1 tablespoon olive oil

½ teaspoon salt

½ teaspoon freshly ground black pepper

1. In a small bowl, combine the garlic, pepper, cinnamon, ginger, allspice, nutmeg, and salt and mix well. Rub the spice mixture into the steak on both sides. Put the steak in a large resealable plastic bag and add the red wine. Seal the bag and shake to coat the steak. Refrigerate for at least 15 minutes (or as long as 2 hours), turning once.

2. To make the sauce, heat the olive oil in a medium skillet over medium heat. Add the onion and cook, stirring frequently, until the onion is soft and golden brown, about 10 minutes. Transfer to a bowl or plate.

3. Meanwhile, in a small bowl, stir together the wine, figs, cinnamon, ginger, allspice, salt, and pepper. »

4. Remove the steak from the marinade, discarding the marinade. Add the remaining tablespoon of oil to the skillet and heat over medium heat. Sear the steak in the skillet for about 3 minutes, until browned on the bottom. Flip over and cook another 2 to 3 minutes until browned on the second side. Reduce the heat to low and let cook another 5 minutes or so for medium-rare. Remove the steak to a cutting board, tent with aluminum foil, and let rest for 10 minutes.

5. Meanwhile, add the onions and the wine mixture to the skillet and bring to a boil. Cook, stirring and scraping up any browned bits from the bottom of the pan, until the sauce thickens, about 2 minutes.

6. Thinly slice the steak across the grain and serve drizzled with the sauce.

PER SERVING: CALORIES: 493; TOTAL FAT: 24G; SATURATED FAT: 7G; CARBS: 15G; PROTEIN: 48G; SODIUM: 972MG; FIBER: 3G

SPAIN

SMOKED PAPRIKA AND LEMON MARINATED
PORK KABOBS

Serves 4   Prep time: 10 minutes, plus 4 hours to marinate   Cook time: 10 minutes

DAIRY-FREE | GLUTEN-FREE   *Smoked paprika adds an extra hit of smoke to these grilled pork kabobs. Pork tenderloin is very lean, so marinating the meat is important to keep it moist and give it flavor. Serve this simple dish with salad, couscous, quinoa, or other simple sides.*

⅓ cup finely chopped flat-leaf parsley

¼ cup olive oil

2 tablespoons minced red onion

1 tablespoon lemon juice

1 tablespoon smoked paprika

2 teaspoons ground cumin

1 clove garlic, minced

¼ teaspoon cayenne pepper

½ teaspoon salt

2 pork tenderloins, each about 1 pound, trimmed of silver skin and any excess fat, cut into 1¼-inch cubes

1 lemon, cut into wedges, for serving

1. In a large bowl, whisk together the parsley, olive oil, onion, lemon juice, smoked paprika, cumin, garlic, cayenne, and salt. Add the pork and toss to coat well. Cover and refrigerate, stirring occasionally, for at least 4 hours (or as long as overnight).

2. Soak bamboo skewers in water for 30 minutes.

3. Preheat the grill to high heat.

4. Remove the meat from the marinade, discarding the marinade. Thread the meat onto the soaked skewers and place the skewers on the grill. Cook, with the lid closed, turning occasionally, until the pork is cooked through and browned on all sides, about 8 to 10 minutes total.

5. Transfer the skewers to a serving platter and serve immediately with the lemon wedges.

PER SERVING: CALORIES: 447; TOTAL FAT: 21G; SATURATED FAT: 5G; CARBOHYDRATES: 3G; PROTEIN: 60G; SODIUM: 426MG; FIBER: 1G

CALABRIAN BRAISED BEEF
WITH CARAMELIZED ONIONS AND POTATOES

Serves 6 to 8   Prep time: 10 minutes   Cook time: 4 hours and 30 minutes

GLUTEN-FREE   *This southern Italian-style beef braised with caramelized onions, tomatoes, potatoes, and fresh herbs takes a while to cook, but the hands-on time is minimal. Serve it with crusty Italian bread for dunking in the sauce.*

5 tablespoons olive oil, divided

3 medium onions, thinly sliced

4 cloves garlic, very thinly sliced

1½ teaspoons salt, divided

2 pounds top sirloin steak

½ teaspoon freshly ground black pepper

2 tablespoons chopped fresh thyme, divided

3 medium potatoes, peeled and thinly sliced

2 sprigs fresh rosemary, leaves picked and finely chopped, divided

¼ cup grated Parmesan cheese, plus 4 tablespoons, divided

1 (28-ounce) can crushed tomatoes

1. Preheat the oven to 325°F.

2. Heat 2 tablespoons of olive oil in a large skillet over medium heat. Add the onions and garlic along with ½ teaspoon of salt, reduce the heat to medium-low, and cook, stirring frequently, until they become very soft and golden brown, about 20 minutes. Remove from the heat.

3. Add 1 tablespoon of olive oil to a Dutch oven over medium-high heat. Pat the meat dry with paper towels and sprinkle with the remaining 1 teaspoon of salt and the pepper. Brown the meat on both sides in the Dutch oven, about 10 minutes.

4. Place about half of the cooked onions on top of the meat in an even layer. Sprinkle 1 tablespoon of thyme over the onions, then top with half of the potato slices, arranging them in an even layer. Drizzle with 1 tablespoon of olive oil, and top with half of the rosemary, and 2 tablespoons of cheese. Pour half of the tomatoes over the top. Repeat with the remaining onions, thyme, potatoes, the remaining tablespoon of olive oil, rosemary, 2 tablespoons of cheese, and the tomatoes. Place the lid on the Dutch oven and cook in the preheated oven for about 4 hours, until the meat is very tender. Sprinkle the remaining ¼ cup of cheese over the top and cook under the broiler for a few minutes, until the cheese is melted and golden brown. Serve hot.

★ TIP: This is a great make-ahead dish, as the flavor gets even better after a day or two in the refrigerator. To reheat, place the covered pot in a 325°F oven for about 1 hour, or until heated through.

PER SERVING: CALORIES: 481; TOTAL FAT: 19G; SATURATED FAT: 6G; CARBS: 29G; PROTEIN: 48G; SODIUM: 924MG; FIBER: 7G

MEDITERRANEAN STAPLES

SPAIN

SHERRY VINAIGRETTE

Makes about ¾ cup   Prep time: 5 minutes   Cook time: None

VEGETARIAN | DAIRY-FREE | GLUTEN-FREE | QUICK & EASY   *Sherry vinegar is typically made from Spanish sherry, and like the fortified wine it's made from, it possesses a wide range of subtle flavors including nuts and caramel. This simple vinaigrette highlights the flavor of the vinegar and makes a fantastic dressing for a simple green salad, tomato salads, or even bean or rice and pasta salads.*

⅓ cup sherry vinegar
1 clove garlic
2 teaspoons dried oregano
1 teaspoon salt
½ teaspoon freshly ground black pepper
½ cup olive oil

In a food processor or blender, combine the vinegar, garlic, oregano, salt, and pepper and process until the garlic is minced and the ingredients are well combined. With the food processor running, add the olive oil in a thin stream until it is well incorporated. Serve immediately or store, covered, in the refrigerator for up to a week.

★ TIP: You can find sherry vinegar in many supermarkets these days alongside the wine and balsamic vinegars. Look for one that is imported from Spain to ensure the most authentic flavor. If you don't have sherry vinegar, you could substitute red wine vinegar, but the flavor won't be the same.

PER 2-TABLESPOON SERVING: CALORIES: 74; TOTAL FAT: 8G; SATURATED FAT: 1G; CARBS: 0G; PROTEIN: 0G; SODIUM: 194MG; FIBER: 0G

CYPRUS

TAHINI SAUCE

Makes about ¾ cup   Prep time: 5 minutes   Cook time: None

VEGETARIAN | DAIRY-FREE | GLUTEN-FREE | QUICK & EASY   *Tahini sauce is made from ground sesame seed paste (tahini) combined with garlic, lemon juice, and olive oil. It's a popular condiment throughout the Mediterranean, especially in Turkey, Syria, Israel, and Lebanon, where it is used in wraps and sandwiches, as a dip for bread or vegetables, and as a sauce for falafel and other dishes.*

½ cup tahini
1 clove garlic, crushed
½ teaspoon salt
2 tablespoons olive oil
¼ cup lemon juice
1 tablespoon chopped flat-leaf parsley

1. In a small bowl, combine the tahini, garlic, salt, olive oil, and lemon juice and stir to mix well.

2. Stir in the parsley.

3. If the mixture is too thick, add a tablespoon or two of water and stir to mix well. Serve immediately or store, covered, in the refrigerator for up to a week.

★ TIP: You can buy tahini in most supermarkets, either in the international foods aisle or near the nut butters; it is also available in specialty markets and online.

PER 2-TABLESPOON SERVING: CALORIES: 81; TOTAL FAT: 8G; SATURATED FAT: 1G; CARBS: 2G; PROTEIN: 2G; SODIUM: 110MG; FIBER: 1G

GREECE

TZATZIKI SAUCE

Makes about 2 cups   Prep time: 10 minutes, plus 20 minutes to drain cucumber   Cook time: None

VEGETARIAN | GLUTEN-FREE | QUICK & EASY   *Tzatziki is a Greek condiment made of thick, Greek-style yogurt, grated cucumber, garlic, and fresh herbs. It is used as a dip for bread or vegetables or as a sauce for gyros or grilled meats. This recipe calls for fresh dill, but you can substitute any fresh herb or herb combination you like, such as mint, basil, oregano, or parsley.*

½ a large English cucumber or 2 small
   Persian cucumbers, seeded
½ teaspoon salt, divided
1½ cups plain Greek yogurt
2 cloves garlic, finely minced
2 tablespoons olive oil
1 tablespoon white vinegar
1 tablespoon minced fresh dill

1. Grate the cucumber on the large holes of a box grater. Place the grated cucumber in a fine-meshed sieve and sprinkle with ¼ teaspoon of salt. Let the cucumber drain over the sink for 20 minutes or so, then transfer to a clean dish towel and squeeze out as much excess water as you can.

2. In a large bowl, stir together the yogurt, garlic, olive oil, vinegar, and the remaining ¼ teaspoon of salt. Add the grated cucumber and the dill to the yogurt and stir to mix well. Taste and add additional salt, if needed. Cover and refrigerate until ready to use. Can be stored in the refrigerator for up to 3 days.

PER 2-TABLESPOON SERVING: CALORIES: 38; TOTAL FAT: 3G; SATURATED FAT: 1G; CARBS: 2G; PROTEIN: 1G; SODIUM: 88MG; FIBER: 0G

SPAIN

ROMESCO SAUCE

Makes about 2 cups   Prep time: 5 minutes   Cook time: 30 minutes

VEGETARIAN | DAIRY-FREE   *Romesco sauce is a smooth, rich sauce made from roasted vegetables and nuts, thickened with bread, and spiked with sherry vinegar. As versatile as pesto, it can be served as a sauce for grilled meat or fish, used to top crostini for a quick appetizer, or used as a dip for shellfish or vegetables.*

¼ cup olive oil, plus more for brushing

2 red bell peppers, halved and seeded

3 (½-inch-thick) slices baguette

4 cloves garlic, unpeeled

½ cup slivered almonds

3 medium tomatoes, halved crosswise and seeded

2 tablespoons sherry vinegar

1 teaspoon salt

⅛ teaspoon cayenne pepper

2 tablespoons chopped fresh parsley

1. Preheat the oven to 375°F.

2. Brush a large, rimmed baking sheet with a bit of olive oil.

3. Arrange the bell peppers, baguette slices, garlic cloves, almonds, and tomatoes, cut-side down, in a single layer on the baking sheet. Roast until the bread and almonds turn golden, about 5 minutes. Remove the bread and almonds and continue roasting the vegetables until the skin of the peppers becomes charred and blistered, the garlic softens, and the tomatoes begin to break down, about 25 minutes more.

4. Peel the skins off the tomatoes, bell peppers, and garlic.

5. In a food processor, process the garlic, bread, and almonds until finely ground. Add the tomatoes, bell peppers, and vinegar and process to a smooth purée. With the food processor running, add the oil in a thin stream and process until the mixture is emulsified. Transfer to a serving bowl and stir in the salt, cayenne, and parsley. Serve immediately or store, covered, in the refrigerator for up to 3 days.

PER ¼-CUP SERVING: CALORIES: 116; TOTAL FAT: 10G; SATURATED FAT: 1G; CARBS: 7G; PROTEIN: 3G; SODIUM: 311MG; FIBER: 2G

SOUTHERN ITALIAN-STYLE
TOMATO SAUCE

Makes about 3 cups   Prep time: 5 minutes   Cook time: 15 minutes

VEGETARIAN | DAIRY-FREE | GLUTEN-FREE | QUICK & EASY   *This simple tomato sauce is quick to make and delicious on any type of pasta, either strained or left chunky. Top it with a grating of Pecorino Romano cheese for an extra Southern Italian touch. Make a large batch to freeze so that you'll always have some on hand for a quick meal.*

3 cups canned whole tomatoes, drained
¼ cup plus 2 tablespoons olive oil
4 cloves garlic, lightly crushed
½ teaspoon salt
¼ teaspoon freshly ground black pepper
1 tablespoon finely chopped fresh basil
    or flat-leaf parsley

1. Remove and discard the tomato seeds. Place the tomatoes in a medium bowl and crush them with a fork or potato masher.

2. Heat the olive oil in a medium saucepan over medium heat. Add the garlic and cook, stirring frequently, until it softens and turns golden. Stir in the tomatoes, salt, and pepper. Simmer for 15 minutes. Discard the garlic cloves and stir in the basil just before serving. For a smoother sauce, use an immersion blender to purée the sauce or put it in a food processor, countertop blender, or food mill.

★ TIP: This sauce stores well in the refrigerator or freezer. Simply omit the fresh herbs, cool the sauce to room temperature, then cover and refrigerate for up to 5 days or freeze for up to 3 months. Reheat the sauce and stir in the herbs just before serving.

PER ¼-CUP SERVING: CALORIES: 66; TOTAL FAT: 7G;
SATURATED FAT: 1G; CARBS: 2G; PROTEIN: 1G; SODIUM: 99MG; FIBER: 1G

PIRI PIRI SAUCE

Makes about 1 cup   Prep time: 5 minutes, plus 3 days to cure   Cook time: None

VEGETARIAN | DAIRY-FREE | GLUTEN-FREE   *Piri piri chiles, also known as African bird's eye chiles, are abundant in Africa, where Portuguese settlers came across them a few hundred years ago and created this addictive sauce. If you can't find them (they're not generally available fresh in the US), substitute cayenne, New Mexico, or pequín chiles.*

4 to 8 fresh hot, red chiles, stemmed
    and coarsely chopped
2 cloves garlic, minced
Juice of 1 lemon
Pinch of salt
½ to 1 cup olive oil

1. In a food processor, combine the chiles (with their seeds), garlic, lemon juice, salt, and ½ cup of olive oil. Process to a smooth purée. Add additional oil as needed to reach the desired consistency.

2. Pour the mixture into a glass jar or non-reactive bowl, cover, and refrigerate for at least 3 days before using. Store in the refrigerator for up to a month.

PER 2-TABLESPOON SERVING: CALORIES: 84; TOTAL FAT: 10G;
SATURATED FAT: 1G; CARBS: 0G; PROTEIN: 0G; SODIUM: 13MG; FIBER: 0G

SOUTHERN ITALY

MINT PESTO
WITH PECORINO ROMANO

Makes about 1 cup   Prep time: 5 minutes   Cook time: none

VEGETARIAN | GLUTEN-FREE | QUICK & EASY   *Traditional basil pesto—a paste made of fresh basil, garlic, pine nuts, olive oil, and Parmesan cheese—is a northern Italian specialty, hailing from the region of Liguria. In the south, bright fresh mint is used as a seasoning as often as basil is. Using mint instead of basil in a classic pesto makes it a refreshing alternative. This recipe also calls for Pecorino Romano cheese instead of Parmesan since the sharp, dry sheep's milk cheese is a southern specialty.*

1 tablespoon toasted walnuts
2 cups packed fresh mint leaves
1 clove garlic
1 tablespoon lemon juice
½ teaspoon lemon zest
¼ teaspoon salt
⅔ cup olive oil
½ cup grated Pecorino cheese

1. Place the walnuts, mint, and garlic in a food processor and pulse to mince finely. Add the lemon juice, lemon zest, and salt and pulse to grind to a paste.

2. With the processor running, add the olive oil in a thin stream. Process until the mixture is well combined.

3. Add the cheese and pulse to combine.

★ TIP: Pesto keeps well in the freezer. If you are planning to freeze it, leave out the cheese and spoon the pesto into an ice cube tray. Freeze overnight or until solid, and then transfer the cubes to a freezer-safe resealable plastic bag and store in the freezer for up to 3 months. Add the cheese to the defrosted pesto.

PER 2-TABLESPOON SERVING: CALORIES: 113; TOTAL FAT: 12G; SATURATED FAT: 3G; CARBS: 1G; PROTEIN: 3G; SODIUM: 234MG; FIBER: 0G

MOROCCO

PRESERVED LEMONS
WITH MOROCCAN SPICES

Makes 4 preserved lemons   Prep time: 10 minutes, plus 1 month curing time   Cook time: none

VEGETARIAN | DAIRY-FREE | GLUTEN-FREE   *Preserved lemons are commonly used in Moroccan and other North African cuisines to add a boost of flavor to sauces, dressings, marinades, and dishes of all kinds. This version is spiced with cinnamon, bay leaf, clove, coriander, and black pepper, but you can leave these out for a more straightforward result. While it will only take about 10 minutes to prepare the lemons, they'll need at least one month to fully cure. But don't worry, a little goes a long way, so once they're ready they'll last for a long while.*

1 cup lemon juice, divided
3 tablespoons salt, divided
4 lemons
1 cinnamon stick
1 bay leaf
2 whole cloves
3 coriander seeds
3 black peppercorns

1. Place ½ cup of lemon juice and 1 tablespoon of salt in a glass jar that is just large enough to hold the lemons.

2. Cut the lemons into 6 wedges each, without cutting all the way through at the stem end (so that the wedges are still attached at one end). Sprinkle salt into each opening and then close each lemon back up.

3. Place the lemons into the jar, pressing them down to pack them in. Add the cinnamon stick, bay leaf, cloves, coriander seeds, and peppercorns along with the remaining ½ cup of lemon juice and the remaining salt.

4. Cap the jar and store it in the refrigerator for at least 4 weeks before using. The lemons will keep for months in the refrigerator.

5. To use the lemons, rinse them well under running water and then remove and discard the flesh. Slice, dice, or mince the rind.

PER LEMON: CALORIES: 144; TOTAL FAT: 14G; SATURATED FAT: 2G; CARBS: 8G; PROTEIN: 1G; SODIUM: 1,983MG; FIBER: 2G

WHOLE-WHEAT PIZZA DOUGH

Makes 1 pound   Prep time: 10 minutes, plus 1 hour and 10 minutes to rise
Cook time: 10 to 12 minutes

VEGETARIAN | DAIRY-FREE   *These days most supermarkets carry refrigerated or frozen pizza dough, but they are usually made with refined white flour. For a healthier version, make this simple yeasted dough that replaces half of the all-purpose flour with whole-wheat flour.*

¾ cup hot tap water

½ teaspoon honey

1 envelope quick-rising yeast, (2¼ teaspoons)

1 tablespoon olive oil, plus more for oiling the bowl

1 cup whole-wheat flour

1 cup all-purpose flour

1 teaspoon salt

1. Preheat the oven to 500°F.

2. In a non-reactive bowl, stir together the hot water and honey. Sprinkle the yeast over the top, stir to mix, and let sit for about 10 minutes, until foamy. Add 1 tablespoon of olive oil.

3. In a food processor or the bowl of a stand mixer fitted with a dough hook, combine the whole-wheat and all-purpose flours, and the salt. With the food processor or mixer running, slowly add the yeast and water mixture until the dough comes together in a ball. The dough should be quite soft and tacky, but not overly sticky. If it is too dry, you can add warm water 1 tablespoon at a time, mixing after each addition, until the right consistency is achieved. Likewise, if it seems too wet, you can add all-purpose flour, 1 tablespoon at a time, until the desired consistency is achieved. Process for about 1 more minute to knead the dough.

4. Oil a large bowl lightly with olive oil. Put the dough in the bowl and turn to coat with oil. Cover the bowl with a clean dish towel and set it in a warm place (like on your stovetop or in a sunny spot on the kitchen counter) and let rise for 1 hour, during which time it should double in size.

5. Using your hands or a rolling pin, shape the dough into whatever shape you like. Top as desired and bake in a preheated oven for 10 to 12 minutes, until crisp and lightly browned.

★ TIP: The pizza dough can be wrapped in lightly oiled plastic wrap and stored in the refrigerator for up to 2 days. Bring it to room temperature by letting it sit out on the countertop for 45 minutes before using.

PER RECIPE: CALORIES: 1,061; TOTAL FAT: 17G; SATURATED FAT: 2G; CARBS: 196G; PROTEIN: 29G; SODIUM: 2,334MG; FIBER: 8G

MOROCCO

MOROCCAN CHERMOULA

Makes about 1½ cups   Prep time: 5 minutes   Cook time: None

VEGETARIAN | DAIRY-FREE | GLUTEN-FREE | QUICK & EASY   Chermoula *(also called* charmoula*)* *is a spicy North African condiment made of fresh herbs, spices, chiles, lemon juice, and olive oil. There are many different recipes for chermoula and they all use slightly different combinations of herbs and spices. This one uses cilantro and parsley, along with paprika, cumin, and cayenne.*

1 cup packed cilantro leaves
½ cup packed flat-leaf parsley leaves
4 cloves garlic, peeled
⅓ cup lemon juice
1 tablespoon paprika
2 teaspoons ground cumin
½ teaspoon cayenne pepper
1 teaspoon salt
½ cup olive oil

1. In a food processor, combine the cilantro, parsley, and garlic and pulse until finely minced.

2. Add the lemon juice, paprika, cumin, cayenne, and salt and pulse to combine.

3. With the food processor running, add the olive oil in a thin stream and process until the sauce is smooth and well combined. Use immediately or store, covered, in the refrigerator for up to 3 days.

PER 2-TABLESPOON SERVING: CALORIES: 40; TOTAL FAT: 4G; SATURATED FAT: 1G; CARBS: 1G; PROTEIN: 0G; SODIUM: 99MG; FIBER: 0G

MOROCCO

GREEN OLIVE TAPENADE
WITH HARISSA

Makes about 1½ cups   Prep time: 5 minutes   Cook time: None

VEGETARIAN | DAIRY-FREE | GLUTEN-FREE | QUICK & EASY   *Tapenade is another dish that is made in many different Mediterranean cuisines. It sometimes includes anchovies, capers, dried fruit, or other ingredients. This simple version gets Moroccan flavor from* harissa, *a spicy red pepper paste popular in northern African cuisines.*

1 cup pitted, cured green olives
1 clove garlic, minced
1 tablespoon harissa
1 tablespoon lemon juice
1 tablespoon chopped fresh parsley
¼ cup olive oil, or more to taste

1. Finely chop the olives (or pulse them in a food processor until they resemble a chunky paste).

2. Add the garlic, harissa, lemon juice, parsley, and olive oil and stir or pulse to combine well.

★ TIP: Harissa is available in Middle Eastern markets or online. If you can't find it, you can substitute 1 teaspoon chili-garlic paste, which can be found in Asian markets or in the Asian foods aisle of many supermarkets.

PER ¼ CUP SERVING: CALORIES: 215; TOTAL FAT: 23G; SATURATED FAT: 3G; CARBS: 5G; PROTEIN: 1G; SODIUM: 453MG; FIBER: 2G

14

DESSERTS

MINTY CANTALOUPE GRANITA

Serves 4   Prep time: 10 minutes, plus 4 hours to freeze   Cook time: 5 minutes

VEGETARIAN | DAIRY-FREE | GLUTEN-FREE   Granitas *are the ideal dessert for balmy Mediterranean summer days. This one uses cantaloupe, but you could substitute another melon such as honeydew or watermelon, if you like. It is sweetened with honey and flavored with a hint of fresh mint.*

½ cup plus 2 tablespoons honey
¼ cup water
2 tablespoons fresh mint leaves, plus
   more for garnish
1 medium cantaloupe (about 4 pounds)
   peeled, seeded, and cut into
   1-inch chunks

1. In a small saucepan set over low heat, combine the honey and water and cook, stirring, until the honey has fully dissolved. Stir in the mint and remove from the heat. Set aside to cool.

2. In a food processor, process the cantaloupe until very smooth. Transfer to a medium bowl. Remove the mint leaves from the syrup and discard them. Pour the syrup into the cantaloupe purée and stir to mix.

3. Transfer the mixture into a 7-by-12-inch glass baking dish and freeze, stirring with a fork every 30 minutes, for 3 to 4 hours, until it is frozen, but still grainy. Serve chilled, scooped into glasses and garnished with mint leaves.

★ TIP: For best results, do not stir the granita once it is past the frozen state. If the ice crystals get too small, it becomes a solid block that can no longer be stirred. Granita should be slightly slushy.

PER SERVING: CALORIES: 174; TOTAL FAT: 0G; SATURATED FAT: 0G; CARBS: 47G; PROTEIN: 1G; SODIUM: 9MG; FIBER: 1G

RICOTTA WITH BALSAMIC CHERRIES
AND BLACK PEPPER

Serves 4   Prep time: 10 minutes, plus 1 hour to chill   Cook time: None

VEGETARIAN | GLUTEN-FREE   *With its creamy texture and mild flavor, ricotta cheese is a common ingredient in Italian desserts. Processing it in a food processor gives it a silky-smooth, mousse-like texture that is just dreamy, especially when topped with sweet-tart balsamic-marinated cherries. A pinch of freshly ground black pepper gives this dessert an unexpected kick.*

1 cup (8 ounces) ricotta
2 tablespoons honey
1 teaspoon vanilla extract
3 cups pitted sweet cherries (thawed if frozen), halved
1½ teaspoons aged balsamic vinegar
Pinch of freshly ground black pepper

1. In a food processor, combine the ricotta, honey, and vanilla and process until smooth. Transfer the mixture to a medium bowl, cover, and refrigerate for 1 hour.

2. In a small bowl, combine the cherries, vinegar, and pepper and stir to mix well. Chill along with the ricotta mixture.

3. To serve, spoon the ricotta mixture into 4 serving bowls or glasses. Top with the cherries, dividing them equally and spooning a bit of the accumulated juice over the top of each bowl. Serve chilled.

PER SERVING: CALORIES: 236; TOTAL FAT: 5G; SATURATED FAT: 3G; CARBS: 42G; PROTEIN: 7G; SODIUM: 93MG; FIBER: 1G

SOUTHERN ITALY

GREEK YOGURT PANNA COTTA

Serves 6   Prep time: 10 minutes, plus 3 hours to chill   Cook time: 10 minutes

GLUTEN-FREE   Panna cotta *is a dish of northern Italian origins, but this version uses distinctly Mediterranean ingredients for a Southern Italian twist. Greek yogurt is substituted for the usual heavy cream, making it lighter without sacrificing any of the creaminess.*

1 envelope unflavored gelatin (2¼ teaspoons)
2 tablespoons cold water
1 cup milk
⅔ cup honey, divided
1 vanilla bean
2 cups plain Greek yogurt
¼ cup chopped, roasted, unsalted hazelnuts

1. In a small bowl, sprinkle the gelatin over the water and let it sit for 5 minutes.

2. Combine the milk and ⅓ cup of honey in a small saucepan. Split the vanilla bean and scrape the seeds into the milk mixture. Add the split pod to the milk mixture as well. Bring the mixture to a simmer over medium heat. Remove from the heat and stir in the gelatin mixture until it is fully dissolved.

3. In a large bowl, whisk the yogurt until smooth and then whisk in the milk mixture. Remove and discard the vanilla bean and transfer the mixture to six 4-ounce ramekins. Cover and chill until the panna cotta is firm, at least 3 hours.

4. In a small saucepan, heat the remaining ⅓ cup of honey over medium heat until it is runny. Stir in the chopped hazelnuts and remove from the heat.

5. Gently dislodge the panna cotta by running a knife around the inside of each ramekin. Invert each ramekin onto a serving plate. Drizzle some of the warm honey and hazelnuts over each panna cotta and serve immediately.

PER SERVING: CALORIES: 232; TOTAL FAT: 7G; SATURATED FAT: 4G; CARBS: 39G; PROTEIN: 6G; SODIUM: 73MG; FIBER: 0G

MOROCCO

DATE AND HONEY
ALMOND MILK ICE CREAM

Serves 4   Prep time: 10 minutes, plus 15 minutes to soak dates, 1 hour to chill,
and 30 minutes to freeze in the ice cream maker   Cook time: 5 minutes

VEGETARIAN | DAIRY-FREE | GLUTEN-FREE   *Native to the Mediterranean, dates are so naturally sweet that they're like candy that grows on trees. Using them to sweeten a dairy-free ice cream made with almond milk makes for an exotically flavored and sweet frozen treat that needs no other sweeteners.*

¾ cup (about 4 ounces) pitted dates
¼ cup honey
½ cup water
2 cups cold unsweetened almond milk
2 teaspoons vanilla extract

1. Combine the dates and water in a small saucepan and bring to a boil over high heat. Remove the pan from the heat, cover, and let stand for 15 minutes.

2. In a blender, combine the almond milk, dates, the date soaking water, honey, and the vanilla and process until very smooth.

3. Cover the blender jar and refrigerate the mixture until cold, at least 1 hour.

4. Transfer the mixture to an electric ice cream maker and freeze according to the manufacturer's instructions.

5. Serve immediately or transfer to a freezer-safe storage container and freeze for 4 hours (or longer). Serve frozen.

★ TIP: You can serve this ice cream straight out of the ice cream maker, but the texture will be similar to soft-serve ice cream. For a more traditional solid ice cream, freeze the mixture for at least an additional 4 hours.

PER SERVING: CALORIES: 106; TOTAL FAT: 2G; SATURATED FAT: 0G; CARBS: 23G; PROTEIN: 1G; SODIUM: 92MG; FIBER: 3G

GREECE

PEARS POACHED IN POMEGRANATE AND WINE

Serves 4   Prep time: 5 minutes   Cook time: 60 minutes

VEGETARIAN | DAIRY-FREE | GLUTEN-FREE   *Pomegranates are a quintessentially Mediterranean fruit. Here, the tart juice is cooked down to a syrup with sweet wine. It gives both flavor and a gorgeous ruby hue to the pears.*

4 ripe, firm Bosc pears, peeled, left whole, and stems left intact

1½ cups pomegranate juice

1 cup sweet, white dessert wine, such as vin santo

½ cup pomegranate seeds (seeds from about ½ whole fruit)

★ TIP: Use a bowl of water to easily seed a pomegranate. With the fruit submerged in the water, slice off the crown end and lightly score the fruit into 4 segments. With the fruit still submerged, break the segments apart and gently separate the seeds from the inner membrane and pith. Drain the seeds in a colander and discard the peel and pith.

1. Slice off a bit of the bottom of each pear to create a flat surface so that the pears can stand upright. If desired, use an apple corer to remove the cores of the fruit, working from the bottom.

2. Lay the pears in a large saucepan on their sides and pour the juice and wine over the top. Set over medium-high heat and bring to a simmer. Cover the pan, reduce the heat, and let the pears simmer, turning twice, for about 40 minutes, until the pears are tender. Transfer the pears to a shallow bowl, leaving the cooking liquid in the saucepan.

3. Turn the heat under the saucepan to high and bring the poaching liquid to a boil. Cook, stirring frequently, for about 15 to 20 minutes, until the liquid becomes thick and syrupy and is reduced to about ½ cup.

4. Spoon a bit of the syrup onto each of 4 serving plates and top each with a pear, sitting it upright. Drizzle a bit more of the sauce over the pears and garnish with the pomegranate seeds. Serve immediately.

PER SERVING: CALORIES: 208; TOTAL FAT: 0G; SATURATED FAT: 0G; CARBS: 46G; PROTEIN: 1G; SODIUM: 7MG; FIBER: 7G

NUT AND HONEY
BAKLAVA

Makes about 24 pieces   Prep time: 45 minutes   Cook time: 1 hour and 45 minutes

VEGETARIAN   Baklava *is a sweet dessert popular throughout the Mediterranean, with variations by region. At its most basic, though, baklava is a dessert made of thin, flaky sheets of pastry (phyllo) layered with chopped nuts and soaked in a sweet syrup made either of sugar or honey, or a combination of the two. This version combines both walnuts and pistachios and uses only honey as a sweetener.*

1 cup honey
¾ cup water
Finely grated zest of ½ lemon
1 (16-ounce) package frozen phyllo
   sheets, thawed
2 sticks (½ pound) unsalted butter,
   melted, divided
2 cups (about 8 ounces) walnuts,
   coarsely chopped
2 cups (about 8 ounces) pistachios,
   coarsely chopped
1 teaspoon ground cinnamon

1. Preheat the oven to 325°F.

2. In a small saucepan, combine the honey, water, and lemon zest and bring to a boil over medium-high heat. Reduce the heat to low and simmer the mixture, stirring occasionally, for 25 minutes. Remove from the heat and set aside to cool.

3. Brush the bottom and sides of a 13-by-9-inch baking pan with butter.

4. Trim the phyllo sheets to fit your pan. You'll need 40 sheets, roughly 9-by-14 inches.

5. In a medium bowl, stir together the walnuts, pistachios, and cinnamon.

6. Layer 10 sheets of the phyllo into the prepared baking pan one at a time, brushing each one all over with butter before adding the next. Sprinkle ¾ cup of the nut mixture evenly over the top. »

7. Top with 5 more layers of phyllo, again brushing each sheet all over with butter before adding the next. Sprinkle with another ¾ cup of the nut mixture. Do this until you have 4 layers of 5 buttered phyllo sheets and nuts. Top with 10 layers of buttered phyllo sheets. Brush the top layer with butter.

8. Cut the pastry into strips 1½ inches wide and 13 inches long. Next cut the strips diagonally to form diamond-shaped pieces.

9. Bake in the preheated oven until the top is golden brown, about 1 hour and 15 minutes.

10. Spoon the cooled honey syrup over the top of the baklava immediately after removing it from the oven. Set aside to cool completely. Serve at room temperature.

★ TIP: To keep your phyllo sheets from drying out while you construct the baklava, lay them on a dry, flat surface. Cover them with a sheet of plastic wrap and then a damp dishtowel. Pull out one sheet at a time as you need it and re-cover the rest with the plastic wrap and damp towel.

PER PIECE: CALORIES: 291; TOTAL FAT: 20G; SATURATED FAT: 6G; CARBS: 26G; PROTEIN: 6G; SODIUM: 147MG; FIBER: 2G

SOUTHERN ITALY

HONEY-SWEETENED
POLENTA CAKE

Serves 12   Prep time: 10 minutes   Cook time: 30 minutes

VEGETARIAN   *This cake is lightly sweetened with honey and carries the sweet flavor of corn from the polenta. For a citrus-flavored cake, add the grated zest and juice of a lemon or half an orange to the batter. Whipped cream with a bit of citrus zest makes a lovely topping as well.*

2½ cups all-purpose flour
1 cup uncooked finely ground polenta
2 tablespoons baking powder
1 teaspoon salt
1 cup unsalted butter, melted
1¾ cups milk
¾ cup honey
2 eggs, lightly beaten

1. Preheat the oven to 325°F and lightly oil a 13-by-9-inch baking pan.

2. Combine the flour, polenta, baking powder, and salt in a large bowl.

3. In a small bowl, whisk together the butter, milk, honey, and eggs. Gently mix the wet ingredients into the dry ingredients and mix until just incorporated.

4. Pour the batter into the prepared baking pan and bake in the preheated oven for 25 to 30 minutes, until a toothpick inserted into the center comes out clean.

5. Invert the cake onto a wire rack and cool completely. Serve at room temperature with a drizzle of honey or a dollop of lightly sweetened whipped cream, if desired.

PER PIECE: CALORIES: 372; TOTAL FAT: 17G; SATURATED FAT: 10G; CARBS: 51G; PROTEIN: 6G; SODIUM: 334MG; FIBER: 1G

GREECE

BANANA-NUT PHYLLO ROLLS
WITH CHOCOLATE-DATE SAUCE

Serves 4   Prep time: 10 minutes   Cook time: 30 minutes

VEGETARIAN   *Wrapping bananas in flaky, buttery layers of phyllo dough interspersed with chopped walnuts gives this dessert Greek flair. The chocolate sauce—sweetened with dates—is a luxurious touch, but you could substitute a sprinkling of ground cinnamon, if you prefer.*

8 sheets phyllo dough
   (about 9-by-14 inches)
2 tablespoons melted butter
¼ cup finely chopped walnuts
4 large ripe bananas
½ cup boiling water
4 medjool dates, pitted and chopped
1 tablespoon cocoa powder

1. Preheat the oven to 375°F.

2. Brush a baking dish lightly with melted butter.

3. Place one sheet of phyllo on your work surface (keep the rest covered with plastic wrap and a damp dishtowel). Brush the phyllo all over with the melted butter and then sprinkle with 1 tablespoon of nuts. Place a second phyllo sheet on top of the nut layer and brush with butter. Sprinkle another tablespoon of nuts over the top. Lay one of the bananas along one of the narrow ends of the sheet and roll the phyllo dough up around it, folding in the sides to make a packet. Cut in half and place, seam side down in the prepared baking dish. Repeat with the remaining banana, phyllo sheets, nuts, and butter. Brush the tops of the rolls with the last of the butter.

4. Bake in the preheated oven for 25 to 30 minutes, until the bananas soften and begin to release syrupy juices and the phyllo is golden brown.

5. While the bananas are baking, make the chocolate sauce. In a small, heat-safe bowl, pour the boiling water over the dates in a bowl. Let stand for 10 minutes. Transfer the dates and their soaking water to a blender and add the cocoa powder. Process until very smooth.

6. Place one roll on each of 4 serving plates and drizzle with a tablespoon or two of the chocolate sauce. Serve immediately.

PER PIECE: CALORIES: 457; TOTAL FAT: 13G; SATURATED FAT: 5G; CARBS: 94G; PROTEIN: 7G; SODIUM: 227MG; FIBER: 8G

THE DIRTY DOZEN
AND THE CLEAN FIFTEEN

2015

DIRTY DOZEN	CLEAN FIFTEEN
Apples	Asparagus
Celery	Avocados
Cherry tomatoes	Cabbage
Cucumbers	Cantaloupe
Grapes	Cauliflower
Nectarines	Eggplant
Peaches	Grapefruit
Potatoes	Kiwis
Snap peas	Mangoes
Spinach	Onions
Strawberries	Papayas
Sweet bell peppers	Pineapples
	Sweet corn
	Sweet peas (frozen)
	Sweet potatoes

In addition to the Dirty Dozen, the EWG added two foods contaminated with highly toxic organophosphate insecticides:

Hot peppers
Kale/Collard greens

A nonprofit and environmental watchdog organization called Environmental Working Group (EWG) looks at data supplied by the US Department of Agriculture (USDA) and the Food and Drug Administration (FDA) about pesticide residues and compiles a list each year of thTX flushe best and worst pesticide loads found in commercial crops. You can refer to the Dirty Dozen list to know which fruits and vegetables you should always buy organic. The Clean Fifteen list lets you know which produce is considered safe enough when grown conventionally to allow you to skip the organics. This does not mean that the Clean Fifteen produce is pesticide-free, though, so wash these fruits and vegetables thoroughly. These lists change every year, so make sure you look up the most recent before you fill your shopping cart. You'll find the most recent lists as well as a guide to pesticides in produce at EWG.org/FoodNews.

CONVERSION TABLE

Volume Equivalents (Liquid)

US STANDARD	US STANDARD (OUNCES)	METRIC (APPROXIMATE)
2 tablespoons	1 fl. oz.	30 mL
¼ cup	2 fl. oz.	60 mL
½ cup	4 fl. oz.	120 mL
1 cup	8 fl. oz.	240 mL
1½ cups	12 fl. oz.	355 mL
2 cups or 1 pint	16 fl. oz.	475 mL
4 cups or 1 quart	32 fl. oz.	1 L
1 gallon	128 fl. oz.	4 L

Oven Temperatures

FAHRENHEIT (F)	CELSIUS (C) (APPROXIMATE)
250	120
300	150
325	165
350	180
375	190
400	200
425	220
450	230

Volume Equivalents (Dry)

US STANDARD	METRIC (APPROXIMATE)
⅛ teaspoon	.5 mL
¼ teaspoon	1 mL
½ teaspoon	2 mL
¾ teaspoon	4 mL
1 teaspoon	5 mL
1 tablespoon	15 mL
¼ cup	59 mL
⅓ cup	79 mL
½ cup	118 mL
⅔ cup	156 mL
¾ cup	177 mL
1 cup	235 mL
2 cups or 1 pint	475 mL
3 cups	700 mL
4 cups or 1 quart	1 L
½ gallon	2 L
1 gallon	4 L

Weight Equivalents

US STANDARD	METRIC (APPROXIMATE)
½ ounce	15 g
1 ounce	30 g
2 ounces	60 g
4 ounces	115 g
8 ounces	225 g
12 ounces	340 g
16 ounces or 1 pound	455 g

REFERENCES

Altomare, Roberta, Francesco Cacciabaudo, Giuseppe Damiano, Vincenzo Davide Palumbo, et al. "The Mediterranean Diet: A History of Health." *Iranian Journal of Public Health* 42 no. 5 (May 1, 2013): 449–457. Accessed April 14, 2015. www.ncbi.nlm.nih.gov/pmc /articles/PMC3684452/.

Estruch, Ramon, MD, PhD, et al. "Primary Prevention of Cardiovascular Disease with a Mediterranean Diet." *New England Journal of Medicine* 368 (April 4, 2013): 1279–1290. Accessed April 14, 2015. www.nejm.org /doi/full/10.1056/NEJMoa1200303.

Fuster, Valentine and Antonio M. Gotto. "Risk Reduction." American Heart Association. *Circulation* Accessed May 18, 2015. circ.ahajournals.org/content/102/suppl_4 /Iv-94.full.

Giacosa, Attilio, Roberto Barale, Luigi Bavaresco, Piers Gatenby, et al. "Cancer prevention in Europe: the Mediterranean diet as a protective choice." *European Journal of Cancer Prevention* 22. no. 1 (May 2012). doi: 10.1097 /CEJ.0b013e328354d2d7 www.researchgate .net/profile/Vincenzo_Gerbi/publication /225073470.

Godman, Heidi. "Adopt a Mediterranean Diet Now for Better Health Later." *Harvard Health Blog* November, 6, 2013. Accessed April 14, 2015. www.health.harvard.edu/blog /adopt-a-mediterranean-diet-now-for-better -health-later-201311066846.

Jin, Zi-Yi, Ming Wu, Ren-Quiang Han, Xiao-Feng Zhang, et al. "Raw Garlic Consumption as a Protective Factor for Lung Cancer, a Population-Based Case–Control Study in a Chinese Population." *Cancer Prevention Research* May 8, 2013. Accessed April 14, 2015. cancerpreventionresearch.aacrjournals.org /content/6/7/711.full.

Kromhout, Daan, Alessandro Menotti, Huge Kesteloot, and Susana Sans. "Prevention of Coronary Heart Disease by Diet and Lifestyle: Evidence from Prospective Cross-Cultural, Cohort, and Intervention Studies." American Heart Association. *Circulation* Accessed April 14, 2015. circ.ahajournals.org/content /105/7/893.full.

Lourida, I., M. Soni, J. Thompson-Coon, N. Purandare, et al. "Mediterranean Diet, Cognitive Function, and Dementia: a Systematic Review." *Epidemiology* 24 no. 4 (July 24, 2013):479-89. doi: 10.1097 /EDE.0b013e3182944410. Accessed online April 14, 2015. www.ncbi.nlm.nih.gov /pubmed/23680940.

Mayo Clinic. "Mediterranean Diet: A Heart Healthy Eating Plan." Accessed April 14, 2015. oldwayspt.org/sites/default/files/images /Med_pyramid_flyer.jpg.

Panagiotakos, Demosthenes B., Christina Chrysohoou, Gerasimos Siasos, Konstantinos Zisimos, et al. "Sociodemographic and Lifestyle Statistics of Oldest Old People (>80 Years) Living in Ikaria Island: The Ikaria Study." *Cardiology Research and Practice* 679187 (February 24, 2011). Accessed April 14, 2015. www.ncbi.nlm.nih.gov/pmc/articles /PMC3051199/.

Parikh, Parin, Michael C. McDaniel, Dominique M. Ashen, Joseph I. Miller, et al. "Diets and Cardiovascular Disease: An Evidence-Based Assessment." *Journal of the American College of Cardiology* 45, no. 9 (May 2005) Accessed May 18, 2015. content. onlinejacc.org/article.aspx?articleid=1136572.

Salas-Salvadó J., M. Bulló, N. Babio, M. Martínez-González, et al. "Reduction in the Incidence of Type 2 Diabetes with the Mediterranean Diet: Results of the PREDIMED-Reus Nutrition Intervention Randomized Trial." *Diabetes Care* 34, no. 1 (January 2011): 14–19. Accessed online April 14, 2015. www.ncbi.nlm.nih.gov /pubmed/20929998.

The Seven Countries Study. "Cross-cultural findings of the Seven Countries Study." Accessed April 14, 2015. sevencountriesstudy.com/study-findings /cross-cultural.

Sofi, Francesco, Francesca Cesari, Rosanna Abbate, Gian Franco Gensini, and Alessandro Casini. "Adherence to Mediterranean Diet and Health Status: Meta-Analysis." *British Journal of Medicine* 337:a1344 (September 11, 2008). Accessed April 14, 2015. www.bmj.com /content/337/bmj.a1344.

Sofi, Francesco, Rosanna Abbate, Gian Franco Gensini, and Alessandro Casini. Importance of diet on disease prevention." *International Journal of Medicine and Medical Sciences* 5, no. 2 (February 2013): 55–59. Accessed April 14, 2015. www.academicjournals.org/journal /IJMMS/article-abstract/D35D81C320.

Szmitko, Paul E. and Subodh Verma. "Red Wine and Your Heart." American Heart Association. *Circulation*. Accessed April 14, 2015. circ.ahajournals.org/content/111/2/e10.full.

World Health Organization. "Cancer Mortality and Morbidity." *Global Health Observatory Data*. Accessed May 18, 2015. www.who.int/gho/ncd /mortality_morbidity/cancer_text/en/.

RESOURCES

Books

Acquista, Angelo. *The Mediterranean Prescription: Meal Plans and Recipes to Help You Stay Slim and Healthy for the Rest of Your Life.* New York, NY: Ballantine Books, 2006.

The Mediterranean Diet for Beginners: The Complete Guide—40 Delicious Recipes, 7-Day Diet Meal Plan, and 10 Tips for Success. Berkeley, CA: Rockridge Press, 2013.

Ozner, Michael. *The Complete Mediterranean Diet: Everything You Need to Know to Lose Weight and Lower Your Risk of Heart Disease.* Dallas, TX: BenBella Books, 2014.

Online Resources

Amazon
www.amazon.com

Amazon sells ingredients and cookware from all over the world, including the Mediterranean.

BuyPortugueseFood.com
www.buyportuguesefood.com

An online market carrying Portuguese ingredients from bacalhau (salt cod) to linguiça, chouriço, and piri piri sauce.

Daynae. Market Mediterranean Foods
www.daynasmarket.com

This online market carries Mediterranean ingredients like spices, tahini paste, olives, and olive oil.

Ditalia
www.ditalia.com

A gourmet online retailer of all things Italian. Ditalia carries fresh and cured meats, oils and vinegars, cheeses, olives, pasta, rice, jarred tomatoes and sauces, canned fish, honey, and more.

La Tienda
www.tienda.com

This online Spanish market carries Spanish specialties including imported cured meats like jamón serrano and chorizo, Spanish cheeses, bomba rice for paella, and Spanish wines. They also carry paella pans and other Spanish cooking essentials.

Odysea
www.odysea.com

Carries Mediterranean ingredients, with an emphasis on products from Greece, including olives, olive oil, spices, honey, and sauces.

Spanish Table
www.spanishtable.com

The Spanish Table has three retail shops in Seattle, WA; Berkeley, CA; and Mill Valley, CA. They carry Spanish (and Portuguese) ingredients including cured meats, jarred fish, dried beans and rice, olives, olive oil, spices, and condiments. They also carry wines from the region as well as cookware and tableware.

Zamouri Spices
www.zamourispices.com

This online retailer specializes in Middle Eastern and North African ingredients. They carry ras al hanout, harissa, Moroccan olives and olive oil, as well as tagines and other cookware.

RECIPE INDEX

INDEX

CPSIA information can be obtained
at www.ICGtesting.com
Printed in the USA
BVOW10s0757050416

442993BV00013B/25/P

SOME STILL WANT THE MOON

A Woman's Introduction to Tantra Yoga

By Vimala McClure

SOME STILL WANT THE MOON
A Woman's Introduction to Tantra Yoga
by Vimala McClure

Illustrations and book design by Michael B. McClure.

Acknowledgments:
The author wishes to thank Joni Zweig, Tom Barefoot, Christina Davis, and Barbara Parham for their help and support.

For information and instruction:
The Progressive Women's Spiritual Association offers classes and personal instruction in meditation, yoga, vegetarian diet, and spiritual philosophy. For further information, write to: PWSA, C/O 97-38 42nd Ave., Corona, N.Y. 11368-2145

Published by NUCLEUS Publications, Rte. 2, Box 48, Willow Springs, MO 65793. Send for free catalog.
First printing 1989

Library of Congress Cataloging in Publication Data

McClure, Vimala, 1952—

    Some Still Want the Moon: A Woman's Introduction to Tantra Yoga by Vimala McClure
                p.   cm.
      Includes index.
      ISBN 0-945934-00-9 : $9.95
        1. Yoga. 2. Tantrism. 3. Women—Conduct of life. I. Title.
    B132. Y6M373 1989
    181' .45—dc 19
                                88-15181
                                CIP
                                (Rev.)

Printed in the United States of America

Dedicated to P. R. Sarkar

An Invitation

In 1971 I was nineteen years old. After a tumultuous adolescence I was searching for some positive direction for my life. A creek ran by the small house where I lived and I sat by it every day that summer, trying to unravel the truth about life and my place in it. I began reading books about yoga, which led me to an interest in adopting a vegetarian diet. One day in the health food store I saw a notice for a free yoga class. I took the class and was so impressed by the instructor and by the changes that a simple daily yoga/meditation routine brought into my life that I continued to study and practice. Eventually I began to teach.

Many years and many changes have occurred in my life since then, but one constant is my daily practice. Tantric meditation has provided me with a spiritual base upon which I have built the rest of my life. It is a daily alchemy, turning the dross of my mind's wanderings into the golden treasure of spiritual realization. I cannot imagine my life without this treasure. I have not had an easy life, nor have I always understood the meaning of its trials. But my meditation has always brought me into focus, provided me with strength to prevail over pain and loss, and inspired me to continue to find my way to health and positivity. It has nurtured my desire to contribute whatever I can to the betterment of my world, and helped me to find creative ways to do so. The intuitive capabilities I have developed and the love I feel for people which allows me to communicate well with parents and babies (with whom I work as an educator and counselor) are a direct result of my daily spiritual work.

A book like this one introduced me to Tantra Yoga, its underlying philosophy, and the benefits of meditation. I wrote this book with a desire to provide other women with an invitation. No one can walk your spiritual path for you; each step must be taken consciously, by you alone. No guru, guide, or channel can do the inner work that is necessary to develop your higher capabilities and bring you to the realization that answers your deepest questions. Make yourself very still, and listen quietly with openness. You will be led to what you need at every point along the way.

Table of Contents

Chapter One:
Your Perfect Nature

Some people,
no matter what you give them,
still want the moon.

—Denise Levertov
(from *"Adam's Complaint"*)

Consciousness

Gaze, for awhile, at the vast expanse of the ocean. Its surface is turbulent, waves crashing, spewing millions of water droplets into the air. But as you dive deeper the turbulence subsides; at its depths is silence and peace. Ordinarily you may experience only the surface of your mind's potential —the crashing waves of emotion, millions of thoughts like tiny drops of water flying in every direction. Meditation helps you to dive deeply into your mind, and in the process uncover hidden treasures.

As you discover the deeper aspects of your mind, you become better able to control your thoughts, your actions, and your reactions to the external world. "Who am I?," "Where did I come from?," and "Why am I here?" are questions whose answers are revealed as your feeling of individual existence merges in infinite awareness.

In another way, your mind is like the ocean reflecting the image of the moon. It is possible to see the reflection of the moon on the water only when the water is calm, not when the waves are turbulent. Similarly, when your mind is calm and still, when the agitated waves of thought and desire cease, only then is pure consciousness revealed.

The old materialistic concepts about the origin and composition of mind and matter are dissolving as we learn that matter is nothing but bottled-up energy, a pattern of waves in endless motion. Everything from matter to thought is made up of these waves. Physicists are beginning to recognize that intelligence is at the source of all creation. Physicist Lincoln Barnett was perhaps speaking of the connection between matter and spirit when he said, "In the evolution of scientific thought one fact has become impressively clear: there is no mystery of the physical world which does not point to a mystery beyond itself." Through intuitional science, or the practice of meditation, you explore these mysteries, discovering the subtle substance from which the universe evolves, which we call infinite consciousness, or *Brahma.*

Your Perfect Nature

There is a hunger for limitless freedom and happiness within every person. We seek freedom from the bondage of time, place, and person. We want to surmount time, replacing walking with supersonic travel; we try to expand our spatial boundaries with instantaneous communications and transport systems, stretching even into outer space. We attempt to surpass our personal limitations with dramas, masks, stories, personal love (trying to merge with another) and with endless attempts to create the "new me." All these attempts lead to exploration, invention, and efforts at social, political, economic and sexual freedom. But the only absolute freedom is to go beyond material progress and reach for expanded consciousness.

This reaching, this search for something greater, is our innate nature, our *dharma*. Everything in the universe has its nature. Dharma is that which maintains the structural solidarity of something, without which that entity could not exist. The innate nature of fire is its capacity to burn. The nature of most of the animal kingdom is to eat, drink, procreate, and sleep; various species have their species-specific dharma, such as the honey-making nature of bees.

The most significant quality which sets human beings apart from animals has to do with the evolution of our minds; we can call it our "perfect nature." We, too, have the animal instincts for self-preservation. But we also have a longing for the Great. It is that part of you which remains unsatisfied with appeasing the animal instincts, which propels you toward fulfilment —the search for infinite happiness.

But unending happiness and self-actualization can never be yours by simply fulfiling your desires with material things or intellectual ideas which are finite. Even personal relationships are temporary; your family and dearest friends will one day pass away. The only way the desire for infinite happiness can be fulfiled is by establishing yourself in the infinite, by merging your consciousness with all-knowing supreme consciousness. Whether you consciously know it or not, this is your goal. This is where your perfect nature is taking you.

The four parts of your perfect nature

There are four components of your perfect nature: expansion of mind, vibrational flow, selfless service, and consciousness. Meditation is the practical means whereby your perfect nature can be realized. Meditation helps you, step by step, through specific practices, to achieve that realization.

First you learn the practice of mental expansion. As you go about your day-to-day activities the mind is absorbed in countless objects and sense impressions. No matter how hard you try, you will find that it is impossible to stop this natural flow of your mind. It is always jumping from one thing to another, often in such a manner as to work itself into a frenzy, creating both physical and mental stress. The Indian saint Ramakrishna once characterized the mind as "a mad monkey stung by a scorpion." The mind must always have an object; you use this natural tendency and give it an "infinite object" on which to focus.

The ego, or the part of the mind which can say, "I exist," is always focused on the external world. The consciousness —that part of you which can say, "I *know* I exist"—witnesses the ego's activity. When you meditate, you reverse the outward-going process, training your mind to focus instead on the infinite, beyond form or thought.

The ego makes you feel as if you are a separate individual entity. It must have a finite object or thought with which to be involved in order to maintain its existence. Given infinite consciousness as its object, the individual sense of "I" merges with the infinite "I." It is unable to contain this feeling of infinite awareness within the limited scope of its existence. What evolves from this practice is a state of absolute peace which is beyond description because it is beyond the busy workings of the mind.

The outward expression of mental expansion is the realization of the oneness of all creation. This universal outlook prevents you from encouraging any division in humanity. You are inspired from within to work for the unity and upliftment of all

4

and to remove the barriers which separate living beings from one another. Expansion of mind lends compassion to your outlook and enables you to accept the problems of the world as your own.

The second aspect of your perfect nature can be called "vibrational flow." This sounds a little esoteric. What does it mean?

Everything in the universe is composed of vibration.

According to Tantra your mind, as well as the physical universe, is made of the thought waves of infinite consciousness. Nothing is truly external. In each being, the combination of all its wavelengths —physical, mental, emotional —is its individual vibration. Each of us, because of our previous experiences, our environment, our desires and stage of development, has an entirely different vibrational expression than any other being. But infinite consciousness is beyond all of our individual tendencies. Being the combination of every vibration in the universe, just as pure white is the sum-total of the rainbow, its vibrational flow is the flow of the entire cosmos.

The second component of meditation, "living meditation," is the practice of merging your individual rhythmic vibration with that of the infinite, trying to keep your mind immersed in that flow at all times. You come to realize that your individual flow is that of the Supreme, and so all of your actions are in harmony with it.

Happiness, attraction, or congeniality results when the vibrational expression of one being is harmonious with that of another. Conversely, irritation, stress, even hatred results when those same vibrational rhythms are opposing or clashing with one another. You've probably experienced a sense of being "in tune" with someone ("I liked you from the moment I met you") —or the opposite ("The minute I saw him, I knew we wouldn't get along"). When you are able to bring your individual vibrational rhythms into harmony with the infinite peace of the consciousness from which everything arises, an inner calm and happiness ensues which is not affected by the limited impact of the finite world upon you. Your understanding of others increases. You are in harmony with the creator of all vibrational expressions, and you are able to adjust your own expressions accordingly. Thus, you are no longer tossed about by attraction and repulsion, but empathy, understanding, and deep love for all creation gives you a pleasure much finer than you have ever experienced.

The third part of your perfect nature is selfless service. Service is giving fully of yourself without expectation of reward. It is the result of mental expansion and vibrational flow. The person who meditates regularly eventually gains the expansion of mind to perceive consciousness in all creation and the harmonious relationship with the universe which enables her to work selflessly for its upliftment.

Service and meditation are like two lovers who are never happily separated. It is impossible to progress in meditation without developing the impulse to care for others; the universal love that grows as a result of the mind's expansion compels us to serve. Service is an extension of meditation; "I am an expression of infinite consciousness, serving the infinite in you." This thought helps to uplift the mind and prepare it for meditation. When you serve, your thought is that "Infinite consciousness has manifested before me in this form in order to give me a chance to serve." In this way the limited ego is kept in perspective, the mind is immersed in the thought of oneness, progress in meditation is assured, and your service ensures the progress of your fellow beings.

The fourth and final aspect of your perfect nature is actually the goal —infinite consciousness. It is your very essence. It is perfection. Although *every* living being, *every* atom, cell, and electron, *every* rock, *every* plant, *every* quark of the universe is in essence that consciousness, we humans have the unique capacity to know our divinity, to realize our perfection in the spiritual realm. This faculty also gives us a responsibility to the world in which we live. We begin to want to develop ourselves to fulfil our great potential.

This sense of oneness with the infinite is more than "mood-making." Fritjof Capra writes, in *The Tao of Physics*, "The basic oneness of the universe is not only the central characteristic of the mystical experience, but is also one of the most important revelations of modern physics." Many physicists and others who study the origins of the universe are coming to the conclusion that oneness is the natural state from which everything arises.

Attitude

Meditation is not a magic cure-all that can be taken in doses and work overnight. Your approach is decidedly an important factor in your self-realization. Though in meditation there is no failure, your attitude can make the difference between ease and difficulty. Cultivating the right frame of mind is very helpful if you are serious about continuing your practice, because it supplies the internal inspiration and enthusiasm that will fuel your meditation and color your thoughts and actions throughout each day.

The essence of Tantra Yoga is the joyous affirmation that "there is nothing whatever that is not divine." Instead of proclaiming, like many traditional philosophies, "God is not this, God is not that," the Tantric affirms, "All is God; I am God." Recognizing that all forms in the universe are manifestations of the same consciousness, your attitude is positive and dynamic. You see the universe as the arena for spiritual endeavor. Perceived and utilized properly it reveals, not veils, God. Rather than concentrating on admonitions of "don't be this way, don't do that," you concentrate on the positive, using all your physical, mental, and spiritual potential as part of your path. Meditation is not a process of elimination, but a taking-in, expanding your awareness of that consciousness infinitely.

Discrimination and Non-Attachment

You might think that to such a person, discrimination and non-attachment would be negative concepts. But understood properly these two functions of the higher mind are integral to the positive approach of Tantra Yoga.

"In the progress toward truth, let us notice that each step is from particles to waves, or from material to mental; the final picture consists wholly of waves, and its ingredients are wholly mental constructs. It seems more and more likely that reality is better described as mental than material."
—Physicist James Jeans

Discrimination is knowing what is lasting and what is not; being able to perceive the eternal consciousness within the passing show of the material world, and knowing that attachment to finite objects as such can only ultimately bring pain and suffering. In this age, it is increasingly easy for us to remain aloof from suffering and death. Not faced with it every day, we become oblivious to our connection with it. We do not realize that one day we too must die —we too must suffer the pain of loss. The impersonal way in which we are exposed to pain and death, via movies and television, only serves to further separate us from its reality and to desensitize us to the suffering of others.

When we are faced with the shock of loss, we find ourselves longing for some kind of eternal base for our lives —for the knowledge that will enable us to understand these events and thus cope with our fear and loneliness. Many people turn to religion, but turn away again after a crisis has passed and their mental stability has been restored. This is because often religion can offer only a temporary solace that is no real base in itself. Religions that require faith which is not firmly rooted in personal experience or knowledge, which do not give specific practices by which that knowledge is acquired, often fail to offer the continuing growth and real answers that the rational individual seeks.

Meditation is a practical connecting link to the eternal base. Rather than acting as a crutch in times of distress, it is a tool with which you can find real answers from within. The realization achieved through meditation is not faith or belief, but knowledge, and as scientists, psychologists, and philosophers have shown us, fear and all of its accompanying anxiety can only be banished by knowledge. The realization attained through meditation enlightens religious beliefs, enabling you to understand the deeper meaning of your chosen religious teachings and apply them to your life.

When that connecting link is established and you gain some personal experience of your goal, you will begin to gain a sense of discrimination —the ability to place finite events and objects in their proper perspective with the infinite from which they have all evolved.

As it reveals the subtler aspects of your mind, meditation brings you to this fine sense of discrimination, which in turn leads to non-attachment. According to some philosophies, non-attachment means avoidance of the things of the world. Thus some spiritual seekers have mortified themselves to renounce the pleasure and pain of the body, have tried to create aversions in their minds to the natural instincts of eating, sleeping, and sexuality, and have escaped from society to live in jungles or caves far from the "temptations" of worldly life.

Volumes of psychiatric research have shown us that repression is never successful. Such methods of dealing with attachment merely create more obstacles for the practitioner, because they require the mind to be absorbed in negative thoughts rather than in truth. If you adopt such measures you will ultimately turn away from your goal; repression forces your mind to be more deeply entrenched in those things from which you are trying to escape. Although solitude may remove you from the immediate agitations of the world, it does not remove those agitations from the mind, which is their source.

Meditation can reveal truth and calm the agitations of the mind, and meditation can be practiced anywhere. True detachment can never be a negative approach, rather it is a positive attitude of love for the goal, seeing universal consciousness in all forms and attaching the mind to that infinite essence rather than the finite form in which it appears.

Negative interpretations of discrimination and nonattachment developed through the ages as a result of priest-classes controlling spiritual practice and knowledge. It was expedient for them to retain their power and prestige by preventing ordinary family people, especially women, who historically have been most "attached" because of their guardianship of home and children, from practicing meditation. Even today many people avoid meditation because they associate it with solitary asceticism and detachment.

Discrimination also means to understand that pleasure is not the goal of our existence. You can, rather, identify with that which is the broader context within which both pleasure and pain exist as polar expressions. Your attitude is one of dynamic simplicity. You strive without ambition, neither avoiding pain nor seeking pleasure but accepting yourself as you are, letting the process of meditation unfold naturally within you all of your potentialities. Meditation helps you to live your life in balance, and a balanced mind gains deeper realization in meditation.

Motivation

When the realization of oneness develops within, a feeling of attraction for the goal intensifies. As you begin to understand yourself and the universe, as your perfect nature unfolds, you realize that a magnetic attraction to infinite consciousness or truth is the force that has been guiding you from the beginning of your life; it is the same force that is the essential energy of the universe, that keeps everything moving in perfect balance. This realization awakens in you a special kind of love.

Until now, you have been pulled along the path of progress purely by the force of evolution. At a certain point, though, you are bound to discover that the force which is pulling you is infinite consciousness, your innermost being. This discovery is one of great joy, and you begin to use more of your own conscious energy to move toward your goal. It is as if you have been lost in a forest, finding your way home only by vague feelings and memories and landmarks along the way. You wander slowly, carefully, sometimes taking wrong turns, stumbling, confused. But when in the distance the light of home can be seen, you cry out joyfully and run straight for that light, all doubts gone, confusion and loneliness replaced by joyful anticipation and relief. No longer is every fallen log an obstacle, every dark corner a menace, every divergent path a temptation. You return home with speed and confidence. The awakening of devotion (intense love for the higher self) in the heart of the spiritual seeker is just such an experience. With it a new relationship develops between you and your spiritual goal which changes the very quality of your meditative practice.

Psychologist Abraham Maslow described these two stages of motivation as "deficiency" motivation and "growth" or "being" motivation, and the two different kinds of love they produce as deficiency-love and being-love. Deficiency-motivated living is based on needs which must be met from without, by others, e.g., the need for security, respect, and acceptance. It is an attitude of defending and preserving oneself, of fending off attack rather than reaching out for fulfilment. Deficiency-love (called *kama* in yoga terminology) is based on the need of the limited ego; it can be grasping, fearful, insecure. It is an emptiness that must be filled.

Growth or being-motivation is something different; however, it is not contra-dictory. One passes into the other as childhood passes into maturity. The growth-motivated individual has seen the light of home and no longer has the kind of emptiness previously felt. Secure and self-directed, you are able to fully give of yourself because you are no longer motivated by fear. This change does not, however, mean you are exempt from conflict or unhappiness. The growth-motivated person is better able to deal with conflict through meditation and self-searching. Thus, from this perspective you are better able to see problems clearly and be open to accepting help, when necessary, from outside sources. Being-love, or *prema* is fearless. You love the essence, the "being" rather than its changing physical attributes or its capacity to fill the ego's needs. It is open and selfless, and ultimately, beyond the limitations of the emotions or the physical body.

The infinite consciousness within you seeks expression. When you begin to live your life in a way that allows your higher nature to unfold, door after door opens to you. Others begin to seek you out because of your harmonizing energies. You live, work, and play from a center of focused attention that not only allows you to experience limitless energy and tranquility, but draws into your world only the best for you.

Are you bound by fate?

Throw a rock into a pool of still, clear water. What happens? The water reacts. It changes shape, emanating rings of waves which are strongest at the point of contact. The reflection of the moon above is broken up into a thousand moving pieces, unrecognizable.

"Do you love your son? That is perfectly correct. But on the son's death you will have great pain. Isn't that also correct? The son is a finite entity. He cannot live until eternity. He will depart and leave you. But if you treat your son as the expression of God in the form of your son, then there will never be any fear of losing him because God can never be lost. It is present around you in all directions. In that state of mind you will be able to give proper treatment to whatever finite being you come in contact with."
—P.R. Sarkar
in *Idea and Ideology*

The mind is always in a state of motion, experiencing the reactions of previous thoughts and actions, like rocks being thrown incessantly into the peaceful stillness of a pool. Meditation helps you to put down the rock, let the waters settle, and peer in to see the beautiful reflection of your perfect nature. When you experience this oneness with infinite consciousness, you begin to free yourself from the shackles of so-called "fate."

Throughout the ages, people have sought to explain the seemingly random occurrences in their lives. Some religious dogmas teach that God (often perceived as a stern, man-like figure in the sky) rewards and punishes those who are virtuous or who sin. These philosophies must undergo tremendous contortions of logic to withstand the questions of rational people. Hindu "fatalists" assert that every action has its consequences and the sufferings of this life have their prologue in previous incarnations. But because of the limitations of religious dogma, these ideas spawned the caste system in India, whereby millions of people have suffered, kept ignorant and poor by the dictum that it was their fate, decreed by the gods —better luck next life!

Newton's famous assertion that for every action there is an opposite reaction is a basic physical law that applies on the level of mind as well. The mind's balance is constantly being disturbed by thoughts, actions, impressions. It seeks to regain its original state, and strives with force to correct imbalances.

Every thought or action reaps its reaction. Nothing is lost. The universe, according to the theory of relativity, is curved in on itself. If you could throw an object out into space with enough force, it would traverse the universe and come round again to hit you in the back of the head. In the same way, every vibration emanating from you, whether thought, word, or action, will return, with force, to affect your life for good or ill. These potential reactions, or *samskaras,* are the results of thoughts and actions. They remain stored in the mind until they are mature and are then experienced as "the forces of blind fate." According to Tantric teachings, reactive momenta can only mature when the mind is dissociated from its incessant concern with the physical body, as in unconsciousness or death. In the state after death, when the mind is dissociated from the body, momenta from the previous life mature, and when the soul incarnates again in a suitable physical body, those reactions are experienced and new ones are created. Thus the wheel of birth and death turns ceaselessly.

In meditation you momentarily dissociate yourself from concern with the physical body, not in simulation of death, but by identifying with the eternal source of all life. This is another opportunity for reactive momenta to mature. But within your practice lies the key that will stop the relentless turning of the wheel. Each time you meditate, some of the reactive momenta mature. Returning to your everyday life you experience these reactions, reaping what you have sown in this and previous lives. This is why sometimes, especially in the beginning, the new practitioner faces a period of difficulties and obstacles. She undergoes more reactions than the ordinary person. But this phase passes, leaving the meditator freer than before; fewer and fewer potential reactions are created as her meditation gains strength and concentration.

The more you meditate, the more you attain equilibrium in every sphere of your life. You begin to perceive the same infinite consciousness pervading all, and thus your mind is not disturbed by any situation. With no disturbance, there is no need to correct the disturbance; no reaction. Meditation ripens the old reactive momenta and enables you to stop creating new ones. By experiencing your old reactions without attachment, you let them go. Eventually all of your old reactions are exhausted and no new ones wait to be experienced. Your mind has achieved a state of peace, and the body is no longer needed as a vehicle for the expression of reactive momenta. At the end of a practitioner's life her reactions are finished, and, upon leaving her earthly body, her mind merges into infinite consciousness.

There are three types of reactions in potentiality: inborn, acquired, and imposed. The inborn reactions are those which we have acquired in previous lives. The "child prodigy" is one who probably developed a great degree of proficiency in her past life.

Acquired reactions are those which you create of your own will, through action independent of your inborn reactive momenta. A young woman grows up in a family of chefs and has culinary talent from an early age. However, she may acquire momentum to earn her degree in physics and spend her life studying quark symmetries.

Imposed reactions are the impressions created upon your mind by the world in which you live. You acquire these as you are influenced by world conditions, family, responsibility, and education. The young woman in the previous example will always be a good cook because of the momentum imposed by her chef parents.

Peer groups can impose reactive momenta, as can teachers and elders. Thus education and environment are very important to the growing child. The combination of inborn momenta (heredity, through genetic material, is an expression of these) and those which are acquired and imposed are what propel a child into her future as an adult. Acquired and imposed reactions have a tremendous effect on how the inborn ones are expressed. It is crucial that every child have the food, clothing, shelter, education, and medical attention she needs; this is one reason we strive for the upliftment of those less fortunate than ourselves. "Fate" has not decreed the suffering of the poor, the homeless, or hungry. These reactive momenta are forced upon people by their environment and the lack of opportunities to acquire the momentum for physical, mental, and spiritual well-being.

Children are particularly vulnerable to the imposition of reactive momenta and to the altering of their entitative rhythms by constant contact with external forces. For example, a child may come into the world with the momentum for a tremendous amount of physical activity. Her environment, however, will have an impact upon how that activity manifests. She could be a great athlete, or she might be a violent criminal.

As adults we have acquired a certain amount of defensive psychological armor against others imposing upon us. But without the strength and clarity of mind afforded by daily meditation we are still vulnerable to imposition by stronger minds than our own. During Hitler's reign, a few concentrated minds imposed the most ghastly *samskaras* on millions of people.

On a smaller scale, you may find yourself mesmerized every day, often unknowingly following the dictates of a few clever minds which subliminally and subtly impose upon you through advertising, political double-talk, music, and media hype. Meditation helps you gain the clarity to see through the hype and to acquire the tools to defuse its impact in your life and the lives of your children. It inspires you to create uplifting environments and to seek the most expansive expressions in art, music, and literature, for yourself and for all of humanity.

Reactive momenta differentiates one person from another. We are all essentially the same consciousness; the course our lives take is a combination of our free will here and now (momenta we acquire in this life) and what we have chosen in the past. Our desires and prayers can often create reactions which we, with our limited view, cannot perceive in advance, as we earnestly pray for our dreams to come true. A friend of mine once wanted a television. She had a strong mind, having practiced meditation and yoga for several years. Soon after this desire came into her mind, a neighbor knocked on her door.

"My parents are moving today," the neighbor said "and they have a television they don't need any more. I thought maybe you'd like to have it."

"Sure!" said my friend, amazed at how quickly her desire had manifested. They brought the television into the living room and set it down. My friend stared at it, horrified. It was a huge, ugly, old-fashioned television, and it was *pink*. Not only that, but when she turned it on, nothing happened —it didn't work! She kept that pink television for a long time, to remind herself to always be aware of how she used her mind.

Our reactive momenta take us from one lifetime to the next, determining the wavelength of our earthly body (and thus its characteristics, through the genes) as well as the family, environment, and social structure into which we are born. Like

water poured into different cups, consciousness takes the shape of you or me. When the cups are emptied, the water merges, and all is One.

A note on reincarnation

It is not necessary to believe in reincarnation in order to meditate and to lead a spiritual life. An abundance of evidence points to its validity; however, defining the philosophical structure on which it is based is another book and cannot be my intention here. Do your own research, setting aside acquired prejudices in a sincere effort to know the truth. There is no need to commit yourself to a firm belief. Your meditation will eventually reveal to you the truth of all existence. Your spiritual life does not depend on belief, but on practice. The reason for and result of meditation remains the same whether you believe in one life or ten billion.

Recommended reading

The Spiritual Philosophy of Shrii Shrii Anandamurti by Avadhutika Ananda Mitra Acarya.
The Tao of Physics by Fritjof Capra
Einstein's Space and Van Gogh's Sky: Physical Reality and Beyond by LeShan and Margeneau
Reincarnation, a New Horizon in Science, Religion, and Society by Sylvia Cranston and Carey Williams

Chapter Two:
The Circle of Love

We all come from God, and unto God do we return;
Like a stream flowing back to the ocean,
Like a ray of light returning to the sun.
—Quaker hymn

The Creation of the Universe

There is a consciousness in the grass and trees, that animates the tiny amoeba, that manifests in the amazing animal kingdom and in the wondrous richness of human life. This consciousness permeates all creation, within and outside our earth. It controls the movement of the galaxies and it blossoms in the tiniest flower. It creates, it maintains, and it destroys, and yet it is beyond even these. We call it *Brahma.* In the ancient science of Tantra, the creation of the universe is a cycle, called *Brahmacakra* —the "circle of the Supreme."

There are two parts of the cycle of creation —the extroversal phase, or pure consciousness manifesting itself into matter and mind, and the introversal phase, when that consciousness slowly returns to its pure state. Along the way there are temporary reversals, but the essential evolution is from infinite consciousness into static matter and back to consciousness again.

When you begin to understand this cycle, you can begin to perceive the roots of all scientific and religious thought. Researchers, physicists, philosophers and religious teachers through the ages have discovered pieces of the puzzle of creation and have labeled them in many ways; it looks as if there are many distinctly different theories of creation. But if you study carefully, you will begin to see that the pieces of the puzzle fit together. Many creation stories are simply the attempts of early teachers to translate subtle ideas into symbols that people of their day could understand.

Modern thinkers are beginning to fit more of the creation/evolution puzzle pieces together, and what emerges looks very much like yoga philosophy. Ken Wilbur, author of ground-breaking books such as *The Spectrum of Consciousness* and *Up from Eden,* maintains that the force of evolution *is* the drive toward spirit. "The creation did not take place all at once at some time in the distant past," he says. "Creation is occurring now as evolution —ceaselessly novel, ceaselessly driving toward higher and higher unities in search of the absolute Unity, or spirit itself. And that, I believe, is the only way to bring science and religion together."

According to Tantra this ultimate unity is Brahma, and every being, every atom in the universe is moving toward realization of that supreme state.

Try to picture the infinite cycle of creation in your imagination. Go way back, before the beginning, before matter...before mind...oops! You've hit a snag already. How can you, with the mind, perceive that which is beyond the mind? The point between manifest and unmanifest consciousness is the "beginning" of the creation of the universe —a point not in time, but beyond it. Only through deep meditation can you perceive this initial point, and when you do, you merge in it and you are unable to communicate that state in words. A knotty problem!

Speaking of knotty problems, I want to share with you a dilemma I encountered while writing this chapter. Tantric cosmology is fascinating and complex. It combines quantum physics, intuitive insight, and religious metaphor. Much of it is not yet understood in scientific terms. I have tried to get it into simple language and to eliminate as many Sanskrit words as possible, but, quite frankly, it's still rough going. I considered placing it at the end of the book, but these concepts are the foundation upon which the practices of yoga and meditation are built. Understanding the Cycle of Creation is, in my view, very helpful if not essential in motivating you to do meditation and yoga practices every day. It provides a context for the conduct of everyday life.

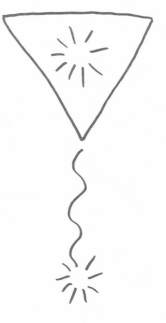

So, it's up to you: You can either read on from here, or skip over this chapter and read the rest of the book, referring back to this one when you need the information. If, on the other hand, you find this explanation of cosmology simplistic, please refer to other sources listed at the end of this chapter for a more in-depth discussion.

What is supreme consciousness made of?

Brahma is composed of cosmic consciousness, called *Shiva,* and cosmic energy, called *Shakti,* and it exists in two states. Like flowers and their fragrance or fire and its burning, Shiva and Shakti are inseparable. Understanding this oneness is essential. Religion often divorces Shiva from Shakti, saying that God and creation are different and separate. But both Tantric science and modern physics contend that consciousness is *one*, whether manifest or unmanifest.

In the very beginning Brahma is so pure that it has no sense of existence. It is beyond anything you can imagine. Shakti, the latent creative force, is composed of three tendencies or forces. The sentient tendency imparts the sense of existence and also the feelings of happiness and relief. It awakens the desire to seek liberation from bondage. It is the force of life, of luster and beauty. The mutative tendency is the sense of action, of growth; it activates the "I." The static force is that which gives the results of action, which binds action to reaction. It is the force of crudification and death.

These transforming qualities are apparent in every object of the created universe. One of these is always dominant, as the play of forces moves from one to the other. The life-force of the mutative tendency is what dominates as a flower blossoms in the spring. As long as the mutative tendency prevails, the sentient tendency glows from within. But when the force of the mutative tendency is spent, the static tendency predominates, and the luster of the sentient tendency fades; the flower wilts and dies.

The creation of cosmic mind

Imagine Shiva, or pure consciousness, to be like the ocean, and Shakti, or creative energy, like the climate. When the climate is stable, or congruent with the ocean, the water flows freely, uninhibited. This is the state before the beginning, the state of absolute peace. The transforming principles of Shakti flow in Shiva without obstruction. But at some point the climatic conditions change and freeze a part of this ocean. The transforming factors gradually form a matrix, and the forces begin to play. The sentient tendency converts to mutative, the mutative to static, the static to mutative and back to sentient again, thus creating a whirlpool of balanced but interacting forces. This interaction becomes a struggle for dominance, and, because it is the most powerful of the three, the sentient force prevails.

At this subtle point, Shakti begins to transform Shiva with its forces and pure consciousness manifests in its first stage: cosmic mind. There begins to emerge in this ocean of consciousness the feeling of existence, "I am." It is only after this self-awareness occurs that creation can begin; the sense of existence is necessary for action. This sense of "I am" has come about as a result of the subtlest transforming factor, the sentient tendency, exerting the first influence upon consciousness.

Now that the "I am" exists, Shakti's energy continues to transform even further with the mutative tendency. The water of our imaginary ocean has gone from free-flowing to dense, and now it is...slush! The influence of the mutative tendency enables cosmic mind to act. "I am" becomes "I do." Now the mutative tendency has full sway over consciousness; the final transforming force takes over. The pressure of the static tendency objectifies a portion of cosmic mind in order to act. This objectified portion is mind-stuff (ectoplasm). Cosmic mind-stuff is the iceberg in the ocean. The subtlest consciousness is now ready to be transformed into dense material forms.

The combination of the sense of "I am," the sense of "I do," and the cosmic ectoplasm is called cosmic mind, and it is through the thought waves of the cosmic mind that the innumerable forms of the created universe come into existence. But the entire creation doesn't just burst forth from the "imagination" of Brahma. It is a natural creative process, and like all creative endeavors, the stage must be set; the requisite conditions must be created first.

Before a baby is born, all of the right conditions exist in its mother's womb. The right temperature, the right time in the mother's cycle, even the pull of the moon can affect the conception, growth, and birth of a child. If conditions are favorable, microscopic cells divide and become an embryo, which in turn unfolds, in a perfectly designed sequence, all of the elements necessary for the development of a human being. So, too, in the creation of the universe, the subtlest factors must first exist before the denser forms which we can perceive can come into being. These are the five fundamental factors, the basic building-blocks of the manifest universe.

The building blocks of the universe

As the influence of Shakti's static principle transforms consciousness more and more, a portion of cosmic mind crudifies and becomes the *etheric factor*, or what we term "space." Space is the stuff in which the universe exists; it is the subtlest substance. It has the capacity to carry the subtlest quality, that of sound.

The static tendency continues exerting more and more influence, qualifying a portion of space and transforming it into the next cruder factor: air. The *aerial factor* can carry the vibrational essences of both sound and touch. Air gives sound the ability to touch the ear; thus, sound becomes audible at this stage. Atoms of hydrogen come into being, and the pressure of the static force draws them together, forming hydrogen clouds. The force of gravity causes the clouds to condense, which drives the atoms closer together, causing friction and heat. This is the first expression of the next cruder factor: luminosity.

The *luminous factor* carries the vibrational qualities of sound, touch, and sight. Thus light comes into being, and stars are born. At this stage, the increasing heat and pressure at the center of a star fuses the hydrogen nuclei together to make helium. Later heavier atoms are fused and each of the elements is created. The space between atoms and molecules continues to decrease, eventually condensing the luminous factor into liquid plasma.

The *liquid factor* carries the sensory qualities of sound, touch, sight, and taste. Further pressure from the static tendency solidifies the liquid factor, and the *solid factor*, carrying the vibration of smell as well, comes into being. At this point, all the factors co-exist simultaneously in the universe. The degree and combinations of these five factors determines the make-up of all material substances, and how the next act in the drama of creation evolves.

The pressure that creates life

Up until this point, the creative process has been extroversal —movement from subtle to dense. Inanimate matter is the crudest form of consciousness. Shakti's static force can transform no further, and its hold must begin to loosen. The introversal phase of creation begins as matter finds its way back to pure consciousness again.

The static tendency exerts so much pressure on the solid factor that a tension of forces is created. The center-seeking force of static Shakti clashes with the exterior force, which is directed from the center outward. These two forces vie for dominance, and a critical climax in the cycle of creation occurs. If the exterior force becomes dominant, the structure can no longer maintain the delicate balance, and it dissociates into millions of particles.

On the other hand, if there is an imbalance of the five factors within the structure, the object contracts more and more, the tension in the solid factor becomes very great, and an explosion occurs. At this point the crudest factor is converted back into subtler factors to "try again." This means, of course, that no factors are lost. The eventual death of the universe, therefore, is impossible. Furthermore, cosmic mind is never imperiled by the explosions in the crude factor; the particles return to their respective factors. Cosmic mind-stuff remains unaffected, and creation continues endlessly.

The alternative course is that which, when it occurs, is the turning point in the cycle of creation. If, in this struggle between the exterior and interial forces, the center-seeking force wins, a resultant force is created which controls all of the factors within the structure. All five factors must be in requisite proportions and the balance of forces within the structure must be such that each factor's energy is controlled and coordinated. The controlling point of all the energies within a structure is called its *vital energy*. With vital energy, the evolution of life begins.

The creation of individual mind

Just as vital energy is the controller of all of the forces within a structure, the vital energy itself must be controlled. Individual ectoplasm, or mind-stuff, emerges to direct the vital energy, controlled by the will of the cosmic mind. Another way of putting this is that the loosening of Shakti's bondage enables the cosmic ectoplasm to reflect, or "show through" as individual mind-stuff. Thus begins the second half of the cycle of creation, the attraction of the unit being toward its "Self," the supreme consciousness. Matter has evolved from mind, and now mind evolves from matter and moves toward merger with consciousness. The mind-stuff of the individual controls its vital energy through the development of instincts. In the most undeveloped life forms, the two basic instincts are self-preservation and reproduction.

Evolution

As reactions are experienced and stored in the mind (a "vibrational record" as it were), behavioral patterns emerge. The entity encounters clash with its environment, which is recorded in the mind, and the structure evolves capacities for overcoming that clash. Thus more and more complex life forms evolve. The sense of existence emerges in the unit mind, and the entity develops a more complex nervous and glandular system to control the more highly developed body with each successive incarnation.

Eventually, from the sense of existence, the ego or the feeling "I act" emerges. The wavelength of the mind becomes more subtle, and ego is formed from a portion of ectoplasm. At this stage, the ego has two functions: determination, or will, and translation into action. Living beings with only mind-stuff act only on mechanical impulses; those with ego as well can make limited decisions about their actions. For example, a worm confronted with a stimulus such as fire can only contract instinctively. An ape, however, when attacked may either fight or flee. This is due to the more highly developed glandular system and the corresponding development of ego.

The human being emerges

Moving on in the course of evolution, the mutative tendency begins to wane and the subtle vibration of the sentient tendency carves a place in the individual mind. The subtlest aspect of mind, the sense of self-awareness, awakens. At this stage, the mind of the living being is a complete reflection, in potential, of the mind of God. At last a conscious awareness of that reflection is possible, and a desire to *know* arises. Who am I? Where do I come from? Where am I going? These are the questions which haunt the human being, and which she alone is capable of asking. The attraction of the supreme nucleus, the longing for the infinite, propels us toward self-realization.

Through the long process of evolution, the individual soul is propelled through many incarnations, moving up the scale of complexity, eventually embodying in a human form. There are three forces of evolution which guide this process and determine the duration and complexity of each structure in each lifetime.

The forces which evolve the mind

First there is the force of *physical clash* by which the crudest portion of mind, the ectoplasm, is developed. It is the result of contact between mind and matter —the resultant clash between the subtle and crude vibrations of the two. As each living being struggles with nature to survive, that struggle refines the mind and helps develop higher capacities for survival. As these higher capacities evolve, the mind needs a subtler structure in which to grow and takes on subtler physical forms. Early humans evolved because of clash with nature. They developed tools, mathematics, science, etc., and as they did so, the human body evolved into a more complex form in order to house the more complex and subtle workings of the mind.

The second force of evolution is that by which the ego evolves —*psychic clash*. This is the association with other minds, with ideas. As the mind struggles to attune itself to the wavelength of a more highly evolved mind, clash occurs and the mind expands. It is said that often domestic animals who have a lot of contact with humans will embody as humans the next life. Constant contact with the vibration of the human mind evolves the animal's ego. In order to maintain parallelism between the physical and psychic wavelength, a subtler form is necessary. Education is a form of psychic clash that helps to evolve the human ego.

The third type of clash which acts as an evolutionary force is *spiritual clash*, by which intuition is developed. This happens only in the later stages of human evolution, when the mind has sufficiently evolved and the longing for the infinite is intense. This is the attraction between the individual mind and the infinite wavelength of supreme consciousness. It creates the tremendous desire and momentum needed to drive the spiritual aspirant to full self-realization.

As the mind evolves, subtler forms are necessary in order that the body's wavelength may maintain a parallel with the mind.

Now you can begin to see the importance of spiritual practices. Yoga postures, food, meditation, right conduct, service, study of spiritual ideas —all of these activ-ities help the body/mind relationship remain in balance as you evolve.

Negative evolution

According to Tantric philosophy, it is possible for humans to de-evolve into other life forms. The free will we have is a result of the full evolution of our minds —we have mind-stuff, ego, and self-awareness; we exist, we act to maintain that existence, and we *know*. We have the capacity to grasp with understanding the universal laws, and we can choose our actions. We are at a critical juncture.

We are attracted by those familiar basic propensities which dominated our existence in animal embodiments —eating, sleeping, procreation, fear. But we also have a sense of greater fulfilment, a dim memory of infinite bliss. Thus many people wander for lifetimes in a state of confusion, vacillating between the pleasures and pains of animal existence and the "unknown" journey toward higher consciousness. If a human's mind becomes completely dominated by animal-like instinct, she may need to go back, temporarily, to an animal body to fulfil that propensity before taking a human form again.

Recommended reading

The Spiritual Philosophy of Shrii Shrii Anandamurti by Avadhutika Ananda Mitra Acarya
Up from Eden by Ken Wilbur
Eternal Dance of Macrocosm by Michael Towsey

28

Chapter Three:
The Psycho-Spiritual Anatomy

*Woman dancing with hair
on fire, woman writhing in the
cone of orange snakes, flowering
into crackling lithe vines
Woman...*

*—Marge Piercy
(from "The Twelve-Spoked Wheel
Flashing")*

The subtle body

In primitive cultures long ago, when someone had a disabling disease it was thought to be the work of a demon who had either projected some object (a dart, a worm, etc.) inside the person's body, or had extracted the patient's soul. The best cure was thought to be "trepanning," or making a hole in the person's skull so the evil spirit or object would come out, or the soul would re-enter.

Later, as recent as the nineteenth century, healers were still convinced that such diseases could be gotten out of the body somehow; they cut arteries or applied leeches to the patient's body in hopes of draining out the "bad blood." All through history, people have disbelieved or misunderstood that which they could not see. Medical science has been greatly aided by the anatomists who dissected and examined animal and human bodies. We were finally able to grasp, after thousands of years of trial and error and superstition, the subtler workings of the physical organs. Yoga experts say that we are as primitive in our understanding of the human body and mind now as those ancient physicians. We have yet to realize that the physical body is only one layer of the human organism, one layer of mind. There are many subtle organs, of a psychic nature, that have yet to find their way into anatomical textbooks.

Yoga practitioners long ago discovered these subtle anatomical parts through deep meditation. They experimented, they observed, and they discovered a body "beyond the body"—a kind of psychic structure, the development of which was found to be essential to spiritual progress. All of the Tantric spiritual practices came out of these discoveries, updated and refined across thousands of years. Yogic physicians of the future will work with the subtle psychic systems as well as our physical organs to help us heal ourselves, to prevent disease, and to correct imbalances that may affect our mental and spiritual well-being. They will look back with horror upon some of the primitive practices of modern medicine; they will probably shake their heads at the astounding ignorance of human beings in the twentieth century.

The physical body and the subtle body are interrelated; they have an impact on one another. For example, a blockage or disturbance in one of the psychic centers can affect the physical health, because the glandular system is intimately associated with and affected by these psychic centers. Similarly, if the glandular system is out of balance, your mental health will be compromised, a disturbance will arise in one or more of the psychic centers, and your meditation will be impaired. As you progress in your meditation, you will have experiences related to the psycho-spiritual anatomy. Your spiritual practices and the higher lessons in meditation will directly involve these subtle systems; it may be helpful to gain a basic understanding of them now.

Kundalini

A prominent aspect of the philosophy and practice of Tantra is Kundalini Yoga – that which brings the dormant spiritual energy in a living being into fruition, to union with its cause —infinite consciousness. According to Tantra, the human structure is a reflection of the universe. The human mind is a reflection, a replica in microcosm, of the cosmic mind.

In the cycle of creation, as you recall, there is a point at the "top" of the cycle, where consciousness is infinite, both within and beyond everything. There is also a point at the "bottom" of the cycle, where the force of static Shakti exerts the most influence possible —the crudest expression of consciousness. It is at this crudest point when evolution, as we know it, begins.

So, too, in the human structure, the evolution of the spirit begins at the crudest point, at the base of the spine. This point is known as "kula" meaning "the container." Within this container is the kundalini or the dormant force of spiritual energy, the expression of cosmic energy in human form. This cosmic energy lies asleep within your psycho-physical structure. All spiritual practices strive to awaken this dormant force and to elevate it to oneness with infinite consciousness —the "top" of the cycle —reflected in the human structure as the "crown center" at the top of the head.

Imagine you are sleeping soundly. Perhaps you have been on a long journey and you haven't slept in a couple of days. Your sleep is so deep you do not notice people going in and out of the room, the sun shining in the window in the morning, the sound of the busy street outside. Then suddenly your alarm clock rings near your ear. It's time to catch your plane home. It takes a special instrument —an alarm, a friend nudging you, a telephone ringing nearby —to awaken you from such a deep slumber.

The kundalini has been sleeping deep inside the kula for eons —since the beginning of evolution. It takes a very special instrument to awaken it. The instrument designed to awaken the kundalini is the *mantra,* a sound vibration repeated in the mind during meditation. It is the key which unlocks the infinite energy and force residing in every human being, and which propels you toward the infinite bliss of self-realization.

An effective mantra is one that has been invested with the tremendous attainment of a teacher who has already achieved what you seek. When the mantra is given correctly at the moment of the initial instruction, its vibration awakens the kundalini. Each time it is repeated in the mind, it vibrates the primordial spiritual energy and the kundalini rises. When repetition stops, it returns again to the kula. It is said that the kundalini, when seen with the "inner eye" is as bright as ten million flashes of lightning, but as soothing to gaze upon as ten million moons.

The kundalini rises through a "psychic canal" called the *susumna,* passing through each of the subtler energy centers. As it does, the practitioner experiences profound states of blissful consciousness, until a total merger with infinite consciousness is attained, when the kundalini energy reaches the topmost center, associated with the pineal gland. You may sense the movement of the kundalini, you may not. You will probably not notice anything unusual until much later, after many months or years of meditation. At that time, glimpses of the forces at work in meditation are taken in stride, and actually paid no heed. The goal of unqualified union with the infinite is firmly implanted, and the experiences along the path are merely signs, like markers on a hiking trail.

Cakras

Remember, for a moment, our discussion of the cycle of creation in the previous chapter. You recall that everything in the universe is composed of the five fundamental factors —solid, liquid, luminous, aerial, etheric. In the living being, these five factors are controlled by the vital energy which in turn is controlled by the mind. The five factors in the body find their controlling nuclei along the route of the kundalini. These are called *cakras* (pronounced "chakras" with "ch" as in "church") or centers of psychic force.

The cakras (cakra means circle or wheel) regulate the subtle energy within the body. There are seven basic cakras, each associated with states of consciousness, control of physical elements, and the seats of psychic propensities or instincts — the longings, desires, and emotions which must be harnessed along the way. The cakras are the controlling points of all the vital elements in your being —physical, mental, and spiritual. They are closely associated with the glandular system, and thus have an impact upon your physical and emotional well-being. Spiritually, the cakras are the stepping stones to attainment. The control of each cakra brings more profound states of consciousness and corresponding control over all the forces in the universe. The cakras are the gateways to oneness with the Supreme.

Virtually every spiritual teaching refers to the cakras. St. John, in "Revelations" wrote of the "seven spirits before the throne," and the "seven seals on the back of the Book of Life." Other early Christians are said to have used the term "seven churches in Asia." The Tibetans call them "Khor-lo"; the Hopi, in their creation story, speak of energy centers; the early alchemists spoke of seven metals by which crude matter was transmuted into "gold."

Chakras

The first cakra

The first cakra is located at the base of the perineum. It controls the solid factor of the body and is related to the excretory functions. It is controlled by the conscious layer of mind. It is here where the spiritual and evolutionary journey begins; this is the crudest expression of creation, where consciousness, both in the macrocosmic universe and in the microcosmic reflection of mind in the individual, has been crudified by static energy to the greatest degree. It is here that the kundalini, the latent force of cosmic energy in the individual, resides.

When the kundalini awakens, you realize "Brahma exists" —a state associated with this psychic center. This realization is one of great joy. It is not an intellectual process, but a state of consciousness in which you sense your oneness with infinite consciousness. You suddenly realize that God is real and exists within your reach, in the core of your own being.

The second cakra

The second cakra is located a little higher, at the base of the pelvis. It controls the liquid factor of the body, is related to the sexual functions, and is controlled by the subconscious layer of mind. As the kundalini pierces this cakra, you realize "Brahma is everywhere, Brahma is all that exists."

The third cakra

The third cakra, located at the navel point, is the controlling point for the luminous factor, the fiery energy of the body, and is associated with digestion. It is controlled by the supramental, or intuitional layer of the mind. You experience the close proximity of your goal as you gain control over this cakra. You can hardly remember a time when the intense desire for self-realization was not the pivot of your life.

The fourth cakra

The fourth cakra is located at the center of the chest. It controls the aerial factor of the body and is related to the body's respiratory and circulatory functions. It is controlled by the subliminal layer of mind. The state of consciousness experienced as the kundalini pierces it is one of divine love. The fourth cakra is often called the "yogic heart" because as the practitioner's attainment rises to this level, she becomes more and more like a lover on fire with devotion to her Beloved. The desires for the experiences, joys, and pleasures of the physical world pale in comparison to the ecstatic, encompassing love your meditation brings. Even the mere contemplation of the infinite brings you an intense joy which seems to give you a special radiance and grace.

The fifth cakra

The fifth cakra, located at the throat, controls the etheric factor and is related to the function of speech. It is controlled by the highest layer of mind, the subtle causal layer. This cakra controls the ones below, thus it coordinates all the energies of the physical body. Control of this cakra brings with it the knowledge of past, present, and future. You hear the cosmic sound, the Aunkara (AUM) in deep meditation. You are one with the cosmic mind, from whom the creation ("A" sound), the operation ("U"), and the destruction ("M") of the entire cosmos resides. You are merged with the pure "I am" —the origin of the universe.

Can there be more?

As realization reaches the next two cakras, all objective reality dissolves. The consciousness of the individual gives way to the universal consciousness, beyond even cosmic mind.

The sixth cakra

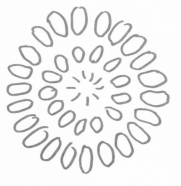

The sixth cakra is called the "seat of mind" and is located at the "third eye," directly above the nose, between the eyebrows. No physical factor is controlled here. Beyond the reach of limitation, having broken the mirror of the ego, you are merged in the consciousness from which the mind of the Supreme originates.

The seventh cakra

The seventh cakra is known as the "thousand petaled lotus" because it is the controlling point for every tendency in the individual. It is here that the kundalini reaches its goal and awareness merges completely in infinite consciousness, the origin of origins. There is no human expression for this state. It is beyond anything we can ever imagine. We know of it only by its after-effects; the waves of ecstasy which follow even a fraction of a moment in that state. When no reactive momenta are left to bind the individual to the physical world, the merger in this state will be complete. Like the salt doll who tried to measure the ocean, you merge in the immeasurable expanse of your own origin. This is the goal of human life.

The layers of the mind

Existence is a continuum, moving from the crude, dense expression of consciousness to the subtle, and then to the unity of infinite consciousness, where all is one. Along this continuum are several "layers," wherein the expression of consciousness in the form of body and mind performs the functions which are necessary to maintain individual existence and progress. The layers of the mind are called the *kosas*. On the following pages, you can see how each functions and how each is developed. The spiritual practices, including yoga postures, meditation, exercise, and regulation of the diet, all contribute to the holistic development of all the layers of the mind.

The physical body

Sanskrit name: *Annamaya Kosa* ("made of food")
Dominating tendency: static
Function: mechanical
Controlled by: conscious mind
Naturally developed by: physical labor
Spiritual practices which develop: yoga postures, diet, exercise

Conscious layer

Sanskrit name: *Kamamaya Kosa* ("desire")
Dominating tendency: static
Function: sensing, through sensory organs; desire or aversion; acting through motor organs
Controls: first cakra
Naturally developed by: physical clash —struggle for existence
Spiritual practices which develop: right conduct

Subconscious layer

Sanskrit name: *Manomaya Kosa* ("mental")
Dominating tendency: mutative
Function: controls conscious mind; memory, contemplation, experience of pleasure and pain, dreams
Controls: second cakra
Naturally developed by: physical clash
Spiritual practices which develop: control of breath

Kosas

The cakras are controlled by the layers of the mind.

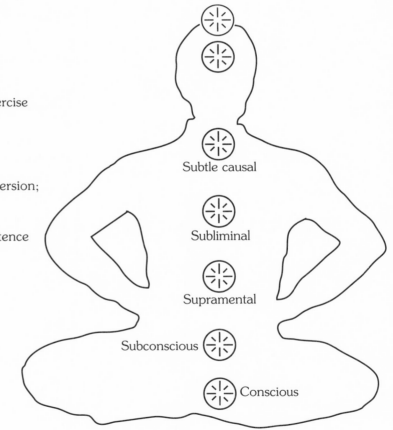

Subtle causal

Subliminal

Supramental

Subconscious

Conscious

Supramental layer

Sanskrit name: *Atimanasa Kosa* ("higher mind")
Dominating tendency: mutative
Function: creative insight, intuition, para-normal phenomena; the "all-knowing" layer
Controls: third cakra
Naturally developed by: psychic clash; contact with more highly developed minds, education, new environments
Spiritual practices which develop: sense withdrawal in meditation

Subliminal layer

Sanskrit name: *Vijinanamaya Kosa* ("special knowledge")
Dominating tendency: sentient
Function: discrimination and detachment
Controls: fourth cakra
Naturally developed by: psychic clash
Spiritual practices which develop: concentration

Subtle causal layer

Sanskrit name: *Hiranyamaya Kosa* ("golden")
Dominating tendency: sentient
Function: yearning for self-realization
Controls: fifth cakra
Naturally developed by: attraction for infinite
Spiritual practices which develop: deep devotional meditation

In summary, the body is composed of the five fundamental factors, which are controlled by the mind. The five layers of mind control, through the vital energy, each of the lower cakras respectively. The fifth cakra, however, is the controlling point for all of these. Spiritual practices such as meditation in its various forms, yoga postures, and right conduct develop each of these systems. If you are able to gain access to the higher layers of mind, you will have the concentration to control, develop, and strengthen the cakras and the bodily functions, leading to greater mental clarity, emotional stability, and physical longevity.

As the body becomes more subtle the cakras are purified, strengthened, and controlled. Refining the body helps you reach the higher layers of mind. Tantra is holistic in that it recognizes the inter-connectedness and interdependence of body, mind, and spirit. You cannot attain enlightenment merely by doing yoga postures; you *will not* if you neglect the body, for at some point the unrefined body will not be able to handle the subtlety of mind, and it will break down.

Psychic powers

As each cakra is controlled, with the intense effort in meditation and spiritual practices which develops the higher layers of mind, you attain access to the infinite storehouse of power and knowledge which we call cosmic mind.

The highly advanced practitioner may develop the ability to levitate, to walk on water, to make things appear and disappear, to infuse fragrance in objects, to cure disease, and any number of "supernatural" powers. Because the cakras are the controlling points for the fundamental factors, control of each of these also gives the yogi access to the manipulation of matter. But she knows that such powers are dangerous deterrents. Great masters may occasionally use these powers to illustrate some aspect of their teachings to their students. But the greatest masters will always point out the dangers of these powers, and will encourage their students to disregard them and keep moving straight toward their goal.

The higher levels of the mind are accessible to all of us; extrasensory perception, precognition, intuition, creative insight, etc. are abilities we all possess. Intense concentration, drugs, or altered consciousness from a shock will often temporarily elevate us to a higher dimension. Some people, because of intense concentration in a previous life, are born with "supernatural" abilities. But without the regular practice of deep meditation with the goal of infinite expansion, these abilities can bring more pain than pleasure. Inspiration from the superconscious mind, without the discrimination instilled by meditation, must filter through the subconscious mind

"Thus yogis have always emphasized the importance of the gradual and careful preparation of the mind and body to receive and control the unlimited powers of the superconscious state. One master told his disciple, who had begged him to give him the experience of higher consciousness, "As a small lamp bulb would be shattered by excessive voltage, so your nerves are unready for the cosmic current. If I gave you the infinite ecstasy right now, you would burn as though every cell were on fire." Through centuries of experimentation, a scientific physical and mental system was developed to safely and easily attain the bliss of higher consciousness and then integrate these expanded states with normal, waking consciousness, to live life with fuller awareness."

—Avtk. Ananda Mitra Ac.
in *Beyond the Superconscious Mind*

39

and can thus become confused with limited sense impressions. The person possessing these abilities not only develops a false sense of power and prestige, but her "guidance" may adversely impact the lives of people she encounters.

Artistic and scientific geniuses often work in a state of superconscious awareness which they then have difficulty integrating into their everyday consciousness; a difficulty which has sometimes led to madness or suicide.

There is little to be gained by hankering after occult powers. Anyway, most of us are a long way from having to be mindful of their dangers. With regular practice you will gradually notice a sharpening of your senses, a keener awareness of the things and people around you, an intuitive insight that you may not have had access to before, and a deepening respect for the unlimited potential of the human mind.

Recommended reading

Baba's Grace: Discourses by P. R. Sarkar
The Great Universe: Discourses on Society by P.R. Sarkar

Chapter Four:
Physical Health

"Woman is the flowering tree.
You are the center of the universe,
of creation, the mother earth.
You need to relearn this and build up your strength."

—Agnes Whistling Elk
Native American Medicine Woman

A balanced approach

Now it's time to learn about the things you can do to help develop all these different aspects of yourself. I will cover, briefly, some of the practices that can help you do this and suggest a starting point. It is important to go slowly. Don't try to do everything at once, or you will soon be frustrated.

In order to develop yourself on higher levels, you'll want to be sure your body is fit and that you know what to do to keep it that way. Certain practices are very conducive to meditation, and there are some things you'll want to cut down on or avoid in order to make your meditation easy, your body more comfortable, and to keep your emotions in balance. For example, a diet heavy in meat and rich foods, cigarette smoking and alcohol consumption can interfere with your concentration and deteriorate your health. You may wish to experiment with cutting down or eliminating some of these and see if your meditation, mental balance, and physical health are affected in any way.

Design your daily program with an all-round equilibrium in mind. What must you do to keep your life in balance? This will change as you grow. For example, when you go through phases of longer and more intensive meditation sessions, you'll also want to pay attention to dietary, environmental, and physical changes which will help you maintain a sense of equilibrium. Doing a lot of meditation without developing the other aspects of your being is courting disaster. The physical, mental, and spiritual aspects of your existence all emanate their particular vibrational expressions. The harmonious rhythm of these is called health. If one changes and the others don't, the lack of parallelism can cause physical or mental illness.

Yoga postures

Thousands of years ago, yogis meditating deep in jungles carefully observed the wild animals that shared their solitude. They began to detect the techniques which nature gives less evolved creatures to keep them healthy, agile, and alert. They watched how different animals instinctively cured themselves and began to experiment with these animal postures upon their own bodies. After long and intensive study, practice, and adjustment, they created a systematic series of physical postures known as *asanas*. Many yoga postures are named for the animals which inspired them: cobra, lion, peacock, fish.

Yoga postures balance the glandular secretions, relax and tone the muscles and nervous system, stimulate circulation, oxygenate the blood, stretch stiff ligaments and tendons, limber joints, massage internal organs, align the spine, and calm and concentrate the mind. The entire body is controlled by hormones. The twisting and bending positions of yoga postures, held for particular periods of time, place continued and specific pressure upon the various endocrine glands, thus regulating their secretions. The endocrine system is intimately related to our emotions. Oversecretion of certain hormones can cause a wide range of emotional imbalances; premenstrual syndrome is a good example of this.

You feel emotions in your body: when you are angry, you might say "My blood is boiling!" When sad, you have a "lump in the throat," fear makes "butterflies in the stomach." When disappointed, you say, "My heart sank." You can control, to a great extent, your emotional reaction to various kinds of stress by controlling the glandular secretions through yoga postures.

Hormonal effects of yoga postures

Hormones regulate the body processes with extreme precision. Irregularities in the timing or levels of their release can lead to disease and mental imbalance. Yoga postures are thus to be practiced carefully and with great precision for the most benefit.

The *adrenal* glands govern sudden bursts of energy and heat and activate the "fight or flight" response to stress. When a person is under stress, the adrenals produce more adrenalin, which increases blood pressure, slows down digestion, and makes the liver shed stored sugar so that muscles have a fuel supply. Overactivity of the adrenals can cause a host of problems and chain-reactions in the body. The

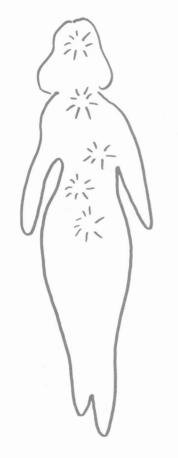

hypothalamus releases corticotropin-releasing hormone (CRH), which prompts the pituitary to secrete adrenocorticotropic hormone (ACTH), which again makes the adrenals produce cortisol, increasing blood sugar and speeding up the metabolism. Cortisol suppresses the immune system, making you more vulnerable to illness. Suicidal people tend to have high levels of cortisol, as do people with manic-depressive illness. Cortisol is also found in higher than average levels in people who are shy and withdrawn.

The adrenals also produce the female sex hormone estrogen, oversecretion of which has been implicated in breast cancer. Oversecretion of the adrenals causes anxiety, tension, and anger. Underactivity causes lethargy, lack of motivation, depression, and inability to handle stress.

The *pancreas* secretes digestive enzymes into the small intestine, and insulin, a hormone which lowers the amount of energy-giving glucose in the blood. If it is unable to secrete sufficient amounts of insulin, blood sugar builds up and diabetes mellitus results. Too much insulin results in hypoglycemia, a condition of trembling and weakness. Native healers have referred to the pancreas as the "seat of woman-courage" and say that it is vitally important for women to control and strengthen this organ. The adrenals and pancreas are associated with the functioning of the third cakra. Strengthening the third cakra helps people who have eating or digestive disorders, anxiety, lethargy, problems with handling power (aggressiveness or passivity), and sleep disorders.

The *ovaries* help govern sexual and reproductive functions. They produce ovum, androgens and estrogens. These hormones interact with other hormones in the body, producing various effects both physiologically and emotionally. Biologists have been unable to find one hormonal mechanism for premenstrual syndrome. It is apparently more complicated than a simple imbalance of estrogen and progesterone levels. One recent study showed that 51 out of 54 PMS sufferers had a thyroid disorder. The ovaries are associated with the functioning of the second cakra. Strengthening the second cakra helps people who have sexual or reproductive disorders, either physiological or emotional.

The *thyroid* gland in the neck controls metabolism —the speed at which the body's chemical processes occur. Like a thermostat, it regulates heat and energy. It controls growth, repair, and waste processes. Oversecretion results in nervous irritability, heart palpitation, digestive disturbances, loss of weight, and manic depressive disease. Undersecretion results in fatigue, low blood pressure, mental dullness, and obesity. Undersecretion has also recently been implicated in premenstrual syndrome. The *parathyroid* glands regulate calcium and phosphorous metabolism. The *thymus* is a gland located behind the breastbone. It is very large during childhood but at puberty begins to shrink. Thymosins, a family of hormones produced by the thymus, regulate the entire immune system, including the production of white blood cells.

The *pineal* and *pituitary* glands are in the head. The pineal body is directly in the middle of the brain and has the largest blood supply for its weight of any organ in the body. Scientists have not yet discovered exactly what the pineal gland is all about. It seems to have some importance in regulating the day-to-day rhythms of the body, and it appears to secrete many substances which have a direct effect on brain function. Yoga science has taught that the pineal body secretes a special substance that contributes to the bliss of certain types of altered states in meditation.

The pituitary has been called the "bandmaster of the endocrine orchestra." It functions as a relay station for impulses arising in the hypothalamus, a structure in the brain which coordinates the nervous system and controls the body's reaction to stress. The pituitary relays messages from the hypothalamus to the other endocrine glands. It also produces growth hormone and ACTH. Each of the yoga postures given in this book can strengthen and balance the endocrine system in specific ways and thus influence your physical and emotional well-being. Spiritually, yoga postures help release blocked energy in the cakras and restore energy in cakras that have been weakened by illness. Yoga postures refine the body and direct its energies toward spirituality.

Rules for Yoga Postures

- after bathing
- before eating
- in a clean, quiet, draft-free place
- in loose, non-binding clothing
- not during menstruation or after the third month of pregnancy

There are thousands of yoga postures. Out of these, only around forty are truly effective for normal people; only a few are necessary for the individual. You need not contort yourself into a pretzel to be a practicing yogi! Because of their profound impact on the endocrine system, your postures should be individually prescribed by a qualified teacher who can analyze your constitution, your level of development, your physical, mental, and spiritual needs. If you have any specific problems, be sure to tell your teacher about them. The postures given here are especially helpful for women, and can be done by anyone.

Breathing

In order to be cleansed of dust and bacteria, air should be drawn in through the nose. The mucous membranes filter it and the germicidal properties of their secretions kill many of the bacteria. In addition, the air is gradually warmed to body temperature by the longer route through the nasal passages. In yoga, long, slow, deep exhalation is emphasized, to remove stagnant air from the lungs and to get the most vital energy from the atmosphere. Slow, regulated breathing results in less work for the heart, lower blood pressure, relaxation of the body, quiet nerves, and a feeling of peace. When you breathe in, feel the air slowly fill your lungs completely, letting your stomach expand. With exhalation, squeeze the air out from the bottom up.

Each yoga posture requires a movement during inhalation, then a pause; a movement during exhalation, then another pause. Move slowly and pause fully, without tension. *Asana* means "a posture comfortably held." To strain or hold the postures in tension defeats their purpose.

Relaxation

The art of deep relaxation has been practiced by yogis since ancient times and by animals and babies instinctively. If you can truly relax for five to ten minutes twice a day, you'll find your need for sleep decreased by as much as two hours. Complete rest refreshes and revitalizes the body in a very short period of time. The stresses of modern life drain your vitality and use up all the energy stored in your body. Russian experiments with Kirlian photography have documented the effect of emotions through the "aura" or the energy field surrounding the body; a picture of the fingertips of an emotionally tense person shows bright flares streaming from her fingertips. More energy actually leaves the body during periods of stress. Experiments have also shown that deep relaxation enhances learning and creativity.

In fact, many of the world's great discoveries were made in a state of total relaxation. For example, Charles Darwin, after years of gathering scientific data, suddenly "realized" his theory of evolution while taking a carriage ride in the country. Einstein developed the theory of relativity after spending an afternoon relaxing on a hillside. He let his imagination drift and found himself riding on a sunbeam on a journey through the universe; eventually his drifting took him outside the realm of his scientific training. Curious, he went back to his study and worked out a whole new mathematical theory to explain what his "imagination" had told him.

Periods of relaxation and play allow the right side of the brain, the part that handles music, color, complex memory, images, and holistic thinking to function more fully and to integrate with the left hemisphere. Integrated hemispheric functioning helps us to think, act, and communicate more creatively.

The deep relaxation pose at the end of your yoga session is very important. In this pose, the mind's attention is gradually withdrawn from the body and absorbed in subtle consciousness. Your body and mind together attain a blissful repose. If you want to be energized by your yoga session, do a short (five minutes) relaxation pose at the end. If your prefer to be calmed and relaxed, do a short relaxation pose between each posture, and longer one (ten to fifteen minutes) at the end.

Your Yoga Session

1. Start with some simple warm-up stretches. In the beginning, if you are stiff or have difficulty doing any of the yoga postures, do these stretches instead. Slowly, as you become more flexible, you will be able to cut down on time spent on the warm-ups. These warm-up stretches can be incorporated into your day if your body is unaccustomed to sitting for meditation; they will limber the legs, back, and knees. They can be done during menstruation and pregnancy, when yoga postures are prohibited. Remember to breathe deeply and relax as you stretch--no bouncing or forcing!

a) Calf stretch
Facing a wall, stand a little distance away and lean your forearms on the wall with hands crossed; lean forehead against your hands. Bend one knee and extend the other leg behind, both feet pointed straight ahead. Slowly move hips forward, keeping feet flat, until you feel a slight stretch in the calf muscles of the extended leg. Hold gently for a count of ten. Your body should be relaxed; don't overstretch. Alternate.

b) Quadricep and knee. Keeping one hand on the wall for support, reach behind and grasp the opposite foot. Hold gently for a count of twenty. Alternate.

c) Groin. Sit on the floor with feet together, hands on your feet, and heels a comfortable distance from your body. Gently pull upper body forward, keeping your back erect, until you feel a stretch. Hold for a count of twenty. Relax arms, shoulders, feet.

d) Hamstrings. Straighten one leg, keeping the other leg bent with the sole of the foot facing the inside of the extended leg. Keep the extended leg slightly bent. Now bend forward slightly, from the hips, with arms relaxed on the floor next to the extended leg, until you feel an easy stretch. Touch the top of the thigh of the extended leg; it should be soft and relaxed. Keep the foot of the extended leg upright, not turned out. Hold for a count of thirty. Alternate.

e) Upper hamstrings and hip. Hold your bent leg to you gently, like a baby, with the other leg extended. Gently pull leg toward you until you feel an easy stretch. Hold for a count of twenty. Alternate.

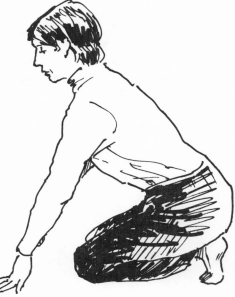

f) Arch. Sit on toes with hands on floor in front for balance. Gently stretch the arches of the feet. Hold for a count of ten.

g) Arms. Hold one elbow with the other hand, over your head. Gently pull, relax and hold for a count of twenty. Alternate.

h) All-over stretch. Standing erect, touch palms together, arms extended forward. (Cont'd. next page)

Bring the arms slowly back to shoulder level.
Then clasp hands behind back with arms extended
straight down. Inhale deeply, pulling shoulders back.
Exhale and bend forward, raising arms over head.

Return very slowly to original position, then slowly twist left and right. Repeat three times.

i) Back. Sit down and bring your knees up to your chest, (ankles crossed) clasping them with both arms. Drop your head down to your knees and roll backwards on your spine. Roll forwards and backwards several times, then side to side several times.

2. First posture (called *Yogasana* or *Yogamudra*): Sit with your legs crossed and your back erect. With arms behind your back, grasp the left wrist with the right hand. Breathe out slowly as you bend forward to touch your forehead to the floor. If you can't reach the floor at first, just hold the posture at whatever point is comfortable. Hold for a count of eight. Breathe in slowly as you rise up again. Hold for a count of eight. Repeat the entire cycle eight times.

3. Second posture (called *Bhujaungasana* or Cobra): Lie down on your chest, with your palms on the floor near your head. Slowly raise up, looking toward the ceiling, breathing in. Keep the navel point on the floor. Hold for a count of eight. Return to the original position slowly, breathing out. Remember to keep your body relaxed as you hold the position. Repeat entire cycle eight times.

4. Third posture (called *Ardhakurmakasana* or *Diirgha Pranam*):
Kneel upright, sitting on heels, supported by extended toes. Joining
palms, extend your arms upward, keeping them close to your ears.
Exhale and slowly bend forward, touching the floor with your forehead,
keeping hips touching your heels. Hold for a count of eight. Slowly
return to the original position, breathing in. Hold for a count of eight.
Repeat the entire cycle eight times. If your arches are not flexible
enough for this posture, you can do it with feet tucked under. Practice
the arch stretch until you can do this posture correctly.

5. Self-massage: A massage following yoga postures conserves the oily secretions of the sebaceous glands (keeping the skin soft and supple), stimulates the nervous system, relaxes the muscles, and enhances the circulation of blood and lymph. Lymph is a vital fluid which purifies the blood. It is not moved along lymphatic vessels by the pumping pressure of the heart; it moves solely by the action of the muscles. Massage thus greatly facilitates the flow of lymph. Special care should be taken to massage the areas of important lymph nodes: the neck, armpit, groin, and knee. Here's how:

a) Massage up the forehead, over the top of the head, and down the back of the head with palms, three times.

b) With the tips of the fingers, massage out across the eyebrows, three times.

c) With pointer fingers, press down in the crease between the top of the eyeball and the eyebrow. Pressure on this spot stimulates the vagus nerve to slow the heart, thus calming and relaxing the body and preparing for the deep relaxation pose. Continue pressing with the fingers, moving them across the top of the eyes, down the temples, in front of the ears, and around the back of the ears. Repeat three times.

d) Massage inside the ears.

e) With the outside edge of your palms, massage from the sides of your cheeks in toward the tip of the nose, three times.

f) With fingertips, massage under the eyes, down the side of the face, then turn the hands sideways and massage the front of the neck. Then massage back across the sides of the neck and around the back, ending by massaging the back of the neck. Repeat three times.

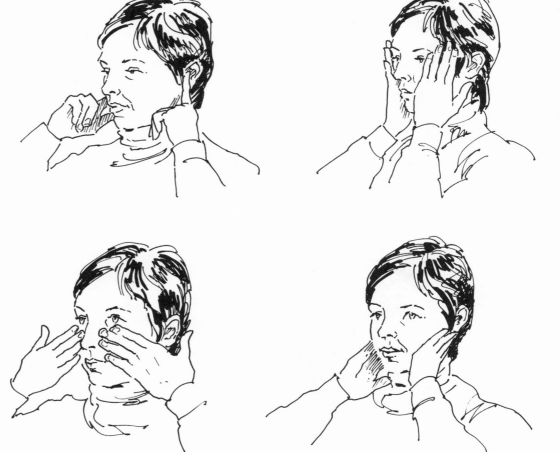

59

g) Massage the upper lip three times.

h) Massage the chin area three times.

i) With two thumbs, massage up inside the jaw starting under the chin and massaging outward toward the sides of the face, three times. This massages the lymph nodes and salivary glands.

j) With the palms pressed against the center of the neck, massage outward. This pressure on the center of the neck also affects the vagus nerve and lowers blood pressure. Repeat three times.

60

k) Raise the arm and massage down the armpit with the fingers, three times. This massages the lymph nodes.

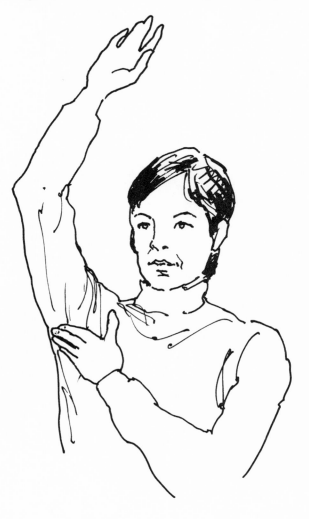

l) Massage over the shoulder and down the upper arm, then use a twisting motion to massage the forearm (follow the direction of hair growth).

m) Massage the back of the hand, the palm, and rotate around each finger.
(Repeat these instructions with other arm)

n) Reaching up over the right shoulder with the right arm and behind the back with the left arm, bring your hands as close together as possible at the mid-back. Massage upward with the right hand and downward with the left. Reverse hands and repeat.

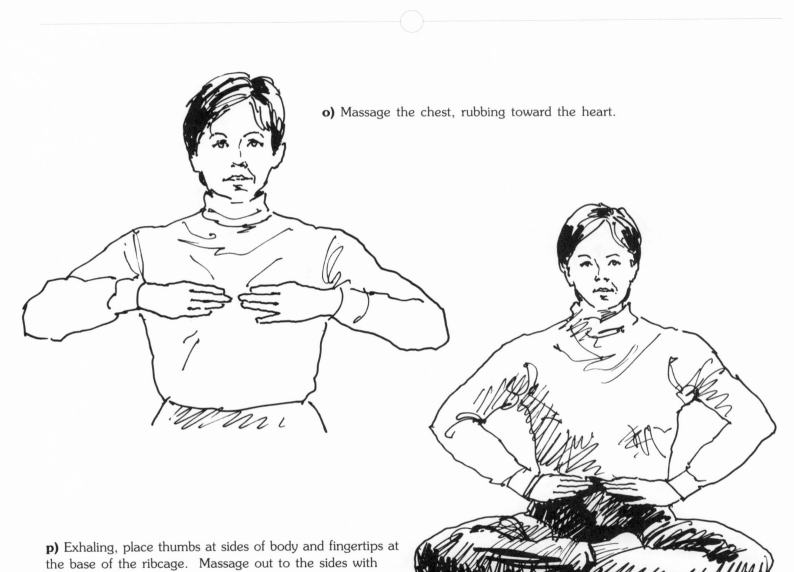

o) Massage the chest, rubbing toward the heart.

p) Exhaling, place thumbs at sides of body and fingertips at the base of the ribcage. Massage out to the sides with fingertips, three times.

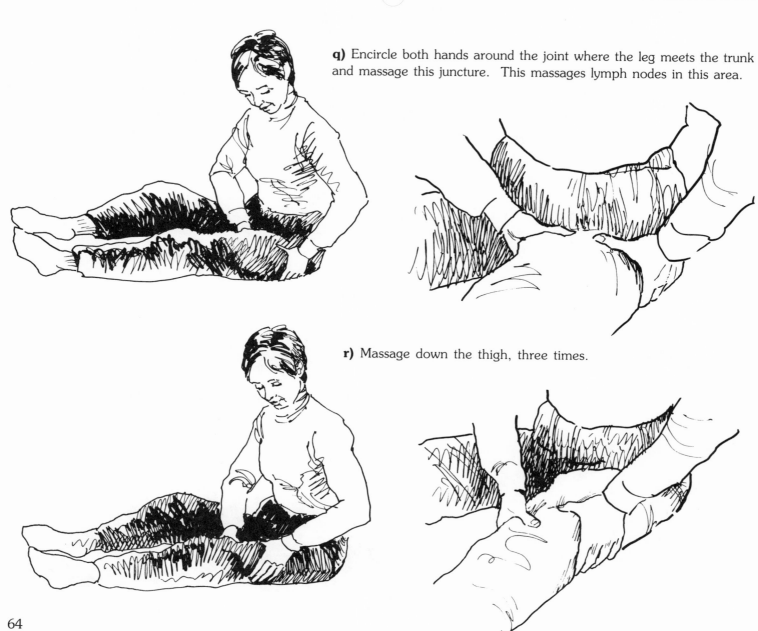

q) Encircle both hands around the joint where the leg meets the trunk and massage this juncture. This massages lymph nodes in this area.

r) Massage down the thigh, three times.

s) Place right palm over kneecap and left hand under. Massage with a combined motion of the two hands. Then massage down the calf, following the direction of hair growth.

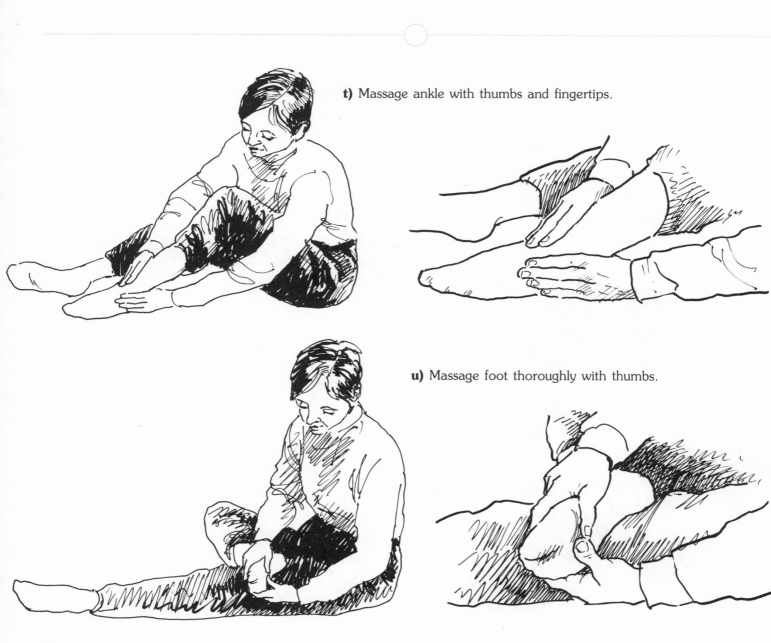

t) Massage ankle with thumbs and fingertips.

u) Massage foot thoroughly with thumbs.

6. Final posture (called *Shavasana*): Lie quietly on the back, palms up. Deeply relax each part of the body, starting with the toes. Practice for five to ten minutes.

Additional Postures

These two postures are for those who are strong and limber. They work on the entire endocrine system, enhance circulation to the brain and thyroid gland, and stretch and align the spine. Do these postures after warm-ups and before the self-massage.

7. Shoulderstand (called *Sarvaungasana*): Lie down on your back. Gradually curl up, raising the body, supported by your hands. Slowly uncurl the legs until your body is in a straight line upward, chin in contact with the chest and feet relaxed. Look at your toes. After two minutes slowly bring the legs back down into a curl, and lower yourself vertebra by vertebra onto the floor. Relax for at least one minute.

8. The Fish (called *Matsyamudra*): Lie down on your back and bring your feet up, one leg over the other, grasping each foot with a hand. Arch the back, with the top of the head touching the floor. Look at the tip of your nose, and rest elbows on the floor.

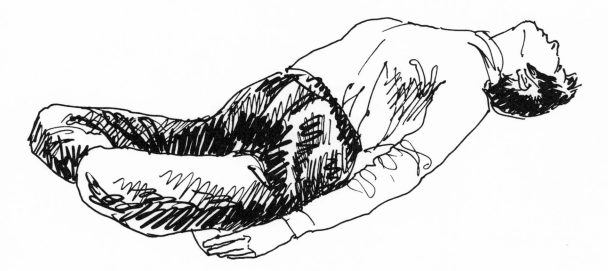

Hold (relaxing as much as possible) for one minute, then stretch out and relax. If you are unable to cross your legs on top, tuck them under you, crossed, holding each foot with the opposite hand.

Exercise

There are two categories of exercise —low intensity exercise and aerobics. Yoga postures represent the first of these. Some type of aerobic exercise (rhythmic activity of the large muscle groups), in addition to yoga postures, will strengthen your cardiovascular system and increase your stamina. There is an exercise in yoga which has this effect and also has the spiritual benefits of yoga postures. It is actually a "dancing posture" and is called *kaoshikii* (pronounced "cow-shee-kee"). It is the "dance of mental expansion." A daily session which includes warm-ups, yoga postures, self-massage, relaxation, and kaoshikii will give you more all-round benefit than any other system of activity, plus the added benefit of directing both the body's and the mind's subtle energies toward your spiritual goal.

Like jogging or other aerobic exercise, kaoshikii should be adopted gradually. It may feel awkward at first, but soon you will feel its rhythm and pace and become comfortable with it. Kaoshikii can be done any time, but the best time is after your yoga postures, when your body is warmed up and relaxed and you are ready for the revitalization of this wonderful exercise.

Kaoshikii combines the benefits of meditation, yoga, and exercise. It has an ideation, that is, a sequence of *thoughts* which accompany the movements. These thoughts, combined with the movements, help strengthen the mind. The hetero-lateral movements, which cross the midline of the body, help enhance left brain functions, while the homolateral movements, which extend the limbs, enhance the functioning of the right brain and bring the consciousness to a sense of surrender to the higher self.

How to do kaoshikii

The dance consists of moving the upper body (with arms up and palms together, bending from the waist) to the right, to the center, left, center, forward to touch the floor, center, backward, and to the center again.

As you do this, you are moving your feet in rhythm: the right foot touches the floor behind the left foot, then hits the floor, flat. Then the left foot touches the floor behind the right foot and hits the floor, flat. The dance ends with each foot stamping flat and the body upright. Repeat the entire cycle as many times as you can (start with three and gradually add more). Kaoshikii is the dance of the spiritual warrior. It prepares you to face the world with strength and courage.

Kaoshikii

Practice this until you feel comfortable with it. Then you can add the ideation:

Ready (arms up, feet a comfortable distance apart): "I seek a link to the Infinite."

To the right: "I request its presence."

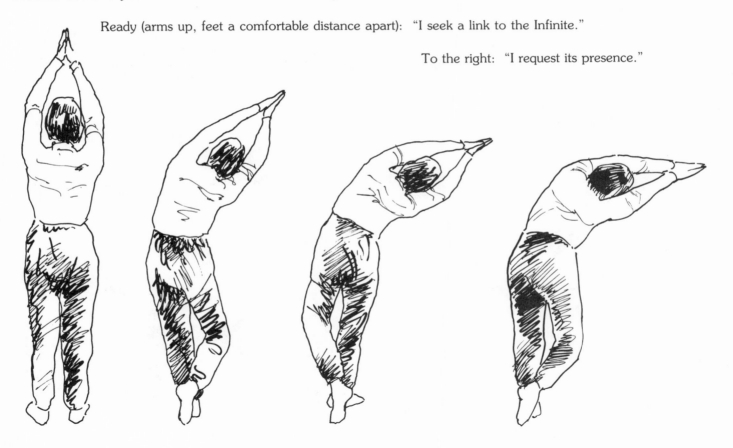

To the left: "I am a willing channel for infinite consciousness."

Forward : "I surrender to my higher self."

Backward: "I am ready to face all obstacles."

Center: "I repeat the cosmic rhythm."

Beauty Secrets of the Yogis

Everyone wants to be beautiful. Most people realize that beauty and attractiveness are essentially inner qualities, not merely related to our physical appearance. If you possess inner beauty there isn't much you have to do to enhance it. However, there are a few habits cultivated by yoga practitioners that will help your natural beauty shine through and which contribute to the all-round health of body and mind. Cleanliness is truly "next to Godliness." Keeping the body clean is the yogi's most important health and beauty secret.

Skin

Take a full bath once every day, using natural castile soaps and scrubbing all over with an abrasive sponge such as a loofa to remove dead cells and enhance circulation to the outer layers of the skin. Finish your bath with a cool rinse, and while your skin is still damp, use a natural lotion or cream to re-moisturize.

Mouth and nose

At least twice a day use a tongue cleaner or spoon to clean accumulations from the tongue. Especially after fasting, in the morning after sleep, and when you are ill, there is a build-up of film from the digestive process. Cleaning the tongue virtually eliminates the need for using a mouthwash, because along with a good brushing of the teeth, it gets rid of the bacteria which can cause breath odor.

It is also helpful to clean the nasal passages, especially when there is any blockage of mucous in the nose and throat. Here's how: Add about 1/2 teaspoon of salt to a bowl of warm water. Bend over, placing your nose into the water, and gently pull some water through your nose. Spit it out, and blow your nose. The salt in the water acts as a germicide and also makes the process comfortable for tender mucous membranes.

Hair

Coconut oil is an inexpensive and natural conditioning for the hair. Once a week or so, comb some coconut oil through your hair and, if possible, take a steam bath (hot steam will help it penetrate). Leave it on overnight, then wash your hair in the morning. A few drops of coconut oil combed through pubic and armpit hair once a day keep these areas cool and clean and act as a natural deodorant. Pouring cool water over the genital area after urinating also helps keep this area cool, clean, and odor-free.

A note on diet

Our food certainly has an impact upon us, both physically and psychologically. A well-balanced diet of fresh foods will aid in your spiritual work. However, food is also intimately tied to lifelong habits and psychological needs. I don't want to turn you away from meditation by telling you how to eat. Start meditating today. You don't need to change your life otherwise; meditation will bring to you intuitively the changes which will help you on your path toward self-realization. If you are interested in dietary changes that might enhance your spiritual practices, the recommended reading will give you a good start.

Recommended reading:

What's Wrong With Eating Meat? by Barbara Parham
Food for Thought by Avadhutika Ananda Mitra Acarya
Stretching by Bob Anderson

Chapter Five:
Mental and Emotional Well-Being

There is no need to run outside for better seeing...
Rather, abide at the center of your being;
For the more you leave it, the less you learn.
Search your heart and see...
The way to do is to be.
(Lao-tzu)

When you begin a regular practice of meditation, your outward-focused energy will become balanced with an inward-turning awareness. There will be times when you encounter, within yourself or as a result of your circumstances, forces which set you off course and require more of your attention. These may be patterns created in childhood, as a result of negative experiences, or fears which have accompanied you from past lives into this one. Sometimes these psychological patterns can be so strong that they hinder your progress in meditation.

Tantra recommends two ways of balancing the mind and emotions —through techniques using *auto-suggestion* and those using *outer-suggestion*.

Auto-suggestion

The term means, simply, change motivated from within. The best form of auto-suggestion is internal repetition of, and ideation upon, the mantra (see Chapter Six). Two other types of auto-suggestion which work very well for the yoga practitioner are visualization and affirmation.

The specific techniques you use will depend upon your personality and what works best for you. First, analyze yourself; do you respond most to seeing, hearing, or feeling? One way to find out is to notice how you phrase things when you talk. Your verbal cues will say a lot about you. People who are very visually-oriented will say things like, "This is how I see it," "You should have seen that," "I see," "I can just picture him doing that," "Show me," "Look." People who are auditory will respond this way: "Tell me about it," "I hear what you're saying," "Listen." Those who are more kinesthetic, or feeling-oriented will say things like, "I feel you're wrong," "He's so touchy," "I lean toward that opinion," "I need to get a feel for it." For example, three friends describe a day at the beach:

Susan: "It was great! You should have seen the waves! The beach was so clean-- pure white sand, and little shells everywhere. I found a beautiful pink one. The sun was so bright, and the sky so blue! Look, I brought a picture of it."

Margaret: "The waves crashed against the shore, and the gulls made such a racket! Then at sunset, everything became quiet and serene."

Ann: "Oh, and the feel of the warm water —it was like rocking in a big womb! The sand was so warm and squishy, and the air so clean and fresh."

Of course, we all use all of our senses to perceive and describe our experiences, but most people do express one more than the others; some people are dominant in two of these modes. In using the following techniques, you'll find that approaches that utilize your orientation will be the most effective. In fact, you can design any system to fit your needs. For example, a "visualization" exercise can include predominantly feeling-images or sound-images.

Visualization

Many diseases have been arrested or cured by the patient's use of imagery. These techniques have been used with particular effectiveness by children, whose defenses and rigidity toward the free-flowing imagination are not yet developed. Meditation, by calming our minds and focusing on the expansive thought of the infinite, helps us revitalize that often dormant part of ourselves. Many of the practices you learn later on include the use of visualization of the cakras and energies of the psychic body.

The imagination is in the realm of the higher mind, where all knowledge resides. By using your conscious mind to direct images inward, you allow the unconscious to function in assisting the lower layers to heal the physical or psychic body. It is a means of getting your programming (those things which you have absorbed or which you have been taught that may not be true) out of the way.

There are as many ways to visualize as there are people. A good way to do it is to write a script for your visualization, incorporating things that are meaningful to you in ways that are pleasing. Then make a tape of your script, and play it to yourself at night before going to sleep or after your yoga postures, as you lie in the deep relaxation pose. Here is one example of a visualization you might use for healing:

A Healing Visualization

Lying in a comfortable position, relax your entire body. Breathe in deeply, then out, several times. You will notice that with each inhalation you become more deeply relaxed, and with each exhalation tension melts away from your body. Starting with your toes and feet, focus your attention gently, and feel your muscles, your tendons, your bones, getting warm and heavy and completely relaxed. Move your attention up to your ankles, then your calves, knees, and thighs, gently focusing, feeling warmth and relaxation in each part of your body. Continue until you have inwardly spoken to every cell of your body, and you are completely, deeply, warmly, relaxed.

Now imagine yourself in a special place —a place that's just for you. It is exactly as you would like it to be, with everything you need available to you. Imagine it in every detail —how it looks, feels, smells. What colors are there? What textures? What objects? Now focus your attention on your body again, and allow it to tell you what it needs to heal. Wait patiently for the answer, each breath relaxing you more deeply.

Now imagine a beautiful light, a beautiful sound, or a beautiful feeling, surrounding and penetrating your body, sinking into your skin, your blood, every cell. This light, sound, or feeling is capable of healing you completely. It is drawn from the universal storehouse, where all things are known, and where perfection resides. It comes from a place where there is no disease, and it has the power to heal you completely. Feel its healing energy. Breathe it in, and out. You can carry it with you, and if you need more, it will always be available to you.

When you wish, gradually return to the conscious world, comfortable in the knowledge that everything you need is already with you.

Affirmations

An affirmation is a positive statement. It is used to replace negative assumptions which can block your progress. The subconscious mind, being very absorbent, often takes as truth statements or past experiences which may not be helpful to you here and now. Your internal belief system can be based on these, and thus your own beliefs can undermine you, short-circuiting the new information that outdates these assumptions. For example, if someone is told again and again in childhood that she can't do math, it is very likely that she will grow up with this belief very deeply entrenched in her mind. It becomes an imposed momentum. Every time she is faced with a mathematical problem, she will be uncomfortable, perhaps even panicky, and she will again hear that voice droning, "*You can't do math.*"

A mantra is a kind of affirmation. It gives new information to your mind, countering old assumptions that you are limited, "only human," that perfection isn't possible. Affirmations are fun to use and can help you keep your mind in the open, positive state which is conducive to growth and success. To use them effectively, you'll want to find statements which ring true to you and which challenge a part of your beliefs that you sincerely want to change. Obviously, parroting a statement which is too far from what you believe is possible will not help.

In an exercise which helps identify and change false assumptions, we'll use the example of our sister, the mathematician —call her Sandra. Sandra would use two sheets of paper; the left one is for her affirmations, the right one for her subconscious responses. She writes "I love math, and I'm good at it," on the left-hand paper. Immediately, she'll probably hear an annoying voice, let's call it "Aunt Nettie" (if you have a wonderful Aunt Nettie, use another name, please) from her subconscious mind say something like, "Yeah, and I'm the Queen of England!" Sandra writes that down on the right-hand paper.

Again, she writes the affirmation on the left, and there's that voice again: "*You can't do math!*" She writes it down, and says something like, "Thank you for your

input," to Aunt Nettie. Then she writes her positive statement again. She continues to do this until Aunt Nettie gives way. Perhaps after awhile, Aunt Nettie will say something like, "Well, maybe you've improved over the years." Later she might concede, "I suppose it *is* possible." And finally, she'll agree, "Okay, so I was wrong. You *can* do math." Sandra tears up the list of negative responses and continues to write her affirmation *every* day for a few weeks. If she's really determined, she might draw it in big, colorful letters and post it on her refrigerator. She might record it on tape and play it to herself on the way to work. Then she can forget about it and enjoy being good at math for the first time in her life. If she's really motivated, she can begin taking math courses to sharpen her skill, confident that her subconscious mind will assist rather than hinder her.

This simple principle can be used in a variety of ways. You might want to identify obstacles in your meditation; perhaps they are assumptions rather than realities. Try to get to the bottom of whatever gets in your way; is it that you don't have time, or is some underlying fear the real reason you haven't set aside time for meditation? You can use visualizations and affirmations to help change your "self talk" when you feel stuck.

Making your own affirmations

Following this section I've included an example of an affirmation exercise you might use. I've filled in the "Clearing Responses" side (that's good old Aunt Nettie) so that you can see what it might look like. Do five to ten sets in the first, second, and third person, once a day for a week. When your "Clearing Responses" have tapered off, make a cassette tape for yourself, repeating the affirmations in the first, second and third person. Say the affirmation slowly, changing the feeling-emphasis each time you say it; wait a few seconds before repeating it again. If you have two tape players, you might try playing your affirmation tape along with a tape of music. Baroque classical music has been proven to be an aid in accelerated learning. Why? Because its heartbeat pace induces deep relaxation and breathing; when you are deeply relaxed and breathing freely, information is easily absorbed by the deeper layers of your mind. Vivaldi's "Four Seasons" or Pachelbel's "Canon in

D" are perfect; adagio, larghetto, or largo movements from concertos by baroque composers usually have the 60-beats-per-minute rhythm that is most conducive for this type of learning.

AFFIRMATION	CLEARING RESPONSE
I, (your name) enjoy meditating twice a day	It's so hard to sit there.
I, (your name) enjoy meditating twice a day	I can't concentrate at all.
I, (your name) enjoy meditating twice a day	I don't have the time to do it right, so I shouldn't do it at all.
You, (your name) enjoy meditating twice a day	My back hurts.
You, (your name) enjoy meditating twice a day	I should have started a long time ago.
You, (your name) enjoy meditating twice a day	It is nice sometimes.
(Your name) enjoys meditating twice a day	I do sleep better when I meditate regularly.
(Your name) enjoys meditating twice a day	It makes me feel good about myself.
(Your name) enjoys meditating twice a day	Who knows, maybe I'll have one of those "peak experiences" I've heard about!
I, (Your name) enjoy meditating twice a day	Yes, I do!

Affirmations work best if they are short, simple, and phrased in the present tense; "I am strong and confident" is better than "I will be a strong and confident person." Also, phrase your affirmation in the positive —"I am strong and confident" rather than "I am not weak."

Sample affirmations

"The more receptive I am, the more I receive."
"I am able to focus effortlessly on anything I choose."
"I have an infinite supply of energy and draw on it continuously."
"I speak only with good intention."
"I naturally enjoy and share my feelings."
"All that I give is given to me."
"I keep only thoughts that are supportive to me and others."
"Every negative thought automatically triggers three positive thoughts in my mind."
"I nurture and support myself."
"Each and every day I become more loving, more open, and more effective."
"I keep my agreements effortlessly."
"I am clear and straightforward in speech and action."
"All problems are opportunities to grow."
"I am infinite consciousness every moment."

Outer suggestion

Outer-suggestion consists of things and people outside of you that can help you achieve mental and emotional well being. These include books, tapes, therapies, and the advice and instruction of a teacher. When you find something in yourself that needs to change, you have a wealth of information and support available to you. Sometimes talking to a counselor or psychotherapist can help you sort things out and find solutions to problems that come up. When choosing someone with whom to share your personal journey, choose wisely. Interview several people recommended by others you trust and do not settle for less than you deserve —someone who supports your spiritual journey and can communicate well with you. In Tantra, there are several types of outer suggestion —aids in adjusting the subjective approach of meditation with the objective world. These include a code of ethics, a set of guiding supports, and the comraderie of others in a spiritual community.

The Tantric Code of Ethics

The way you conduct your outer life compliments your meditation. With a balance of inner development and outer restraint, a sense of strength, of peace and clarity, stays with you all the time. Right conduct is the foundation of spiritual practice. Meditation without morality is useless; morality alone, though admirable, is not the goal of life. Because right behavior is often a struggle, the strength of mind afforded by regular meditation is a must. The guidelines below are thousands of years old, developed by the yogis as a way of bringing spiritual realization into a social context. They are not "commandments" but guides which must be deeply contemplated and rationally adjusted.

1) *Non-harming.* Not intentionally inflicting pain upon anyone by thought, word, or action.

2) *Benevolent truthfulness.* To use the mind and speech with the spirit of benevolence toward all.

3) *Non-theft.* Not to take what belongs to others, in thought, in action, or in non-action (depriving others of their due).

4) *Remembrance.* To look upon everything as a manifestation of the same consciousness and to keep the mind attached to this one universal truth.

5) *Non-accumulation.* To abstain from accumulating more material comforts than you need, using your excess for the upliftment of those less fortunate.

Supports

These may be considered the other half of the code of ethics —things you can do to help you maintain the clarity you need to lead a conscious life.

1) *Purity.* To keep your body, your environment, and your mind as clear and clean as possible at all times.

2) *Contentment.* To keep desires in check, feeling gratitude for what you have, while striving to better yourself and others.

3) *Sacrifice.* To regularly sacrifice some of your own comfort in the service of

others less fortunate.

4) *Understanding*. To study spiritual subjects, trying to grasp the underlying significance, not accepting superficial dogma.

5) *Goal*. To keep self-realization as the goal of your existence, adjusting all things in your life to this objective.

Community

You will find that it is much easier to continue your spiritual practices if you are able to meditate with other people regularly. Association with others, especially those who have been meditating longer, will have a positive effect upon your own meditation. If there is no on-going group meditation in your area, you may want to form your own group, gathering together women with a common goal to strengthen and care for one another in the spirit of oneness.

Begin your group meditation with music. Singing, chanting, or listening to someone singing uplifting songs can help bring everyone into the frame of mind conducive to meditation. Simple songs or chants with a universal theme such as "We are one in the spirit," or "We all come from God," work well to bring everyone together. The beauty of group meditation is in the powerful energy created by one focus on the infinite.

There is an ancient Sanskrit chant, used by some groups for this purpose:

Samgacchadhvam, samvadadhvam
Samvomanamsi janatam
Devabhagam jatapurve
Samjanana upasate
Samaniva akuti
Samana hrdaya nivah
Samanamastu vomano
Jatavaha susahasati

Translation:

Let us come together
Let us sing together
Let us come to know our minds together
Let us share like sages of the past
That all people may enjoy the universe.
Our hearts are as one heart
Our minds are as one mind
As we, to know one another, become one.

Suggested Reading:

The Intuitive Edge by Philip Goldberg
A Guide to Human Conduct by P.R. Sarkar
Woman Spirit: A Guide to Women's Wisdom by Hallie Iglehart

Chapter Six:
Spiritual Growth

---

*It is not only for an exterior show or ostentation
that our soul must play her part, but inwardly
within ourselves, where no eyes shine but ours.*
                                        —Montaigne

Components of meditation

Tantric meditation is taught in several components, each having a specific impact upon your mental and spiritual being, each helping you to gain access to the deeper layers of mind and to reach oneness with infinite consciousness. You receive these instructions when both you and your teacher feel you are ready for them.

The Guru

The Guru is that which leads to the goal. Ultimately, the only Guru is Brahma, the consciousness within us. But in the life of every person who treads the spiritual path, there comes a time when some external help and guidance is needed. "Guru" means "dispeller of darkness." Having mastered the path, the Guru can provide you with many insights, show you the pitfalls, and give you the instruction and correction which is vital to your development.

It is through meditation that an internal relationship with the Guru is first established. Most people, when they meet their Guru in person, realize that a relationship already exists which has been wrought through their meditation. This relationship is very deep and very subtle, and, for the most part, it cannot be described. The Guru cannot be sought after. An old yogic saying is, "When the student is ready, the teacher appears." In the depth and stillness of meditation, at the time that is right for you, the Guru will make himself or herself known.

Initiation

The Tantric scriptures say, "Initiation is the first ladder to the terrace of liberation." As the word implies, initiation is a rite of sorts, a time when the door is opened for you to enter your spiritual path. In Tantra Yoga, initiation is the name given the first step of meditation, when you are instructed in your meditation process, in private, by your Guru or an appointed teacher. However, as the teacher will tell you, it is not she, but infinite consciousness, the true Guru, whose presence is manifest through the process you receive.

Mantra

A mantra is a collection of sound vibrations that is uttered silently in the mind as a part of the meditation process. As was discussed earlier, the mind must always have some sort of object to which it attaches itself. You use this characteristic of mind in meditation by giving it an infinite object to dwell upon, to identify with, and ultimately to become. The mantra is your tool in this process. The sound of the mantra helps to still the mind, and contemplating its meaning helps to expand the scope of the mind infinitely.

The vibrational wavelength of the mantra is very subtle and so it has the capacity to still the mind and bring it into harmony with the infinite. This is achieved through rhythmic sound vibration and repetition. The mantra is the linking vibration between the cosmic rhythm and the individual rhythm. Another important quality of the mantra is ideation. Ideation, in its simplest sense, is to associate meaning with the mantra as it is repeated in the mind during meditation. It is not so much "thinking about" the meaning of the mantra as it is uniting thought and feeling and directing them toward identification with the infinite, at the same time that you are fully attending to the sound vibration of the mantra itself. These are not separate, as would be saying the mantra and then thinking its meaning or translation.

In the beginning you may simply associate the peaceful feeling of sitting by a mountain stream with the mantra; as your meditation progresses your perception of the goal is expanded and limited concepts fall away. Ideation is perhaps the most important aspect of the process; the feeling with which you approach your meditation can greatly help or hinder it. Half-hearted or mechanical repetition of the mantra will get you nowhere, but if your meditation is saturated with love you will be successful.

Once there was a great yogi walking along the shore of a river. He heard a woman, obviously advanced in yoga, chanting a mantra incorrectly. He thought it was his duty to correct this unfortunate person, so he crossed the river in his boat

to the place where the woman was meditating. He corrected her, and she thanked him. He felt very self-satisfied; after all, it is said that someone who could repeat the sacred mantras correctly could even walk on water. As he was thinking this, he suddenly saw a strange sight. From across the river, the woman was coming toward him, walking on the surface of the water.

"My brother," she said when she was close enough, "I am sorry to bother you, but I must ask you again what is the proper way to repeat the mantra; I can't seem to remember it."

This story illustrates the significance of an intuitive approach. I don't mean to say, however, that correctness in form is not important. Though the most important aspect of a piece of music may be the feeling it evokes, the sound of the music is indispensable to the conveyance of that feeling. To express the highest intentions of the composer, every musician in the orchestra must be in perfect attunement with every note of music she plays. So, though ideation may be the most important aspect of the use of the mantra, its pulsative and incantative qualities are equally indispensable.

The process of meditation involves more than the repetition of the mantra. Each individual is also prescribed a specific posture, method for relaxing and withdrawing the mind from the external world, and mental processes that are preliminary to and involved with the proper use of the mantra. The infinite consciousness, the soul of Self may be thought of as a room with many doors. Regardless of which entrance we use, we all find ourselves in the same room. Your personal entrance is the doorway of individual consciousness, and your key is the mantra. To unlock the door it must be the correct mantra, you must pronounce it correctly and ideate upon it with feeling.

When you are given your mantra you will be asked not to utter it aloud. To speak the mantra is unnecessary, for its power lies in silent repetition and ideation. Keeping it sealed within your heart is a way of preserving its sanctity in your mind. Moreover, sharing your mantra with someone may encourage her to use it.

Another mantra may be more suitable for her; thus, you would be doing her a disservice.

Full Meditation (the First Lesson)

This is the actual "initiation" into the regular practice of meditation, and is the foundation upon which all the other instructions build. You might have begun meditating with a simpler process before receiving this one, in order that you may accustom your body and mind to a new experience and easily incorporate meditation into your life. Your real meditation will begin with this practice. It consists of techniques to withdraw the mind from external concerns, from the body and from everyday mental activity, then finally identifying and unifying yourself with infinite consciousness. Concentration, visualization, and the use of your mantra enable you to do this.

This First Lesson is the only practice you need to attain a blissful state of consciousness. However, long before you experience this oneness, the benefits of your daily practice will be apparent to you. Often people say that though the actual meditation is "hard work," the effect it has on the personality and behavior, the increased energy and the sense of inner strength and clarity gained throughout the day are the real benefits.

Living Meditation (the Second Lesson)

As you build a rich inner life through regular meditation, as your powers of concentration and visualization increase, so does your ability to actualize yourself in the outer world. Your mind becomes a very powerful tool. Earlier we discussed the mind's power to create, to impose, and to react, and the resultant samskaras. Living Meditation is a special mantra which is used in daily activity; it keeps the mind in harmony with the universe and reminds you of the oneness of all things. Keeping this vibrational rhythm and ideation of unity in the mind enables you to avoid creating further binding reactions by your thoughts and actions. It gives you a source of *real* power from which to act —not the limited power of the personal ego, but the limitless source of universal power which enables you to think clearly, act decisively, and give selflessly.

Another component of Living Meditation is related to this consciousness of unity, but specifies an even deeper awareness —a surrender of the limitations of the ego to the limitless divinity within. It is called "Guru Puja" —offering to the Guru —and is performed following meditation. Through visualization you offer all past, present, and future thoughts and actions, all the "colors of the mind," to the Guru (which is infinite consciousness —your "higher self") —releasing all your attachments and qualities, both positive and negative, back to their source. It is an act of clearing the mind, of flinging open all the doors and windows in your temple of consciousness to let a fresh breeze flow through and all the built-up mustiness dissipate.

By letting go again and again you begin to feel and realize that nothing is truly outside of you. You can never be truly alone. For example, you have a deep attachment to your child. The love you feel for her is a positive and dynamic force, and is essential to her growth and well-being. But the kind of attachment which can make you overly fearful, dominating, protective, or clinging can be detrimental to both of you individually and to your relationship.

People often fear that by letting go internally, they may lose the object of their attachment. Actually, what you will find is a deepening, an enrichment of feeling when the limits of a relationship are expanded by surrender of the ego's false sense of control. Guru Puja and the Living Meditation mantra (called "Guru Mantra") help you to feel oneness and freedom from limitation.

Cakra Cleansing (the Third Lesson)

Earlier we discussed the "psycho-spiritual anatomy" and covered, briefly, the role of the cakras, or energy centers, in spiritual development and physical/mental health. The Third Lesson is a technique which helps regulate and control the cakras and unblock the psychic "canal" known as the *susumna*. The meditator sits in a prescribed pose and concentrates her mind while internally visualizing the color, shape, and qualities of each cakra and its controlling sound.

Breath Control (the Fourth Lesson)

It is very important, as we grow through meditation, to keep the body and mind in parallelism, or balance. Thus, in meditation we work with every system, physical and psychic, so that our growth is harmonious. The vital energy is the controlling mechanism for all the forces in a living being. Called the *pranendriya,* it is a psychic "organ" which analyses information received from the senses. It is what we often call the "sixth sense."

Our mind-stuff draws its sustenance from the vital energy of the pranendriya. Control over this vital psychic faculty increases the mind's ability to learn and retain. Keeping the pranendriya controlled is the science of the breath, called *pranayama.* You regulate the flow of breath through the nostrils after deep concentration has been attained. Concentrating on a specific cakra, you use the mantra and its ideation to direct energy there. Respiration is the physical result of the pranendriya's activity; both ideation and respiration are controlled in the practice of pranayama. The result is greater mental concentration and retention and control over the mind's and body's processes. Pranayama should not be practiced without the guidance and supervision of a qualified teacher.

Strengthening the Cakras (the Fifth Lesson)

Here again, you work with the cakras, using visualization, concentration, and the power of the mantra to strengthen and purify them. The Fifth Lesson is an important prerequisite to the depth of meditation achieved in the Sixth Lesson. It provides stability and balance to body and mind.

Deep Meditation (the Sixth Lesson)

Deep Meditation is a process which culminates in unqualified union with the Infinite.

The appellation of "hard" or "soft" that you give to a person on the basis of your knowledge of the hardness of iron and the fluidity of water is also due to your pranendriya or vital sense. A "hard" man does not mean that the man is hard to the touch.
—P.R. Sarkar

It is only effective when you have reached the stage when your inner relationship with the Guru is strong and constant and your devotion to self-realization is unswerving. This process enables you to open the door of your heart fully, to experience total communion with the divine.

Where, when and how?

Create a space, somewhere in your house, for your daily practices. It should be quiet, if possible, where people won't walk over it. It will become a sacred place for you —a place of peace and power. It can be a whole room, or just a corner. Place things there that will focus your spirit and which make you feel good; a nice rug, a small table where you can place a candle or incense or some treasured items, a folded blanket on which to sit for meditation. Go to this special place every day —twice a day if possible —to nourish your body, mind, and spirit. People usually find the best times are early in the morning (an hour before breakfast) and/or in the evening. In the beginning, if you are unaccustomed to meditation and yoga, start easy. Reward yourself for consistent practice and increase gradually, if possible, from twenty minutes of meditation to half an hour.

Cool your body first with a "half bath"—splashing cool water over the lower legs, arms, and face. This refreshing yogic technique helps accelerate circulation while decreasing the workload of the heart; scientists call it the "diving reflex," and it energizes at the same time it relaxes the body. You may find that cooling off before meditation helps you concentrate and center yourself more easily as well.

Unplug the phone and let friends and family know that during this time you do not wish to be disturbed. Close the door, close your eyes, and leave the ordinary world behind.

"The short cold bath is more useful and desirable in changing the functions of the body than any other form of therapeutics...It stimulates the thyroid to normal activity. It keeps the bone marrow functioning properly. It is an important prophylaxis against colds...It should be utilized more frequently than it has been."
—from *Home Remedies* by Agatha Thrash, M.D. and Calvin Thrash, M.D.

How to meditate

If you have not yet been initiated and received your own method and mantra, you can still begin practicing meditation. I will not give you a mantra, for I believe that mantras cannot be taken from books and used with any degree of success. The intonation and pronunciation are very important, and it is impossible to convey them here.

Sit erect, cross-legged, on the floor if possible, with hands folded in your lap. This position is best for meditation because it "locks" your energy in your body, enabling you to withdraw from the outer world. If it is uncomfortable for you to sit this way, find another position —preferably upright but relaxed. Take a deep breath, filling your lungs completely with air. Hold for a moment, then slowly blow the air out, releasing tension with it. Repeat this process a few times, until you feel relaxed. Now imagine yourself in a special place, a place that makes you feel good. It could be near the ocean or in the mountains, anywhere. Imagine the air is full of *prana* —the vital energy of the cosmos, and you are breathing it in and out. Become one with all that is around you. Keep your attention gently on your breath, moving in and out. Let thoughts come and go without disturbing you; imagine your thoughts are birds, flying through the clear blue sky of your mind. They come, you are aware of them, and they fly away. Keep your attention gently on your breath and your ideation on "oneness" or "peace."

Suggested schedule for beginners

Morning

1 (15 minutes) Upon rising, take a bath. If you find it helpful, sing or put on some soothing music while you bathe, to get your mind into a meditative mood. Greet the new day, offering your gratitude and blessings to all those who have gone before, who have given so much to the world to make life easier for you.

2 (20 minutes) Sit in your special place; greet your inner self. Meditate for twenty minutes. Some people find it helpful to set an alarm so that they aren't concerned with the time.

3 (20 minutes) Do warm-ups, yoga postures, self-massage, and the deep-relaxation pose.

4 (3 minutes) Do three rounds of kaoshikii.

Evening

1 (5 minutes) Perform a half-bath with cool water.

2 (5 minutes) Sing or listen to music as you stretch, relax, and prepare your mind and body for meditation.

3 (20 minutes) Meditate.

4 (20 minutes) Do warm-ups, yoga postures, self-massage, and deep relaxation pose.

5 (3 minutes) Do three rounds of kaoshikii.

You will be amazed at the changes this simple program will make. Soon you'll find yourself with more energy, vitality, and an increased awareness of your body's rhythms. Your concentration and alertness will be heightened. You'll sleep less and more deeply. You'll find a calmness and clarity within that helps guide your decisions and your relationships with others.

A final note: On self-acceptance

People in the western cultures tend to become discouraged when they don't achieve instant results. Actually, we are not qualified to say whether we had a "good" meditation or a "bad" one. Every meditation is good, because an effort has been made to calm and control the mind. It is this consistent effort, every day, which forges your character and develops in you a deep inner strength which will guide you through all the peaks and valleys of your life. Accept yourself at every point along your spiritual path, acknowledge how far you've come; then take the next step.

Recommended Reading:

Beyond the Superconscious Mind by Avadhutika Ananda Mitra Acharya
Woman Spirit: A Guide to Women's Wisdom by Hallie Iglehart
The Relaxation and Stress Reduction Workbook by Davis, McKay, and Eshelman

Chapter Seven:
Changes

In the house with the tortoise chair
she will give birth to the pearl
to the beautiful feather.

—Aztec poem for birthing

A woman's life is not static. It changes with every moon, every season, and those changes are profound. Often women who begin their journey on a spiritual path become frustrated, even guilty, about their seeming inability to stick to a rigid program. It is not innate inability, but the inflexibility of male-oriented discipline which can cause these feelings, and can often cause women to abandon their spiritual practices altogether.

Psychologist Georgia Witkin Lanoil, in her book *The Female Stress Syndrome,* says that because girls are more often raised to be "good," that is, they are rewarded most when they conform and are considerate, women end up with an adulthood of impossible struggles. We try to be the perfect wife, mother, employee and friend, often to our own detriment. When we adopt a spiritual path, we often try to be the perfect spiritual person. Unfortunately, the definition of perfection often excludes the natural phenomena of women's lives.

The stresses that women experience are different from those of men. Women must cope with radical bodily changes —menstruation, pregnancy, childbirth, menopause. Psychological stresses arise from society's double messages: a homemaker feels pressured to have a career, a working mother feels pressured to spend more time with her children; a single woman is pressured to marry; the childless are pressured by time running out; the young mother worries about missing work and falling behind.

Women are often responsible for entertaining, chauffeuring, and their children's school and recreational activities in addition to housework, career, and marriage. Life changes such as marriage, divorce, and childbearing impact women much more profoundly because of the choices these changes force upon them. And women, every day, are subjected to the subtle but pervading stresses of unequal pay, double-duty work, sexual harassment and sexism, all of which deplete, deny, and distract us. Statistics bear this out. The death rate for women has stayed the same since 1950, while that for men has dropped. Though there has been a radical improvement in health care in the last thirty years, mortality for women has risen in proportion to it. The incidence of cancer and heart disease has risen for women as they have entered the work force and face the exhaustion and frustration of trying to "do it all."

External and internal stresses aggravate the natural stresses of bodily changes. For example, additional stress such as a deadline to meet or a sick child to care for just before menstruation can intensify premenstrual symptoms such as acne or headaches. Stress affects the glandular secretions which, in turn, cause many of these symptoms. Post-birth depression is very common and is often due to the combined impact of rapid hormonal shifts, changing roles and expectations, new financial worries, loss of freedom and choices, and lack of sleep. Menopause is another phase when women can be vulnerable to stress. Again, on top of other pressures, shifts in brain chemistry can cause anxiety and depression. Women are more often socially stigmatized by aging, and since we live longer and earn less than men, the financial pressures increase once again.

Our society has created a difficult life for women, a situation which we, being over half the population, have the power to change. The stresses in our lives can be transformed by changing our perceptions and by finding new ways of relating to the world. Meditation, yoga, and other practices can help us balance our lives, eliminate unnecessary stress and mentally re-frame those stressors which we can use for our development. Spirituality can give us a strong center from which to work to change the pressures and prejudices that now work against us.

Your body changes with the cycles of the moon —so should your practices. Menstruation, pregnancy, nursing babies, raising small children, menopause —these are all times which change you not only physically but mentally and spirit-ually as well. Every woman will have her own way of growing through these changes, and I firmly believe in a flexible, intuitive approach. I've compiled here some guidelines for the woman on the path of Tantra as well as some philosophical points of view from women who have "been there"—women whose years of spiritual discipline have been challenged by family life.

Monthly cycles

If you don't chart your monthly cycles on a calendar, start now. Observe the effect that a shifting hormonal balance has on your energy, your vitality, your emotions, and your meditation. Many women experience a "heaviness" in their meditation a few days before menstruation begins, even if they perceive no other changes. Notice if your attitude toward meditation shifts during your period; are you more inclined toward it, or less? Knowing your natural inclinations can help you design your spiritual practices in a way that will assist rather than oppose you during this time.

Yoga postures should not be done during your period, a time when the delicate hormonal balance in your body shouldn't be disturbed. If you have menstrual difficulties such as irregular cycles, heavy bleeding, cramping, or PMS, they can be addressed through yoga postures done regularly throughout the rest of the month. The postures and warm-ups in this book are very good for balancing women's hormones and strengthening the lower back and pelvic floor.

Kaoshikii can be done throughout the month and is very helpful as an energizing exercise before and during your period. Native healers have often spoken of menstruation as a woman's "time of power." As you become more attuned to the divine within, you will find this to be true. Kaoshikii strengthens the physical body, centers the mind, and channels the tremendous spiritual force coming through you at this time. Don't believe a culture that says you are weak and crazy once a month! Just the opposite is true. Your period can be a time of expanded awareness, when intuitive realization comes more easily. It is a good time to focus greater attention on your meditation. If because of physical discomfort you find meditation difficult, use the time for other things that will help nurture your spirit in solitude: reading, writing, walking in the woods or by the ocean.

Pregnancy

Pregnancy can be one of the most spiritually alive times in your life; after all, having a little person unfolding inside of your body is living proof of the miracle of the universe. It is also a time when you'll get the most advice about the intimate details of your life from total strangers. I'll leave all that to the hundreds of other books on the subject and confine myself to the "how-to" (or not to, as the case may be) do your spiritual practices during this time, and how to keep your inner life growing amid the radical changes a new child brings.

First trimester

In the first three months of your pregnancy, you may find yourself falling asleep at odd times, emotionally on edge, nauseated at different times of the day, and/or otherwise physically uneasy. Often women experience the same kind of difficulties they have had just before menstruation. All of your spiritual practices can continue during this time, but you may want to alter your schedule a bit, to allow yourself to sleep later in the morning and go to bed earlier at night. During my pregnancies, I became so tired by evening that I found it easier to do my first meditation in the morning and the second one at noon. This is a time to be especially mindful of your diet and to get plenty of fresh air and exercise. Increase your protein intake from combinations of beans, legumes, grains, nuts, seeds, and dairy products. Boost your vitamins with fresh fruits and vegetables and their juices.

Second trimester

In the second few months, many of the physical discomforts of the early days disappear. You'll begin to feel the baby move; often a sense of well-being and positivity are the hallmarks of this trimester. Yoga postures should stop, again because of the drastic hormonal shifts taking place and to avoid putting unnatural pressure upon the womb. Gentle stretching exercises can help ease discomforts and keep your body feeling good; Sandra Jordan's *Yoga for Pregnancy* is a good resource for these. You can continue practicing kaoshikii. This is the time to shore up your spirit with a lot of meditation. The baby needs spiritual energy, and you do too, in preparation for the big job of parenting, when time for quiet meditation is hard to find.

It's time to begin communicating with your baby, and what better way than through your meditation? Set aside a certain time every day for your special meditation. Sit somewhere comfortably, close your eyes, and relax deeply. Place your hands on your belly and relax them. Feel your hands getting warm. Visualize your baby, and imagine the connection between you to be like a beautiful golden figure-eight of light. Feel the love moving back and forth between you, getting stronger and stronger. Talk to your baby. Say whatever comes to mind, and wait for a response; after awhile, you'll start to feel your baby responding to you. It may be just a sense, or it may come in your mind as a voice or in pictures, or you may feel baby move in a way that indicates response. Have no doubt that this communication is real, and that you have the spiritual power to connect with your baby deeply, even at this early stage.

What does your baby need? Imagine yourself in that little body, growing inside the womb; what do you need? When you feel the link between you and your baby, you can even ask him or her, "What do you need? What can I do for you?" and get an answer. You may want to write down your experiences from these meditations; you may perceive messages that you don't understand at the moment, but that you will upon looking back.

Third trimester

In the last few months physical discomfort may return as the baby uses more of your energy for that last growth spurt, and as his/her weight imposes more on your resources. Your special meditations will become very strong these last few months; already you have established a strong bond of communication and respect between you that will help you understand your baby after he or she is born.

When you sit for your regular meditation, you may want some added support; an extra pillow underneath or the support of leaning against a wall should help ease the discomfort of sitting. Kaoshikii, though a bit cumbersome, is one of the best child-birth preparation exercises. It strengthens and stretches all the supportive muscles around the pelvis and back and helps open up the pelvic floor. In addition, you'll want to do extra back-strengthening exercises and squatting movements to help loosen any tightness in the pelvic area.

Schedule yourself for an all-body massage several times during this last trimester. Not only will it help you relax, but studies have shown that a mother who is touched and massaged regularly during her pregnancy is more confident handling her baby later on. Massage your belly every day with a light, natural oil such as almond or avocado oil. Feel your hands massage your baby, sending loving, relaxing energy to him or her. Pay attention to your dreams and intuitive insights during this period —write everything down. Surround yourself with beauty in color, nature, music. Read inspiring books, and sing. The preparation of your spirit for the coming of your child is at least as important as physical and mental preparation, if not more.

Birth

The birth of your baby is an event attended by such an overwhelming amount of advice, I'll refrain. It is important, of course, to prepare for it physically, mentally, and spiritually, to try to plan the most gentle and loving welcome possible; at the same time, to surrender to whatever your samskaras may bring, being willing to make beautiful whatever circumstances unfold at the final hour. The birth is important, but more significant are the next twenty years of your relationship with this new companion on your path.

A newborn in the house

There is a Native American story that goes like this:
There was once a great Indian chief who had done everything, who had seen everything, and who was very, very proud. He walked through the village saying,

"I am the greatest chief there is."

An old woman came up to the chief and said, "No you're not. I know a greater chief than you." "What do you mean?" thundered the chief. "I am the greatest chief. There is no chief greater than me." The old woman challenged him. "If you come to my hogan tomorrow at noon, I will introduce you to this great chief." "Very well, Grandmother," said the chief. "I will be there tomorrow at noon."

The chief went home and slept very soundly in order to gain strength and beauty during the night. In the morning he put on his finest clothing, his eagle headdress, his medicine beads and his buckskin leggings. When he was finished he knew that if it were a contest of strength or beauty, he would win. He went to the woman's house and said, "Grandmother! I am here. It is noon."

He went inside and there was the old one, and a baby crawling around on the floor. He looked around and said, "Where is the great chief of whom you spoke?"

"You see him in front of you, o chief," returned the woman. "What do you mean?" the chief blustered. "This is a baby. Are you trying to play a trick on me?" The baby was frightened by the sudden, angry loud voice and started to cry. The chief became very flustered and pulled off his eagle headdress, brushing the baby's cheeks with the feathers. He pulled off his medicine beads and dangled them in front of the baby's nose; he pulled off all of his baubles and bangles and jingled them in the baby's ears.

At last the baby stopped crying, and the grandmother said, "See? The baby won the battle. Even you, the great chief, had to stop talking to care for the baby. In every hogan, the baby is the greatest chief, for everyone loves and obeys the baby implicitly."

"You are right, Grandmother," the chief replied. "You and the baby chief have taught me a great lesson." He put on his beads and feathers and turned to go, and as he did, the baby called out, "Goo!" So ever since then, babies all over the world say "Goo." It means, "I am the greatest chief!"

For the first year of his or her life, your baby is "chief." This is a special time, and it passes quickly, never to return. More than anything, your baby needs your physical proximity —to hear your voice, to feel your touch, to be welcomed, reassured and loved. Often parents will find that the baby wakes up or starts to fuss when they begin to meditate. Perhaps the baby senses your withdrawal and feels afraid or lonely. There are several remedies —you'll have to experiment to find something that works for you. Some parents are so taxed by the baby's demands and household work those first months that they cannot sit down for regular meditation. Others find that meditation helps keep them centered and increases their stamina, so they make it a priority. If possible, have a partner look after the baby while you do your meditation, at least once a day.

You can continue your special meditations. While nursing or massaging your baby, imagine the energy of love between you, feel your connection to the whole universe. In this way, your baby won't feel shut out by your spiritual practices, but will be a part of them.

Sometimes parents who are overly attached to their disciplines will inadvertently establish an adversarial relationship with their babies by insisting upon keeping rigid schedules regardless of the baby's needs. This is unfortunate, because often our children are much more spiritually evolved than we are; if we include them, if we respect them, we can learn from them. If not, we risk alienating them and miss the point of our spiritual effort altogether.

You can resume yoga postures, if all is well, when your baby is around four to five months old.

Life with young children

Many women experience drastic changes in their spiritual lives with the birth of their children. Some say that withdrawal of the mind in meditation becomes painful or impossible, with a mother's eyes, ears, and heart so attuned to her children. This is especially true with children under five or six years of age; it does change as they grow older. You may need to alter your expectations during this period. Each phase of life brings a different kind of growth, demands a different kind of practice. The early years of parenthood require much more the practice of "living meditation" than other times in your life, when you might place those same energies into your sitting meditations. Each phase, if approached with a sincere desire to grow, will offer the precise tools you need at the moment.

During the hectic years of early parenthood you may long for the tranquility of peaceful meditation without the bonds of love and responsibility which seem to tie you to the earth. But this earth, too, requires mastery; those loving responsibilities, too, move you toward the goal. When you long for the world beyond and worry that you may have lost your spiritual discipline, take a moment to look at your life in a broader context. What are you learning right now? How is your life teaching you spiritual lessons that you will use later? You will probably discover that these earthly "bondages" are some of your most powerful teachers. When you are able to sit for meditation again, you will find a one-pointed concentration has developed during those years of "scattered" energies. A deeper ideation is possible because of the work you have done at the level of the heart. You are able to truly give yourself to your spiritual quest because you have learned how to give.

Sexuality

The word Tantra means "liberation through mental expansion" or "liberation from crudeness and stagnation," depending upon how the syllables are translated. The basic tenet of Tantric philosophy is that absolute reality is neutral, having two aspects —pure consciousness (Shiva) and operative principle (Shakti). This universe is the result of the union of Shiva and Shakti; manifestation occurs as Shakti binds

Shiva into different forms. In human beings, Shiva is predominant and Shakti's power wanes until, through spiritual practice, Shakti again merges totally in Shiva. Ancient teachers described this subtle concept in terms which people could understand; the symbol of man and woman joining in sexual communion. People could relate to the profundity of "two-in-one" through their own experience. Tantra originated in matriarchal times in India, when women were teachers who passed secret knowledge down through generations. Shakti was "Mother," the supreme cognitive force, Shiva was the operative principle. The goal of spiritual practice was, as it is today, to merge in that pure blissful consciousness. Sexuality was a natural symbol of that merger.

With the invasion of the patriarchal war-like Aryan tribes, things began to change. The caste system came about, whereby lighter-skinned people placed themselves above the darker-skinned natives who worshipped the Mother Goddess and had originated Tantric traditions. The interpretation of symbols began to change; eventually Shakti (seen as feminine) was the operative principle, subordinate to Shiva (seen as masculine). The idea was to throw off the shackles of nature (Shakti) in order to merge in Shiva. A split between nature and spirit emerged, and women symbolized the "demoness" nature which held consciousness (men) in bondage.

In ancient religions sexuality was very much a part of life, not hidden or unclean, and could be a means to spiritual development. This changed with the advent of patriarchal domination, and women, whose bodies symbolized the power of nature and sexuality, were seen as enemies of spiritual enlightenment, to be subjugated and controlled by the men who had usurped their spiritual power.

Though the ancient symbols still live in thousands of confusing forms, interpretations, and dogmas, modern Tantrics are reaching beyond the masculine/feminine symbology to a holistic, humanistic view of creation and the spiritual journey. Woman are reclaiming their place on the spiritual path and bringing feminine power back into the picture. A balanced, progressive outlook and philosophy is thus bound to emerge. When nature is no longer perceived as the enemy to be conquered, and light-skinned males are no longer the accepted rulers of religion and society, a radical shift will have taken place that allows the growth and development of humanity in cooperation with all the other creatures on our planet.

There are several different schools of Tantra, and many practical approaches as well. One form of Tantric practice, called "The Five M's" is the basis for the so-called "Tantra of Sex" that you may have heard or read about. The Five M's are a portion of ancient Tantric ritual which had both physical and spiritual meanings. Some scholars say the literal version was meant as a steppingstone for those who were unable to do a more subtle form of practice —those whose animal instincts were still quite strong. It was meant to spiritualize the things of everyday life. Thus, the activities of everyday life such as sexuality could come to be an expression of spirituality, of worship.

The Five M's

1) *Mamsa Sadhana.* Literal meaning: ritual consumption of meat. Subtle meaning: to control the tongue (speech).
2) *Matsya Sadhana.* Literal meaning: ritual consumption of fish. Subtle meaning: to control the respiration (pranayama).
3) *Madya Sadhana.* Literal meaning: ritual consumption of wine. Subtle meaning: to control the nectar which, it is said, is secreted by the pineal gland when the body becomes very subtle, and creates an ecstatic feeling.
4) *Mudra Sadhana.* Literal meaning: the use of symbols in ritual. Subtle meaning: to control the propensities through spiritual practices such as yoga postures.
5) *Maethun Sadhana.* Literal meaning: ritual sexual intercourse. Subtle meaning: the mystic union of Shiva and Shakti through deep meditation.

There is debate as to whether the literal translations of these practices were actually religious doctrine or, more likely, codes which referred to the subtle practices. Much of Tantra has been passed down through thousands of years from teacher to student in code. Tantra provided, and still provides, a context in which all of life is spiritualized. Tantra is not the "yoga of sex"—it is the yoga of *every-thing*. Tantra does not favor suppression of the instincts, but rather control, whereby the mind is always directed toward spirituality. Freud spoke of the libido (sexual energy) as a force which has not necessarily a sexual goal; in this, he was in agreement with Tantric teachings. The powerful energy which may be expressed in sexual intercourse can also be utilized for spiritual attainment. Casual sex can be harmful physically, emotionally, and spiritually, just as are drugs, liquor, or food in excess. Used with addiction like an intoxicant, sex becomes crudi-fying, drawing off vital energy which can be used in creative and spiritual pursuits. Sexuality can be a much higher expression than this. Between two lovers who deeply care for one another and whose spiritual and emotional sensitivity is mature, sexual communication can reinforce spiritual goals and commitment. It is then a sacred enactment of the essential spiritual drama —the bliss of universal oneness.

Later life

The saying "life begins at forty" has never been so true for women as it is today. The myth that menopause is a negative experience is dispelled as women claim their personal power. A new life can open up as children grow and we find more time to direct our inner and outer lives toward our own goals. As Margaret Mead once said, "The most creative force in the world is the menopausal woman with zest." Later life can be a time when a new spiritual awareness grows. Experience and wisdom augment new possibilities; a greater self-assurance allows us to place priority on our self-development.

Physical and emotional discomforts that may be experienced during menopause can be greatly alleviated by good nutrition, yoga, exercise, and meditation. Many health professionals now recommend these natural techniques to augment —even replace —estrogen supplements. If you do take estrogens, you might consider consulting with your doctor about reducing the dosage once you are established in daily yoga, exercise, and a healthy vegetarian or semi-vegetarian diet supplemented with calcium and vitamins. You may find that you can be comfortable on a low dose or none at all, and thus reduce the risks from the long-term use of these drugs.

What an exciting time! No longer do women face the "empty nest" and a rocking chair as later life approaches. Rather, with the strength and inner beauty afforded by a regular meditation practice, we can begin a new phase of physical, mental, and spiritual fulfilment.

Recommended reading

Yoga for Pregnancy: 92 Safe and Gentle Stretches by Sandra Jordan
Essential Exercises for the Childbearing Year by Elizabeth Noble
Infant Massage, a Handbook for Loving Parents by Vimala Schneider McClure
Whole Child Whole Parent by Polly Berrien Berends
Menopause Naturally: Preparing for the Second Half of Life by Sadja Greenwood, M.D.

About the author

Vimala McClure is a writer and infant parenting educator. She lives with "a wonderful husband, three rambunctious children, a trio of furtive cats, a perfectly normal dog and assorted wildlife" in the Ozarks of southern Missouri. Her books include *Infant Massage, a Handbook for Loving Parents* (Bantam Books), *The Infant Massage Instructor's Manual,* and *Discovering Our Heritage: Bangladesh* (Dillon Press).

Vimala is the founder and president of the International Association of Infant Massage Instructors and she writes for several magazines in the U.S. She is a professional member of the Renaissance Artists and Writers' Association, The Society for Children's Book Writers, and the Pre- and Perinatal Psychology Association of North America. Vimala has been practicing Tantra Yoga since 1971.

Glossary

ASANA(S) —physical exercises which harmonize the glandular system and thus make the body fit for meditation.

AUNKARA —(AUM) The sound of creation; sometimes heard in deep meditation.

BRAHMA —The infinite consciousness from which everything arises.

BRAHMACAKRA —The cycle of creation; the movement of consciousness from its infinite state into matter and then from the dense to the subtle, merging again in pure consciousness.

CAKRA(S) —nuclei located throughout the body's subtle structure; foci of psychic force.

DHARMA —"innate tendency." That which propels every living being toward oneness with the Creator.

GURU —"That which dispels darkness." According to Tantra, the only true Guru is infinite consciousness.

KAMA —limited desires.

KAOSHIKII —a dancing exercise which vitalizes the body, focuses and mind, and strengthens the will.

KOSA(S) —The layers of the mind.

KUNDALINI —Spiritual energy residing in every living being.

MANTRA —a collection of sound vibrations used as a focus in meditation.

PRANA —vital energy.

PRANAYAMA —control of the vital energy through the practice of meditation with breathing exercises.

PRANENDRIYA —the "sixth sense," actually a type of psychic organ which regulates mental and physical functions.

PREMA —limitless love.

SAMSKARA(S) —inborn, acquired, or imposed reactive momenta from past thoughts and actions, stored in the mind and expressed as "fate."

SHAKTI —"operative principle." That which binds infinite consciousness to finite form.

SHIVA —infinite consciousness, unbound. Also, the name of a great Tantric Guru who lived in ancient India.

SUSUMNA —the "psychic canal" through which the kundalini energy is channeled.

TANTRA —the ancient spiritual discipline upon which yoga is based.

YOGA —"union" of the self with infinite consciousness.

Index

Notes